Inferno in Chechnya

INFERNO IN CHECHNYA

THE RUSSIAN-CHECHEN WARS, THE AL QAEDA MYTH, AND THE BOSTON MARATHON BOMBINGS

Brian Glyn Williams

ForeEdge

ForeEdge
An imprint of University Press of New England
www.upne.com
© 2015 Brian Glyn Williams
Manufactured in the United States of America
Typeset in Utopia and Aller by
Passumpsic Publishing

For permission to reproduce any of the
material in this book, contact Permissions,
University Press of New England, One Court Street,
Suite 250, Lebanon NH 03766; or visit www.upne.com

Library of Congress Cataloging-in-Publication Data
Williams, Brian Glyn.
Inferno in Chechnya: the Russian-Chechen wars,
the Al Qaeda myth, and the Boston Marathon bombings /
Brian Glyn Williams.
    pages cm
Includes bibliographical references and index.
ISBN 978-1-61168-737-8 (cloth: alkaline paper)—
ISBN 978-1-61168-801-6 (ebook)
1. Chechnia (Russia)—History—Civil War, 1994– 2. Russia
(Federation)—Relations—Russia—Chechnia. 3. Chechnia
(Russia)—Relations—Russia (Federation) 4. War and
society—Russia (Federation)—Chechnia. 5. Jihad—
Political aspects—Russia (Federation)—Chechnia.
6. Qaida (Organization) 7. Terrorism—Europe. 8. Boston
Marathon Bombing, Boston, Mass., 2013. 9. Tsarnaev,
Tamerlan. 10. Tsarnaev, Dzhokhar. I. Title.
DK511.C37W55   2015
947.086—dc23   2015002114

5 4 3 2 1

*For the resilient people of Boston and for all
my friends in the city, including Suki Soltysik,
Dana Fine, Heidi Floerke, Ozge and Eric
Getkin, Ed Fallon, Amy Beuchemin, Josh Ready,
Jenny Murphy, Jason and Molly Seto, Corey
and Leandro Lopez, Steve and Ceren Matteo,
John Lawrenz, Alan Hirshfeld, Michelle Cheyne,
Bob and Pat Getkin, Kevin McWilliams, Laura
Barlow, Brad Pinkos, Scott Gollumcan Levi,
Alan Friedman, Jim Stamos, Ona Ridenour,
Volkan and Tansel Sazak, Marc Yanniello,
Hien Cao, Michelle and Selim Gurel, Len
and Carolyn Travers, Razi Usman, Sue Foley,
Mark Santow, Tim Pakopolos, Pat Gallagher,
Chris and Jill Keough, and my wife, Feyza.*

This is a war for the freedom of a nation.

If the Russians want to call me a terrorist,

a hammer of God, a nightmare creature,

I am happy to be any of these things.

—Chechen field commander turned

notorious terrorist, Shamil Basayev

Contents

Acknowledgments

First and foremost, I would like to thank my parents, Gareth and Donna Williams, for supporting my research on Chechens for the last decade and a half. Their proofreading of this manuscript was, as always, much appreciated. Many thanks go to my wife, Feyza, who patiently supported me in writing this story for the last ten years. I also would like to send my *teshekurs* (thanks) to my in-laws, Feruzan and Kemal Altindag, for providing me with a quiet place to write this book in their seaside town on Turkey's Aegean coast. I would also like to thank my former advisors Uli Schamiloglu and Kemal Karpat for teaching me about the history of Central Eurasia's ethnic groups at the University of Wisconsin and Indiana University. In addition, I would like to thank Norbert Strade for his assistance in helping me understand some of the complexities of Chechnya's recent history and Glen Howard at the Jamestown Foundation for his support over the years. Last, I would also like to thank the Chechens I have met over the last two decades for sharing their homes and tales with me. Their tales inspired me to write this work.

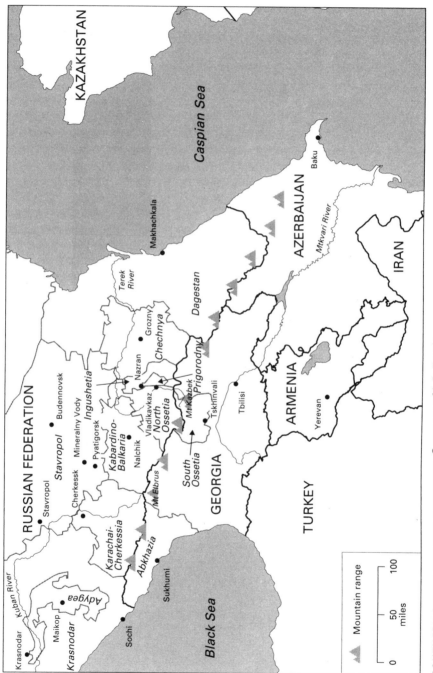

SOUTHERN RUSSIA AND THE CAUCASUS. Courtesy of I. B. Tauris

Introduction

April 15, 2013 — as warm a Patriot's Day for the annual running of the Boston Marathon as anyone could ask for. As the early spring temperature rose to sixty, thousands of cheering spectators lined the sunny route leading to the finish line at Boylston Street. I was among the crowd, watching the runners from a spot on nearby Beacon Street, two blocks from my house. It was a perfect spring day to put aside the memories of the long, cold winter; to cheer on the runners — many of whom were running for local charities; and to join in a celebration of all things Boston.

We had our first inkling that something had gone horribly wrong when a woman next to us received a cell phone call and ran screaming into a nearby bar.

"There's been a bombing at the finish line," she yelled. "There's been a bombing! Oh my God!"

I ran after her into the Publick House, where we all stared in disbelief at the large-screen television on the wall. But all we saw were reassuring images of runners, and we relaxed.

And then the news broke. A clearly distraught local reporter came on TV to announce that there had been two bombings at the finish line. The earlier scenes of a joyous race succumbed to images of panic and horror.

This can't be happening. Not here. Not now!

You expect to see gruesome images of war-torn Baghdad, Beirut, or Kabul, but not in the city we affectionately call "Beantown." As the crowd in the bar stared blankly, several people began to sob while others frantically dialed up friends and family who were right down the street from us at the finish line.

But no one could get through to them. The police had already disabled the cell towers so that the bombers couldn't use their phones to detonate more bombs. Within minutes, several police officers burst into the bar, calling for us to evacuate—just in case. We all left, hurrying down the street toward our homes in stunned silence.

When I reached our house, my wife, Feyza, searched the Internet and found images of maimed victims being rushed to ambulances. Unable to look at them any longer, she broke into tears, damning the terrorists who had inflicted so much senseless pain on—of all days—one of such joy.

Early in the morning, four days later, my phone rang. It was a friend telling me that the authorities had identified the bombers and had launched an unprecedented citywide dragnet to catch them. They were said to be from an ethnic group in Russia known as the Chechens.

Can't be, I thought. The Chechen highlanders were the ancient enemies of Russia, not of the distant USA.

"Don't you teach a class on Chechnya?" my friend asked.

"Yes, at the University of Massachusetts at Dartmouth. Why?"

Because, he told me, one of the bombers, Dzhokhar Tsarnaev, attended that very university and had been seen on campus calmly going about his business several days *after* the bombing.

"My God," I said.

My friend paused before asking me the question that many of the students who took my class on Chechnya would later ask: "Why on earth would Chechens want to attack America?"

Why, indeed. The answer, on the surface, is seemingly "for many reasons." This book is a background journey which explores that perplexing question. It will take readers into the mighty Caucasus Mountains of southern Russia and introduce them to the ancient Chechen highlanders and their centuries-long war with the invading Russians. It will explain the reasons for their hatred of their Russian foes, who chopped down their primordial forests, burnt their villages, raped their women, and waged scorched-earth tactics to break their determined resistance. Most important, this background journey will take readers into the Soviet Union's genocidal decision to ethnically cleanse the entire Chechen people from their ancestral lands in 1944, and their long struggle to return to their beloved Caucasus homeland.

But the heart of this book lies in its retelling of the two bloody wars the Chechen mountaineers fought for independence from post-Soviet Russia. In the process of exploring this blood feud, it will show how Russian and Soviet savagery against this small nation subsequently ignited an Islamist terrorist response among the Muslim Chechens that was to lead to Europe's deadliest terror campaign. Ultimately, it also will demonstrate how the rise of jihadi terrorism in the war-blackened villages of tiny Chechnya spawned a terror plot that reached the shores of America with deadly consequences.

First Blood

The Chechens are a numerous people, but they have no aristocracy. "We are all princes" is the proud contention of the Chechen. They are a people who have no superiority of rank, and never had, and into whose language the word "command" cannot be rendered . . . They are always in a chronic state of feeling themselves insulted by their fellow-creatures, and maintain that nobody can be considerate enough to them as a completely free people.
— Essad Bey, *Twelve Secrets of the Caucasus*, 1930

Cattle-lifting, highway robbery, and murder were in this strange code, counted deeds of honor; they were openly instigated by the village maiden, who scorned any pretender having no such claims to her favor; and these, together with fighting against any foe, but especially against the hated Russians, were the only pursuits deemed worthy of a grown man.
— John F. Baddeley, *The Russian Conquest of the Caucasus*, 1908

Wolves The Ancient Highland Tribes

The Chechen national symbol is the gray wolf, and since the collapse of the Soviet Union, this emblem has appeared in their poems, on their battle standards, and on their national flag, and it has come to symbolize the Chechens' stubborn defense of their homeland. The Chechens like to compare themselves to the gray wolf that has roamed the primeval forests of the Caucasus Mountains since the beginning of time. According to the mountaineers, the gray wolf does not attack humans unless they trespass on its lair, and in this behavior, the Chechens see a parallel to their own relations with the Russians.

As any Chechen will tell you, their ancestors never set out to conquer Russia; the troubles with their empire-minded neighbors began when Russia's generals set their sights on the Caucasus and brought fire and sword to the Chechens' homeland in the late eighteenth century. It was the Chechens' bloody experience of "pacification" at the hands of Russians—to use a nineteenth-century tsarist euphemism for ethnic cleansing, scorched-earth campaigns, and a decades-long war of attrition—that was to poison the relations between these two peoples. While many nonexperts discovered the Chechens after 9/11 and see them only in this context, one cannot claim to know the Chechens without first being familiar with the tragic story of their conquest by Russia's armies in the nineteenth century.

Prior to Russia's imperial adventures in the lands of the Chechens and neighboring tribes, this mountainous land on the distant fringes of Europe had been something of an unknown land for most in the West. Western Christian civilization ended in the lowland shadows of this mighty mountain barrier that separated Europe and the southern borders of the empire of the Orthodox tsars from Asia and the Islamic lands of the Turks and Persians. Forming the highest mountain chain in Europe, the mighty Caucasus range extends 650 miles from the shores of the Black Sea to the landlocked Caspian Sea, and its highest peaks are covered in snow year-round. This rugged rampart dwarfs the Alps in its scale, and its average height is over ten thousand feet.

The massive Caucasus chain has some of the most inaccessible mountain valleys and highland pastures in the world and has served as a refuge for fleeing tribes and ethnic groups since the dawn of history. The hardy highlanders whose cliff-top *auls* (villages) clung tenaciously to the sides of the mountains lived in settlements built on the edges of sheer precipices and guarded by stone towers. In these impenetrable highlands, a village could hold off an army as its warriors defended the narrow path along a dizzying cliff.

In the misty depths of time, when the Indo-Europeans (the forebears of the modern nations of Europe) first arrived in the region, they forced the ancient mountain people already living in the Caucasus lowlands to flee deeper into the wooded valleys of the northern slopes. In the process, the easily defended mountain peaks and impenetrable valleys of the north Caucasus came to serve as a sanctuary for some of the oldest races of Eurasia.

In the twentieth century, long after the older races had been pushed into the mountains, modern anthropologists and linguists would find traces of tribes that had disappeared from history long before the birth of Christ. The origins of some of these races extend back to the ancient peoples of pre–Old Testament Sumeria, Elam and Uratau.

The forest-clad mountains of the Caucasus are home to dozens of ethnolinguistic groups and serve as a storehouse, preserving the ethnic residue of all the passing waves of invaders who have swept through this region since the beginning of time. In some areas each village speaks a different language that, like the pages of history, can be read back in time to provide a historical account of the various tribes of conquerors that ebbed across this tumultuous land. Similar to the rings on a tree, the layers of races in the north Caucasus tell us the history of the mountains.

The Dagestan region, which is located in the northeastern Caucasus to the east of Chechnya, for example, is home to more than thirty different ethnic groups, most of whom speak unrelated languages. The confusing array of languages left by previous invaders in the Caucasus led the medieval Arab Muslim conquerors, who believed that fierce *jinns* (demons) lived in this cloud-covered realm, to name this rugged land the *Jabal Alsuni* (Mountain of Languages).

As history tells us, waves of horse-mounted Scythians, who drank fermented horse milk and wine from their enemies' skulls, Zoroastrian Iranians bringing their ancient worship of fire, savage Huns on their way to ravage Rome, Arab warriors spreading their new Islamic faith, Jewish horse-mounted Khazar nomads, world-conquering Mongol Tatars, empire-building Ottoman Turks, Shiite Persians, and many others lapped up against the mountain barrier of the Caucasus and left remnants of their peoples amid the older races already ensconced in their mountain valleys.

As a result, in the northern Caucasus today you find the half-pagan, half-Christian Ossetians, who worship carved wooden poles in much the same fashion as their distant ancestors, the Alans, who partook in the great barbarian migrations that brought down the Roman Empire. You also encounter the Cherkess, the pitiful remnants of the once-mighty Circassians, who provided slave warriors and the most comely of women for harems of the caliphs of medieval Baghdad. In the eastern plains of the northern Caucasus you also find small pockets of Nogai Tatars, the sheephearding descendents of Genghis Khan's mighty nomadic Mongol armies.

As one leaves the plains of the Nogai steppe and probes deeper into the mountains, however, one finds ancient ethnic groups whose origins are even older than these previously mentioned races. These include the fierce Jewish highlander tribe known as the Tats, whose origin goes back to the original Old Testament dispersal of the Jews in the eighth century BC. You also find other groups who inhabit the bleak mountains of Dagestan (a region whose name translates to "Land of the Mountains"), such as the Dargins, Avars, Lezgins, Laks, Aguls, Rutuls, Tabassrans, and countless others, who fiercely defended their lands against outsiders over the centuries.

Most of these ancient groups, who continued to fight with sabers, shields, and medieval-style armor up until the late nineteenth century, were unknown to the Western world, whose ethno-geographic horizons ended in the more familiar lands of the Orthodox Russians and Ukrainians.

Among the oldest and most powerful of the north Caucasian races are a farming and cattle-breeding people known as the Vainakh, who have inhabited the forested slopes of the northeastern Caucasus for millennia. Made up of dozens of independent *teips* (clans) and known for their industriousness, refusal to submit to any authority, skill in the time-honored sport of cattle raiding, and love of freedom, the unruly Vainakh were divided into two separate tribes by the Russians, who first began to encroach on their lands in the late 1700s. The Russian Cossacks, the "cowboys of Russia," and later Russian imperial administrators called the western Vainakh the "Ingush." Those Vainakh residing in the east, near a village known as Chechen Aul, were called "Chechens." Over time, the two Vainakh tribes, who spoke mutually comprehensible languages, internalized these ethnonyms and became distinct groups. Today the Chechens and the much smaller Ingush people are recognized as separate nations in spite of their close ethnolinguistic links.

When the Russians first shared their accounts of the mysterious Chechen highlanders to the outside world, they spoke of a primordial mountain people who were ruled over by a council of tribal elders known as the *Mehq-Qel* (the Council of the Land). These wise elders were chosen by their clans (*teips*) to represent their interests in community councils. Councils of the people were called to mediate blood feuds, organize the defense of the *ka'am* (the "nation," or more precisely "people" in a premodern sense), and uphold the ancient traditions of the people, which were based on a blend of ancient pagan customs and the later imposition of Islamic law. Traditionally, the Chechens have given great respect to their clan elders, and all Chechens direct their loyalty to their clan first and then to their *tukhum* (their larger tribal alliance).

Interestingly, there was no class of nobility among the egalitarian Chechen people, and one observer noted:

> The equality among the people of the Eastern Caucasus is clear-cut.
> They all possess the same rights and enjoy the same social position.
> The authority with which they invest their tribal chiefs grouped within
> the framework of an elected council is limited in time and power . . .
> Chechens are gay and witty. Russian officers nicknamed them the French
> of the Caucasus.[1]

Islam, it should be mentioned, arrived late in the lands of the Chechen and Ingush, and many of this people did not convert to the religion of the Prophet Mohammed until the late eighteenth and early nineteenth centuries. Even then, Robert Schaefer writes, "Chechnya was not particularly devout."[2] Prior to the advent of Islam, this people worshipped Yalta, the god of wild animals and patron of hunters; Seli, the god of fire; and myriad other supernatural denizens of the snow-covered alpine peaks and forested slopes of the Caucasus. Among the woodland sprites worshipped by the Chechens were ghostly forest creatures called *almas*, who lived in springs and rivers. Lesser gods included Khi-Nama, the "Mother of Water"; Darsta Nama, the "Mother of Snowstorms"; and Moh Nama, the "Mother of Winds."

The Chechens and Ingush owe their submission to Allah to the neighboring tribes of the northeastern Caucasus region known as Dagestan. Dagestan, a foreboding mountainous tableland that separates the more gentle slopes of Chechnya from the shores of the Caspian Sea, had been conquered by the Arabs during their great period of Islamic expansion in the eighth and ninth centuries. For this reason the people of Dagestan were familiar with the preaching of the Prophet Muhammad from an early date. In Dagestan, mullahs (Islamic clerics) who spoke Arabic and Persian delved into the scriptures of the holy Qur'an, the chant of the muezzin (the prayer caller) drifted from the minarets across the mountain valleys, and camel caravans brought the goods of the greater Dar al-Islam (the Islamic Realm) to the villagers inhabiting their well-fortified mountain *auls*.

Over the centuries, mystic Islamic holy men wandered from Dagestan into the neighboring forestlands of the animistic Chechens and preached their tolerant, frontier version of Islam, known as Sufi Islam. Many of these Muslim mystics were purported to have worked miracles in order to convert the pagan Chechens to Islam. The sites of these miraculous events subsequently became places of pilgrimage, although some of these sacred spots were clearly pre-Islamic holy places. The Chechens converted to this mystical Sufi version of Islam, in part, because it allowed them to keep many of their ancient, pre-Islamic traditions.

Muslims from the Middle East who visited the vales of Chechnya in the late nineteenth century found that Chechen women did not wear the full veils worn by women living in Wahhabi-dominated Arabia. On the contrary, the laws of the land were dominated by *adat* (ancient, pre-Islamic custom) more than shariah (Islamic law). In the Caucasus, mystical chants and dances known as *zikirs* were performed to assist the Chechens in attaining Allah's grace and imitate the movement of the cosmos. In this frontier region, tolerance toward neighboring Christian or pagan peoples (such as the Orthodox Christian Cossacks or the animist Ingush, who did not convert to Islam until the mid-nineteenth century) was widespread.

In other words, many of the austere facets of puritanical Wahhabi Islam of the sort being spread by the Saud family in nineteenth-century Arabia were not found on this fluid mountain frontier between Islam, Christianity, and traditional native animism. It was only in response to the Russian conquest that an increasingly xenophobic form of warlike Islam spread among the outnumbered warriors of this tolerant Sufi mountain people.

In addition to their adherence to an indigenous, mystical version of Islam, the Chechens also were known for their fighting skills. In a land where blood feuds (known as *kanli*), raids, and clan warfare were a way of life, Chechen boys grew up mastering the deadly sharpshooter's rifle, the wicked *kinjal* blade, and the hardy mountain steed. The swaggering Chechen highlander who arrived in the Russian lowlands for trade, with his saber dangling from his side, rifle over his shoulder, breast pocket bandoleers brimming with bullets, and tall fur hat placed rakishly on the back of his head, was given a wide berth.

Not surprisingly, this people's culture glorified feats of combat and bravery. Highlander raiders known as *abreks* proved their manhood by engaging in dangerous raids on the neighboring people. While the Russians deplored the highlanders' "evil deeds, raids and robbery," the Chechens lionized famous *abreks*, who proved their daring by slipping past the enemy's patrols and seizing booty. In his analysis of *abreks* in the Caucasus, Russian scholar Vladimir Bobrovnikov writes, "The main hero of their culture—the so called *abrek*, i.e., professional bandit—was a figure who was praised for engaging in a profession that was seen as noble and honorable, in the fashion of Robin Hood."[3]

Another quality recognized among the Chechens was the supreme importance they placed on providing hospitality. A visitor was considered family, and an injury done to a protected guest could lead to a blood feud. In many respects, the premium placed on hospitality by this warlike people, who at the same time prided themselves on their raids on their neighbors, resembles the tradition of hospitality manifested by the Aryan Pashtun tribes of distant Afghanistan.[4]

Thus this proud, warlike, Sufi mountain people may have remained, living in relative isolation on the edges of Christian Europe, engaging in their timeless pursuits of raiding lowlanders and farming. But in the nineteenth century the "White tsars" living in far-off St. Petersburg, Russia, decided to include the Chechens' homeland in their expanding empire and "civilize" the region's wild inhabitants. In so doing, the Russians were to plant the seeds for centuries of violence and begin a war that continues in various forms to this day.[5]

Contact Russia's Initial Probes

The Russians first became involved in the Caucasus following their conquest of the last remnant of the once-mighty Mongol Tatars, the Black Sea state of the Crimean Khanate. After absorbing this troublesome raiding state in 1783, the Russians moved eastward from the Crimean Peninsula and into the plains north of the Caucasus.[6] It was this inexorable progress, which was motivated largely by the urge to gain new lands and glory, that was to leave a bitter legacy between the Caucasian Muslim highlanders and the modernizing Russian Empire.

After the fall of the Muslim bastion of the Crimean Khanate, the Russians began a series of advances into the Caucasus Mountains that culminated in their bold crossing of this range and annexation of the Christian land of Georgia on the southern flanks of the Caucasus. Soon thereafter, Russian settlers began to pour into the foothills of the northern Caucasus and to displace the region's indigenous inhabitants. The first Caucasian people to flee the relentless advance of the Russians were the Nogai Tatars shepherds of the north Caucasian plains. Taking handfuls of soil from the graves of their ancestors, this Turkic Mongol herding people abandoned their native steppes in Europe's last great nomadic migration and settled in the sheltering lands of the Ottoman sultan.[7]

As the Russians probed deeper into the dark forests of the lower slopes of the Caucasus Mountains known to the Chechens as the Bash Cam (Melting Mountains), they clashed with fierce local tribes, who were quick to react to Russia's incursions. It was at this time that the Russians encountered ferocious resistance from the two largest tribal conglomerations inhabiting the north Caucasus flank, namely, the Circassians (in the west) and the Chechens (in the east).

In the initial periods, Russian warfare with the Caucasus's two great raiding peoples took on an almost sportsmanlike quality. Tsarist officers in search of glory, such as the great Russian authors Tolstoy, Pushkin, and Lermontov, cut their teeth in clashes with their respected highlander adversaries. This conformed with the flamboyant highlanders' traditional form of warfare, which consisted of raids, daring skirmishes, personal duels, and martial proofs of manhood that were recounted in the highlanders' colorful epics.

In many ways, the Chechen mountaineers' ritualistic form of warfare resembled the cattle raids of the ancient peoples of Europe, such as the Celts or their descendants the Scottish highlanders. The mountaineers' traditional form of combat was most certainly not the prolonged, regimented sort of warfare of the Napoleonic era or the professional armies of Russia.

In all fairness to the Russians, who have been condemned for their harsh treatment of the Caucasian natives in the nineteenth century, it should be noted that the raids for plunder launched by the Chechens into the lowlands claimed by Russia constituted a perpetual menace to the tsar's newly conquered lands. While these pillaging razzias were considered the honorable pastime of Chechen *abreks*, they took their toll on the lowlanders whom the Russian conquerors claimed as subjects.

Russia's feared frontier generals had no qualms about responding to these raids with an overwhelming display of retaliatory force. Thus the warfare in the Caucasus developed a rhythm that often had little to do with the court of the tsars in distant St. Petersburg. In this respect, it was similar to the warfare that emerged in North America between the Plains Indians and the expanding Americans.

As the tempo of this mounting conflict between cultures accelerated, the Chechens continued to fight in the way of their ancestors. A Chechen ballad from this period, which describes the sad fate of a legendary *abrek* raider, captures the martial spirit of the Chechens, who relished conflict with their Russian neighbors as proof of their manhood:

The bold Hamzad, with the gallant horsemen of Ghikh, crosses the left bank of the Terek [a river that separated the lands of the expanding Russians from the Caucasian foothills] and leaves the river behind him.

The brave Hamzad has crossed the Terek and entered the Nogai Steppes. He has captured a herd of white horses and recrossed the Terek, driving it before him.

At the dawn of day he crossed it and drove the herd into the brushwood of Shirvan on the Hill of the Circassians. There was danger by day, and the riders were tired. They halted at Shirvan-Koulee and hid their spoil in the thicket.

When he had hidden his booty and his companions in the wood, Hamzad ascended a high *kurgan* [ancient burial mound], and looked through his glass to see if the Russians were coming.

Hamzad looks and sees a numerous band darkening the place where he had forded the Terek. As fast as a black cloud driven by the wind that band comes galloping on his traces.

Seeing the multitude he went down from the *kurgan* and said to his companions "They follow as fast as the wind follows the clouds. Be not afraid, we will fight like famished leopards."

And again he said unto them "We will slaughter the horses and the cattle and surround ourselves with them as with a rampart. So shall we be able to defend ourselves."

His companions joyfully gave their consent. They cut the throats of the horses and stabbed the horned cattle and made a strong fence round themselves.

And again Hamzad spoke to his companions and said "The *Naib* [Muslim deputy ruler] of Ghikh, Akhverdi Mahoma, stands likewise no doubt with his men on the [distant] hill-top."

"When he hears the noise of our fighting with the Russians he will fly to our aid like a bird of the air." But this he said but to hearten his companions.

Hamzad sat down with his riders behind the bloody breastwork and ordered one to keep watch on the enemy. The sentinels stand gazing earnestly.

And lo! a horseman gallops out in front of the crowd—[he is] Prince Kagherman—and coming within hail he cries out [to the surrounded Chechens] "What prince's people are you?"

Hamzad laughed "We know no princes nor want to, we are riders from Ghikh, and came for spoil."

"Art thou not Hamzad?" asked Kagherman.

"I am Hamzad!"

"It is a pity, Hamzad, that you came here. A Russian band has overtaken you—overtaken and surrounded you. Unless you can grow wings as of the migrant birds and fly up in the air you cannot escape. The Russian commander has sent me; he will spare you if you surrender without fighting."

To this Hamzad answered "I came not here, oh Kagherman, for want of money; I came to win the death of *gazavat* [holy war]. And were I to surrender to thee, all of the people of Ghikh would laugh me to scorn.

"As a wolf tired and hungry longs to reach the forest, as a horse unfed and mettlesome the fresh clean meadow—so do I and my companions thirst for a fight to the death. Nor do I fear thee, Kagherman. I laugh at all thy force, for our hope is in God, the all-powerful."

And again Hamzad said to Kagherman "Ever we sought booty and gold, but for such a day as this there is nothing so precious as black gunpowder." And again he said "Gold is not money today, today the trusty Crimean flint is pure gold."

Kagherman went back to the Russian commander and told him that Hamzad refused to surrender. And Hamzad returned to his rampart and sat down with his companions.

Then the troops came up and began firing and Hamzad and his riders fired back. Thick was the smoke of their firing, and Hamzad said "May this day be accursed! So hot it is that we have no shade but that of our swords."

And again he said "How thick is the smoke, how dark the day! Our only light is the flash of our guns."

And again Hamzad said "The houris [beautiful women] of paradise look down on us from their windows in Heaven and wonder, they dispute together whose they shall be, and she who falls to the braver of us will vaunt it before her friend—and she who falls to the less brave will blush for shame, and she will close the lattice on him and turn away, and if any of you plays the coward this day may his face be black when he stands before God!"

But Hamzad thought in his heart that while that death was upon him, he could hope no more.

High in the heavens he saw the birds flying and called to them "Oh birds of the air! Give our last greeting, our ultimate salutation, to the *Naib* of Ghikh, Akhverdi Mahoma. Greet also from us the beautiful ones, the damsels fair, and tell them that our proud breasts serve to stop Russian bullets—tell them that our wish was to rest after death in the graveyard at Ghikh, where our sisters would have wept on our tombs, and all the people would have sorrowed—but God grants no such grace. Not the sobbing of our sisters will be heard above us but the howling of famished wolves. Not relatives in troops will gather round, but a flock of ravens swart."

"And tell them too, on the Circassian hill, in the land of the infidel, bare blades in hand, we lie dead. The ravens pick out our eyes, the wolves tear our flesh."[8]

As becomes obvious from both Chechen ballads and Russian records from the frontier, raids such as that commemorated in the ballad of Hamzad were a constant source of tension in this turbulent region. The highlanders in general, and the Chechens in particular, made turbulent neighbors, and the mountaineers engaged in raids for booty and captives on the lowlander populations as a way of life. One nineteenth-century Russian contemporary of the Chechens recorded this people as follows:

Chechens are tall and well built. Their women are beautiful. They are considered to be gay and witty, "the Frenchmen of the Caucasus," and impressionable, but they are less liked than the Circassians, owing to their suspicious, treacherous, and harsh nature—probably from ages of armed struggle. They are known for dauntless bravery, deftness, and hardiness and are cool headed in a fight—qualities long recognized even by their enemies. In time of peace they rob. Cattle rustling and abducting women and children—even it if be at the risk of their lives or having to crawl miles—are their favorite occupation . . .

In the period of independence the Chechens, unlike the Circassians, had no feudal system or class divisions. They lived in free communities governed by people's assemblies. "We are all *uzdeni*," they explained, that is, free and equal.[9]

The following Russian account of the raids of the highlanders brings the turbulent nature of this frontier to life and helps explain the Russian motives for aiming to subdue the predatory mountain tribes:

In 1809 during the attack of a party of Kabardians [a noble Circassian tribe] on the village of Kamennobrodsk, 58 inhabitants were wounded, 51 people were taken captive. By comparison, in repulsing the attack, 12 soldiers died, 19 were wounded, including one officer. In the attacks on the fort of Kruglolsk on the 13th of May 1823, 50 local people were killed, 41 wounded, and 302 were taken captive (the losses to the army—17 killed, 10 wounded). In the attacks of Gazi Mullah [a Dagestani war leader] on the city of Kizilyar [in Dagestan] on the 1st of November 1831, 103 peaceful inhabitants were killed, 29 were wounded and 155 were taken prisoner.[10]

Raids of the sort that were deplored in this Russian record and glorified in the ballad of Hamzad failed to prevent the Russians from systematically establishing forts in the Caucasian foothills to subdue the restless mountaineers. As the Russians moved deeper and deeper into the Caucasus, they established military lines and protected them with wooden forts that resembled those built by the American military in the lands of the nineteenth-century Plains Indians. Among the most important fortresses established by the Russians to control the turbulent highlanders was a fortress city constructed in the lowlands of Chechnya named Grozny, a name that in Russian translates to "The Terrible" or, more accurately, "The Foreboding."

While the highlanders had no way of knowing it at the time, the establishment of Grozny in 1818 was a signal that the Russian conquest of the Caucasus had entered a new stage. Having subdued the Caucasus lowlands, Russia's generals now were preparing to march deeper into the foothills and break the spirit of the troublesome highlanders once and for all. Russia's total war with the Chechens and surrounding tribes was about to begin.

Empire The "Pacification" of the Highlanders

No general was more feared for his brutality in conquering the Chechens than Aleksey Petrovich Yermolov, also known as "the Butcher," who subdued the Chechens in the 1830s.[11] This feared conqueror, whose contempt for the Caucasians led him to engage in all sorts of atrocities against the Chechens, once commented, "Condescension in the eyes of Asiatics is a sign of weakness, and out of pure humanity I am inexorably severe. One execution saves hundreds of Russians from destruction and thousands of Muslims from treason."[12] Yermolov's policy of executing conquered mountaineers to "save them from treason" not surprisingly succeeded in spreading fear throughout a region that had always had a more symbolic form of ritual warfare.

Israeli scholar Moshe Gammer relates, "When he decided to push the Chechens south of the Sunja he surrounded a village and slaughtered all its inhabitants—men, women and children. On other occasions, captured women were sold as slaves or distributed to Russian officers, so that winter quarters 'for the officers, at least, the Commander-in-Chief setting the example, the time passed pleasantly enough in the company of native wives.'"[13]

In the face of Yermolov's brutality, the stunned highlanders initially failed to forge a united front. Those Chechens living in the lowlands of the Caucasus surrendered to the might of the Russian armies in order to preserve their exposed villages from total destruction. Russia's transition from a gradual conquest to a more concentrated effort to subdue the region appeared to be paying off. But as Schaefer points out, "Because Yermolov was only concerned with coercive behavior, he lost the battle for the Chechen hearts and minds, and poisoned entire generations."[14]

It was at this time that many Russian peasants settled in the plains of northern Chechnya, a region known as the above-Terek district, and began displacing the Chechen lowlanders. In the process, the lowlander Chechens became more Russified, their clan system weakened, and they became less prone to joining the uprisings of holy warriors from the mountains. In Russian terms, these lowland Chechens had become "civilized."

After pursuing a successful policy of divide and rule among the lowland Chechens, the Russians subsequently were able to subdue most of the tough fighters of the lands lying to the east of Chechnya in the mountainous land of Dagestan. Like the Chechen lowlanders, the Avars, Darghins, Lezgins, and other Dagestani tribes of the eastern Caucasus sullenly submitted to the might of Russia's professional armies in order to preserve their welfare and their very lives.

In the conquest of Dagestan, however, many local rulers made agreements with the Russians that did not reflect the feelings of their people.

These Russian-dominated quislings quickly earned the contempt of their devout Muslim countrymen, who despised the Orthodox Russian conquerors as infidels. For in Dagestan, Islam was older than in the lands of the Chechens, and the Dagestanis had a deeper attachment to the faith of Muhammad.

But the Russians encountered even more difficulties in the west. The Circassians, from the western Caucasus as previously mentioned, stubbornly refused to submit to Russia's battalions, and the tragic fate of this tribe was to serve as a warning to all its neighbors. In response to the Circassians' stubborn resistance, imperial Russia pursued a scorched-earth policy that saw their homeland ravaged, orchards cut down, fields destroyed, mountain villages burnt, and this once-proud people ethnically cleansed from its ancient hearth. It was to be modern Europe's first genocide. The slaughter and expulsion of as many as three-quarters of a million Circassians, a noble people who had long been respected by their neighbors in the Caucasus, spread ripples of fear throughout the mountains.[15]

The following eyewitness account of Russian operations in Circassia captures the nature of this all-out war, which surpassed the colonial conquests of the French and English in its brutality:

> The mountain *auls* (villages) were burnt by the hundreds. The snow had only just melted away, but it was before the trees had become clothed in their greenery; the crops (of the highlanders) were eaten by the horses or even trampled down. If we managed to catch the inhabitants of the *auls* unawares they were immediately led away under military escort to the Black Sea and then sent to Turkey. How many times did it happen that in the huts which had been hurriedly abandoned upon our approach we found warm gruel with a spoon in it on the table, clothing which was being repaired with the needle still in it, and various children's toys which looked as though they had been spread out on the floor next to a child. Sometimes—to the credit of our soldiers—very seldom, bestial atrocities were committed.[16]

While the above author seemed proud of the fact that Russians rarely carried out "bestial atrocities," such claims are not borne out by other eyewitness accounts. The Russian subjugation of the Circassians was a bloody affair marked by numerous atrocities. One Russian officer quoted in Walter Richmond's groundbreaking work, *The Circassian Genocide*, wrote, "On the road our eyes were met with a staggering image: corpses of women, children, elderly persons, torn to pieces and half-eaten by dogs; deportees emaciated by hunger and disease, almost too weak to move their legs, collapsing from exhaustion and becoming prey to dogs while still alive."[17]

The last pitiful remnants of the Circassians fled from their burning villages and rampaging Russian soldiers to the coastal town of Sochi. There the terrified survivors boarded ships and fled to the sanctuary of the Muslim Ottoman Empire. While few people today are aware of the Circassians because they were largely exterminated, Doku Umarov, the Chechen terrorist leader who took control of the insurgency in 2006 and created the Caucasian Emirate terrorist group, tried to remind the world of their cruel fate. On the eve of the 2014 Winter Olympics held in Sochi, Russia, Doku Umarov lashed out at the Russians and launched three suicide bombings that took the lives of forty people in the nearby Russian town of Volgograd. He warned Russian president Vladimir Putin that holding the Olympics in Sochi was "satanic dancing on the bones of our ancestors."[18]

While the Circassians largely have been forgotten (their survivors peacefully protested Putin's 2014 Winter Olympics), at the time the annihilation of this race caused considerable consternation in Britain. The conquest and total expulsion of this people, the first genocide in modern Europe, was also meant to send a message to all the other highlander tribes. While the Caucasian tribes could sustain a short-term conflict, Russia's massive, professional armies could outlast them in duration and overwhelm them with sheer numbers, determination, and systematic brutality.

As the Russians' unprecedented punitive operations against the Circassians made abundantly clear, resistance to the tsar resulted in total warfare and collective punishment. This mode of warfare applied not just to the warriors, but also to all noncombatants: women, children, the elderly. If a fighter from a nearby village fired on their troops, all the villagers were held responsible for his actions by the Russian conquerors and were punished. Those suspected of providing succor to the highlander *abreks* were held responsible, and whole districts were torched, their cattle driven off, and their crops destroyed in Russia's punitive missions.

With the expulsion of many nineteenth-century Chechens to the Ottoman Empire and the subjugation of the majority of those who remained, the Russians had reason to believe that the north Caucasus had been subdued by the late 1830s. After this date, members of the Russian nobility could ride in carriages through the Chechen villages observing the "quaint local costumes" of "the newly tamed highland natives" and revel in the rugged natural beauty of the empire's latest acquisition.

As the highlanders were to show their Russian "masters" on many occasions, however, they were far from subdued. It took only the smallest of sparks to set off an inferno that could sweep through their valleys and set this "pacified" province on fire. As one British observer ominously noted, "No impartial reader of the Russian accounts of this period can doubt that they [the Chechens] were cruelly oppressed."[19] For in spite of the fact that the Russians had written off the lowlanders as a people who had been humbled by the power of imperial Russia, this proud people seethed under the scepter of Russia and prepared to revolt.

The spark that was to set the conquered mountaineers on the road to holy war against the Russian conquerors was to take the form of a red-bearded Dagestani holy man. That holy man's name was Imam Shamil, the Lion of Dagestan, and his revolt was to cost tens of thousands their lives and to earn the Caucasus the title of "Graveyard of the Russian Empire."

Resistance

It is probably true to say that for the Russian state, Chechnya is a hated obsession, a focus of the deepest wells of ethnic and religious contempt and fear. A strain in Russian thought, voiced by people ranging from the Tsars to the soldiers, has called for the destruction of this entire nation.
— Robert Seeley, *Russo-Chechen Conflict, 1800–2000*[1]

Everywhere there are mountains, everywhere forests, and the Chechens are fierce and tireless fighters.
— General Tournau, 1832[2]

The Flames of Resistance

The Chechens, whose homeland was devastated by the conquering Russians and whose ancient liberty was lost, were more profoundly shaped by their experience of conquest and subjugation than the victorious Russians.[3] In the numbed aftermath of the initial Russian conquest of the north Caucasus, scores of Chechen hamlets had been transformed into smoldering ruins, and the ritual wailing of the Chechens mourning lost loved ones drifted through the mountain vales. Their laments proclaimed to the world that the Chechen highlanders, untamed since the dawn of history, had at long last been subdued.

While a Russian soldier who served on the Russian general Yermolov's staff may have opined "who cares for history?" the proud Chechens have a different relationship with history. Like many conquered peoples, from the Scots and Welsh to the Native American Indians, the Chechens have defined their identity around their past defeats. The Chechens' transgenerational ballads of desperate last stands and holy fighters who were "martyred" provide a residue of ritualized hostility and symbolic grievances whose legacy is still felt in the north Caucasus today.

For over a century, the Chechens have based their collective identity on opposition to the Russian and later Soviet states that conquered and oppressed them. As a result, it is not surprising that their culture glorifies the notion of arms in defense of liberty. In the Chechens' martial culture, the events of the mid-nineteenth century are not relegated to the dustbin of history, they are very much alive today.

For military historians, the nineteenth-century Chechen uprising against the Russians appears as a dress rehearsal for the twenty-first century conflict between the secessionist Chechen rebels and the post-Soviet Russian Federation. As in the Russia of the twenty-first century, in the nineteenth century the occupying tsarist forces arbitrarily arrested many Chechens suspected of being insurgents, launched preemptive sweeps (known as *zachistkas* in the modern wars) in search of rebels, and engaged in a policy of collective punishment.

Having brutally subdued the Chechens and their neighbors, the nineteenth-century Russians also requisitioned their possessions, offended local Muslim sensibilities with their licentious behavior, and supplemented their meager military pay through "taxes" arbitrarily levied on the conquered population. After subduing the Chechen lowlands and neighboring territory of Dagestan, tsarist forces confiscated the natives' crops, attempted to forcefully regulate the mountaineers (who respected no outside authority), and most important, attempted to disarm this war-like people, who considered their weapons to be the supreme marker of their highlander identity.

To the nineteenth-century Chechens and other mountain peoples, arms were both a sign of manhood and an important means of defense against the inroads of neighboring raiders. They were an ancient part of the Chechens' martial culture. Russia's military leaders must have foreseen the outrage their policy of forcefully collecting weapons would cause among the proud highlanders. But few could have foreseen the magnitude of their violent response to this order when it was channeled by one Imam Shamil into a full-blown *jihad* (holy war).

The Russian military's attempt to forcefully wrest the Chechens' weapons from their hands was the straw that broke the proverbial camel's back. This single act transformed the simmering fury of this subjugated mountain people into a full-blown rebellion.

As the Russians launched weapons collection sweeps, the mountain people sought a leader to unite them in expelling their hated oppressors. While most Chechens resembled the famed *abrek* Hamzad in "recognizing no prince," their clan leaders wisely realized that they needed a strong war leader to unify them and help them rid themselves of their tormentors.

It was at this time (1834) that a charismatic imam (a religious leader) appeared among the Avars, the most numerous highlander tribe living nearby in Dagestan. This legendary Avar strategist would succeed, for the first time, in uniting all of the quarreling mountain tribes of the northeastern Caucasus and forming a united fighting force to resist their common Slavic enemy. In the process, Shamil also would succeed in building a short-lived Islamic state uniting the Muslims of the north Caucasus in an alliance that he hoped would enable them to drive the Christian invaders from their lands. It is this state that the Dagestani *jamaats* (military and terror units) and Chechen insurgents in the post-2009 Caucasus aim to reconstruct as part of the so-called Caucasian Emirate.

The nineteenth-century Shamil was a devout Sufi Muslim and a visionary who, like Muhammad ibn abd al-Wahhab (an eighteenth-century puritanical religious reformer in Saudi Arabia who spread an intolerant fundamentalist version of Islam known as Wahhabism), sought to cleanse the pagan corruptions found in Dagestani Islam. As in many Muslim frontier lands that were undergoing encroachment by European colonial powers, Shamil's militant Sufism provided new hope in the face of a creeping sense of defeat. Shamil's anti-Russian Sufi brotherhood also provided a higher sense of spirituality for many Muslims in the region who had never strictly adhered to the tenets of the holy Qu'ran.

Shamil preached a new form of Islam, which sought to cleanse the local versions of Islam of their mystical "corruptions" and pagan holdovers. He also sought to provide the highlanders with a sense of spiritual unity in the face of Russian policies of divide and conquer. As the nineteenth-century Wahhabi Saudi fundamentalists had done in Arabia, Shamil sought to cleanse the Muslim highlanders' beliefs, eliminate their worship of local saints and mystics, and abolish their freewheeling ways, which involved drinking, smoking, and singing. Only by teaching the lax highlanders purified Islam could Shamil transform them into dedicated holy warriors. Shamil clearly understood that the mountain tribes could never withstand the bayonets and cannons of the mighty Russian *kafirs* (unbelievers) if they were divided. But united by a new strict form of shariah Islamic law, they could launch a full-scale guerilla war that would shake the very foundations of the Russian Empire.[4]

As Imam Shamil's message of defensive jihad against the infidels resounded across the valleys of the Russian-occupied Caucasus Mountains, it radicalized the local Islamic culture. It also created a unity of purpose among this divided people, who had never had a fanatical adherence to their faith prior to this. While the easygoing Chechens instinctively disliked Shamil's austere interpretation of Islam, they were willing to submit grudgingly to Shamil's *naibs* (deputies) if it meant expelling the hated Russians. In so doing, their desperate struggle with the Russians over land and freedom took on religious undertones and gradually became a full-fledged holy war.

Mountain Jihad

By 1840 the Caucasus, which many Russian officials had prematurely declared "pacified," was on fire. As the Russians tried to confiscate their guns, the mountain people spontaneously took to the hills and commenced a coordinated guerilla struggle against the tsar's armies under the black banners of Shamil. Even the wild Chechens, who were known for their inability to surrender their prerogatives for self-rule to any man, agreed to submit to Shamil. The Chechens soon formed the most deadly contingent of his trans-Caucasian resistance army.

Having succeeded in uniting the prickly highlander peoples of Dagestan, such as the Avars, Dargins, Lezgins, and Kumyks, with the Chechens, Shamil unleashed a holy war on the Russian Empire. A Russian officer described the electrifying effect of Shamil's call for jihad among the previously disunited mountaineers as follows:

> He threatened the enemy north, east, west and south, kept them continually on the move, dispersed his commandos to their homes, gathered them again as if by magic, and aided by the extraordinary mobility of his mounted troops who required no baggage, nor any equipment or supplies but what each individual carried with him, swooped down on the Russians continually where least expected.[5]

Another officer wrote:

> Establishing a new mode of operations to be constantly followed in the future, almost always successfully, they avoided pitched battle with our forces, thanks to their amazing speed. Our columns were brought to extreme exhaustion by trying to chase them.[6]

Yet another Russian commented:

> We have never had in the Caucasus an enemy so savage and dangerous as Shamil. Owing to a combination of circumstances his rule has acquired a religious-military character, the same by which at the beginning of Islamism Muhammad's sword shook three quarters of the Universe.[7]

The Chechens quickly began to play a prominent role in the united north Caucasian struggle against the Russians. Shamil knew that the resistance to the might of Russia's imperial armies could be sustained only if this people's fierce warriors kept up their struggle side by side with the mountain people of Dagestan. For this reason, Shamil fought tirelessly to convert the Chechens to his puritanical version of Islam and to instill in them a devotion to the cause of the anti-Russian jihad.

Russian commanders on the front lines at the time noticed that many Chechens heeded Shamil's call and joined his *murids* (holy warriors). In Russian terms, these Chechens had become more "fanatical" in their determination to defend their families and villages and their willingness to die for the cause of the jihad.

It became obvious to many Russian officers in the field that Russia's harsh treatment of the Chechens had inspired a new strain of fiercely anti-Russian, xenophobic Islam among the Muslim clans of Chechnya. While it must be stated that the majority of Chechens resented Shamil's representatives for attempting to enforce shariah fundamentalism in their villages, even those who did not join his *murids* were more than willing to join his holy war if it meant destroying the hated Russian occupiers.

Regardless of Chechen society's perceptions of the Islamic fighters, in the nineteenth-century wars, Chechens who took up the novel cause of the jihad proved to be some of the fiercest guerrillas the Russian imperial forces ever had encountered. As the Chechen resistance to the tsar increased in the 1840s, the Russian army commenced a massive deforestation campaign designed to destroy the trees of Chechnya, which provided cover for the Chechen fighters.[8] In addition to systematically chopping down ancient forests, the Russians directly occupied the villages of the Chechen lowlanders and punished those suspected of supporting Shamil's *murids* in the mountains by destroying their farms and livestock.

As the Russians increasingly became frustrated with their failure to destroy Shamil's elusive guerrillas, the differences between the tsar's armies and the Chechen fighters became glaringly obvious. The Russian invading armies were largely made up of serf conscripts taken from the villages of the Russian heartlands and forced to fight in the alien and foreboding mountains of the Caucasus. The Russian conscript soldier, while stolid and able to withstand all sorts of privations, was often not inclined to engage in acts of individual heroism that might reward him with an unmarked grave in the mountains. Rather, his objective was to survive his encounters with the feared Chechen irregulars, who were fighting to defend their homeland.

What the Russians lacked in fighting spirit, however, they compensated for in sheer numbers. Their massive imperial armies in the Caucasus had as many as two hundred thousand soldiers in them by the mid-nineteenth century and dwarfed the seasonal fighting forces of their Muslim highlander adversaries.

While the Russians could throw tens of thousands of Slavic peasants into their imperial enterprise, the numerically inferior highlanders could not afford to sustain the level of losses that Russia's generals found acceptable. What the Chechen fighters lacked in numbers, however, they more than made up for in fighting élan. They were a martial people fighting for the defense of their families, homeland, and increasingly, their faith. The Chechens' ability to fight on against the odds, however, required more than blind devotion. According to one account, their success stemmed largely from the fact that "each fighter was armed and maintained by his family, each fighting unit by its clan. His [Shamil's] 'army' constituted, in essence, a people's volunteer corps."[9]

The average Chechen fighter had more to fight for in the defense of his family and clan than the Russian soldier serving far from his home among the wild tribes of the Caucasus. This is a truism that certainly applies to the sad fate of tens of thousands of frightened Russian Federation conscripts who served in Chechnya during the more recent post-Soviet wars.

In the time of Imam Shamil, the Chechens also employed military tactics that resembled those of their modern descendants in the wars from 1994 to 2015. To make up for their deficiency in numbers, for example, the nineteenth-century Chechen fighters avoided direct combat with the larger Russian armies whenever possible. The mountaineers' warfare usually took the form of ambushes, guerrilla strikes, and attacks on isolated outposts. On occasion, however, the Chechen guerrilla fighters also proved to be capable of launching frontal assaults on Russian columns and formations.

A nineteenth-century account of the highlanders' battle stratagems depicts the sort of fighting skills and tactics that have made the Chechens such feared adversaries to this very day:

It is true that the Caucasian guerrillas rarely expose themselves in a regular pitched battle, and as they are perfectly acquainted with the country and its localities, their losses, compared with those of the Russians, cannot be very great . . . As an irregular soldier, the Caucasian guerrilla has not an equal in any country . . .

Indeed, when we consider the nature of the country, the strength of the defiles, the warlike spirit of the people, their continual wars with the Russians, and [their] determination to maintain their independence at whatever cost, we cannot wonder that, with such training, they should be the most accomplished guerillas any country ever produced, nor that they should undertake the most hazardous and romantic expeditions, and rarely fail of success; for so great is their cunning and address that no enemy can calculate on their movements, appearing to be endowed with the attribute of ubiquity.

In addition to acting in small bodies under their respective chiefs, they prove a constant source of disquietude, and give perpetual occupation to whole brigades of Russian soldiers, even within sight of their own forts; and such is their hardihood, and so great their hatred for the enemy, that, when in want of ammunition, they will lie in wait for days in the thickets till some unfortunate stragglers, or it may be a whole detachment, appear in sight, when they are instantly attacked.[10]

While the Chechen cavalry skirmishers (known as *murtaziqas*) faded away before invading Russian battalions, the Chechen sharpshooters were a constant threat as the Russian battalions marched through the forests of Chechnya. The skilled Chechen marksmen took a heavy toll on the Russian columns that sought to penetrate their land and made sure that the Russians paid a price in blood for every meter of land they conquered.

Prince Bariantsky, a nineteenth-century Russian general tasked with the unenviable mission of conquering the rebellious Chechens, left the following account of losses his men faced to Chechen sharpshooters:

The mountaineers were not to be frightened by fighting. Constant warfare had given them such confidence that a few score men could engage without hesitation a column several battalions strong, and firing one shot to hundred would occasion us more loss than we would them. Fighting implies some sort of equality, and so long as they could fight, the enemy had no thought for submission.[11]

The following account of a Russian campaign, which set out with the intention to "pass through the country, ruining settlements, destroying harvests, raiding herds and flocks, and attacking the enemy wherever they had the audacity to collect in any force," captures the difficulties the Russian invaders faced in attacking the Chechens on their home turf. Once again this eyewitness account could apply to Chechen tactics in the post-Soviet Russo-Chechen Wars. Replace the muskets of the nineteenth century with modern sniper rifles and antitank grenades, and the following account could be a description of the Russian defeat in Grozny at the hands of Chechen guerillas in the winter of 1994–95:

> At that time (1832) we had not yet cut avenues through the forests. In the early "twenties," indeed, Yermoloff had cleared a distance of a musket shot on either side of the road through the well-known Goiten forest, but this had already become overgrown by an impenetrable thicket of underwood, so that we had to face warfare in Chechnya under the most difficult conditions. As opponents the Chechens merited the fullest respect, and amidst their forests and mountains no troops in the world could afford to despise them. Good shots, fiercely brave, intelligent in military affairs, they, like other inhabitants of the Caucasus, were quick to take advantage of local conditions, seize upon any mistake we made, and with incredible swiftness use it for our own destruction . . . .
>
> In the war with the Chechens, one day was like any other . . . Fighting went on from the beginning to [the] end of each march; there was the chatter of musketry, the hum of bullets; men fell; but no enemy was seen. Puffs of smoke in the jungle alone betrayed their lurking-places, and our soldiers, having nothing else to guide them, took aim at that.[12]

In the face of such relentless attacks, the Russians, like a wounded bear, struck indiscriminately at the Chechen civilians, destroying settlements, transferring conquered Chechens to easily controlled regions, settling trusted Cossacks in the pacified lowlands, and destroying the cherished Chechen forests, which offered the guerrillas refuge.

The real conquest of Chechnya actually was achieved not with the bayonet, but with the forester's axe. The denuded foothills of Chechnya are, to this day, unnaturally bare and eloquent testimony to the effectiveness of Russia's systematic campaign of deforestation. Just as the Russian Federation destroyed the "urban forest" of Grozny in its winter 1999–2000 campaign to eradicate Chechen fighters hiding there, the nineteenth-century Russians felled the ancient forests of Chechnya to flush out the guerillas who operated in their dark depths. In so doing, the remorseless Russians finally pushed the Chechens to the brink.

Caucasian Armageddon The Destruction of Chechnya

Time and again a pattern emerged in Chechnya. As the Russians launched brutal attacks on the general populace, embittered Chechens left their burnt forests and villages to join the guerillas. The Russians, in effect, proved to be excellent recruitment officers for Imam Shamil's forces. Many an ordinary Chechen threw down his plow to join the resistance out of a thirst for revenge following a Russian raid.

The great Russian writer Leo Tolstoy, who, like much of the Russian intelligentsia, knew the Caucasus and admired the Chechens for their fierce determination to resist the tsar's forces, left the following account of this process of embitterment among the nineteenth-century Chechens in his famous novel *Hadji Murat*:

> When they returned, Sado [a Chechen] found his house destroyed; the roof had caved in, the door and pillars of the balcony were burnt, and the interior was wrecked. The body of his son, the handsome boy with shining eyes who had thrilled at the sight of Hadji Murat, was brought to the mosque on a horse covered with a cloak. He had been bayoneted in the back . . .
>
> Two ricks of hay that were there had been burnt; the apricot and cherry trees that he had planted and trained were smashed and, worst of all, the beehives were burnt. The wail of women was heard in all the houses and on the square, where two more bodies were brought. Small children howled with their mothers . . .
>
> The fountain was polluted, obviously on purpose, so that no water could be taken from it. The mosque was also defiled, and the *Mullah* was cleaning it with his pupils. No one spoke of the hatred for the Russians. The feelings, which all the Chechens, young and old experienced, was

stronger than hatred. It was not hatred, but a refusal to recognize these
Russian dogs as people, and such a disgust, horror and incomprehension
of the monstrous cruelty of these creatures that the urge to kill them,
like the urge to kill rats, poisonous spiders, and wolves, was as natural a
feeling as the instinct of self-preservation.

The villagers had the choice of remaining in their homes and restoring
with fearful efforts everything that had been built up so laboriously
and so lightly and thoughtlessly destroyed, expecting every moment a
repetition of the same destruction, or, against the laws of their religion
and despite the revulsion and scorn they felt for the Russians, submitting
to them.

The elders prayed and decided unanimously to send envoys to Shamil
asking him for help, and at once started to repair the destruction.[13]

One cannot overestimate the impact that the telling and retelling of
the accounts of such Russian atrocities had on the Chechens' views of
the Russians even decades after these events. The feeling of rage, mingled
with a sense of injustice felt by the Chechens in the aftermath of such
unprecedented destruction shaped future generations that grew up as
subjects of the Russian tsar in the late nineteenth and early twentieth
centuries.

For many Chechens and Dagestanis who were driven to despair by
the ability of the Russians to field larger and larger armies, there was an
almost-millenarian sense of doom as the years of fighting became decades. By the 1850s, the highlanders felt that their way of life was coming
to an end and the fabric of their society was being torn asunder. It was
this sense of doom, combined with a growing sense of spirituality and
fatalism, that drove many Chechens to fight alongside Shamil's ascetic
warriors even as their cause appeared finished.

The following eyewitness account of the destruction of a lowland
Chechen village by a Russian battalion captures the growing sense of hatred, despair, and determination evinced by many Chechens who chose
to fight to the finish rather than accept foreign rule:

The defenders listened to the proposal [to surrender to the Russians],
conferred together, and then a half-naked Chechen, black with smoke
came out, made a short speech, followed by a volley from all the

loopholes. What he said was this: "The only grace we ask of the Russians is to let our families know we died as we lived, refusing submission to any foreign yoke."

Orders were now given to [set] fire [to] the *saklias* [stone houses] from all sides. The sun had set, and the picture of destruction and ruin was lighted only by the red glow of the flames. The Chechens, firmly resolved to die, set up their death-song, loud at first, but sinking lower and lower as their numbers diminished under the influence of fire and smoke.

However, death by fire is a terrible agony, such as all had not strength to bear. There was a flash; a bullet whistled past over our ears, and brandishing his sword, a Chechen dashed straight at us. Artarshtchikov let the raging desperado come within ten paces, quietly took aim, and put a bullet in his bare chest. The Chechen sprang high in the air, fell, rose again to his feet, stretched himself to his full length, and bending slowly forward, fell dead on his native soil.

Five minutes later the scene was repeated; another sprang out, fired his gun, and brandishing his sword, broke through two lines of sharp-shooters, to fall bayoneted by the third. The burning *saklias* began to fall asunder, scattering sparks on the trampled gardens . . . Not one Chechen was taken alive; seventy two men ended their lives in the flame!

The last act of the bloody drama was played out; night covered the scene. Each one had done his duty according to his conscience; the chief actors had gone their way to eternity: the rest, together with the mere spectators, with hearts like lead, sought the refuge of their tents; and maybe more than one, in the depth of his being, asked himself, why must such things be? Is there no room for all on this earth, without distinction of speech or faith?[14]

As scenes of this sort were repeated throughout Chechnya, Shamil's fighters increasingly found themselves hemmed in. Russia's decades-long war of attrition was finally takings its toll on the highland villagers, who paid the price for Shamil's increasingly futile resistance.

In addition to engaging in total warfare against the highlanders, Russia's modern armies had a growing technological advantage over their quasi-medieval opponents. With the aid of sophisticated new weapons, such as faster-firing, quick-loading rifles and, most important, portable field cannons, the Russians were often able to avoid hand-to-hand com-bat with the Chechen fighting men and defeat them at a distance.

In the face of similar superiority in numbers and weaponry, the Che-chen and Dagestani resistance fighters of the nineteenth century found that the villages that supported their struggle were increasingly falling into Russian hands. In the face of relentless Russian advances, Shamil's forces retreated deeper and deeper into the gorges of Chechnya and Dagestan, where Shamil made a desperate last stand.

In 1859 Shamil finally was surrounded by a Russian army and captured, thus bringing an end to the united jihad of the Dagestanis and Chechens. As the mighty Lion of Dagestan was led down from the mountains to cap-tivity in Russia, the highlanders' dream of retaining their ancient freedom came to an end.

Aftermath The Legacy of the Russian Conquest

Largely as a result of the ferocious defense of the highlands by mountain *gazis* (holy warriors), such as Shamil and two earlier imams, it took the Russian Empire not five, or ten, years to subdue the northern Caucasus, but over sixty. This was to be the most drawn-out war the empire ever embarked on. It was with good reason that the Caucasus became known as "The Graveyard of the Russian Empire."

As for the conquered Chechens, when the cannon smoke finally cleared from their burnt and deforested valleys, it left a landscape of toppled minarets, gutted villages, and denuded hills inhabited by an embittered people who dreamed of revenge and freedom. In many ways the following description of the destruction wrecked on the Circassian highland villages by the Russian armies applied to the hamlets of the Chechens as well:

> At the end of the 1830s, when the Russians began to construct coastal strongholds, the entire coast and mountain belt adjacent to it was an elaborately cultivated oasis where, alongside wild, impregnable cliffs and eternal forests (now relentlessly felled in all the more accessible places), nestled fine vineyards and lush meadows, even laid out here and there on artificial terraces supplied with water from man-made canals and protected from heavy downpours by artificial channels.

> But the bloody war drove out and destroyed the mountain people; their culture was exterminated, the artificial canals became choked up, terraces, which had cost so much work, crumbled. The spacious gardens and fine vineyards were partly cut down during the war and the period when the country was settled by the Russians, or became wild and overgrown, so that now it is difficult to determine where the thicket intertwined with wild vines ends, and where the former cultivated area begins.[15]

As this and other eyewitness accounts make abundantly clear, for all of the nineteenth-century Russian authors' musings on the glory of the "civilizing" conquest of this majestic mountain chain, the Russian subjugation of the Caucasus was a cruel and inhumane affair even by the standards of the time. The Russian conquest of Chechnya was a bloody enterprise replete with butchery, ethnic cleansing, total warfare, and every manner of colonial excess. For the nineteenth-century Chechens who surveyed their scorched fields, buried their slain loved ones, rebuilt their desecrated places of worship, and lived with the knowledge that they were no longer a free people, there was cold comfort in the knowledge that they had suffered for the greater glory of the tsar, Orthodoxy, and Mother Russia.

Having recognized the brutal nature of the Russian conquest of the Chechens, it should, however, be stated that the Russian subjugation of the Caucasus was no harsher than the US government's pacification and "resettlement" of the Native American Indians or the European powers' colonization of Africa and Asia. As Russia's burgeoning people spread into the "black lands" of the southern Ukraine and into the plains of the northern Caucasus, they considered it to be their "manifest destiny" to tame the unruly tribes on their southern frontier and open up their lands for Slavic settlement. The constant plundering expeditions of the Chechens into the lands of the Terek Cossacks gave the tsar's frontier generals all the excuse they needed for declaring total war on the mountaineers.

That the nineteenth-century Chechens' raids for plunder and human captives were a threat to the Russian Empire's subjects in the lowlands and neighboring provinces is not disputed here. In the tsarist period, it was Russia's duty to protect her expanding borders from the raids of the

Chechens, and this gave her frontier generals the right then, as now, to subdue the obstreperous highlanders. Furthermore, as Richard Pierce states in his history of Russian expansion in Central Asia, "The idea that it is unethical for one people to control the destiny of another has come late in the development of the human social conscience."[16]

The previous description of the Russian campaigns of conquest in the Caucasus is meant not as a moral critique of Russia's actions in the Caucasus, rather it serves as a means for understanding the Chechens' current perceptions of their shared history with Russia. While the Russians celebrate the conquests of Yermolov, the heroes of the Chechens' history are those who made their conquest of the Caucasus as costly as possible. As a defeated nation, the heroes and martyrs of the past have much greater potency as symbols of resistance among the Chechens today than do the Russians' historical icons from this same period. One cannot understand the Chechens' contemporary relationship with the Russian authorities without understanding this people's countermemory of conquest by, and resistance to, their people's historic "Other," the Russian Empire. This tragic history, more than any mythical alliance with bin Laden's Arab-dominated Al Qaeda, explains the Chechens' rationale for fighting against Russia after the Soviet Union's dissolution in 1991.

Not surprisingly, with the collapse of the USSR in 1991 and subsequent efforts by the Kremlin to regain control of the breakaway province of Chechnya, the Chechens and neighboring Dagestanis have developed something of a cult of personality surrounding Imam Shamil and his nineteenth-century resistance to the tsars. Throughout post-Soviet Chechnya there has been an upsurge of interest in the imam's role in uniting the highlanders of Dagestan and Chechnya against Russia to create a Caucasian Emirate. One of the modern-day Chechen secessionists' most prominent field commanders, Shamil Basayev, for example, openly emulated the anti-Russian exploits of his legendary *gazi* namesake. He tried to duplicate his creation of a unified Dagestani-Chechen *jihadi* state with his 1999 raids into Dagestan. With the defeat of the Chechens in the second war, which officially ended in 2009, there has been the rise of a new Caucasian Emirate based in Dagestan, which is fighting an on-again, off-again terror campaign against Russia. It is a little-known fact that since 2009 Chechnya has been largely pacified, and it is the Dagestani-based terror organization known as the Caucasian Emirate that has carried out most anti-Russian terrorism.

For rogue field commanders such as Shamil Basayev and the terrorists of the modern-day Caucasian Emirate, the glories of Imam Shamil were and are to be emulated in a very real sense. It may have been a desire to follow in Imam Shamil's footsteps that led Basayev to lead a unit of Chechen, Arab, and Dagestani militants in invading the Russian province of Dagestan in August of 1999, thus commencing the fateful Second Russo-Chechen War.

While the memory of Imam Shamil, one of the greatest anticolonial guerillas of the nineteenth century, may have faded away in Russia, he continues to be lionized by the Chechens and neighboring Dagestanis to this very day. Certainly, the memory of Shamil remained alive among the highlanders in the years immediately following their subjugation by Russia. In the decades following Shamil's capture, the Russian imperial officials and later Soviet commissars who entered the Chechen villages to collect taxes, enforce their alien laws, confiscate guns, and arrest potential troublemakers encountered the hostile stares of a conquered population that kept to itself and stubbornly maintained its native traditions. Outsiders who traveled through this newly conquered province entered a land that was to remain the most distinctly "non-Russian" region in the entire Russian Empire right up until that state's collapse during the Russian Civil War of 1917–1923.

While the Russian government claimed the Chechens as *subjects* (or more commonly classified them as *inorodtsy*, "internal aliens"), they were never recognized as trustworthy *citizens*. In many ways, this situation prevailed through the succeeding Soviet and Russian Federation periods as well.

In response, the Chechens kept to themselves. In the timeless mountains of the northern Caucasus, the tsar's new Muslim subjects continued to hold their *zikirs* (mystical chants and dances), visit the holy grave sites of slain *murids* in search of miracles and cures, respect their village elders, and give their loyalty to their Sufi brotherhoods and clans, even as the "infidel" tsarist empire around them entered the turbulent twentieth century.

But the Chechen children, who grew up tending sheep in the shadows of the ruined highland fortresses, recalled the stories of the battles fought there by the great *gazi* Shamil. Many of them dreamed of one day emulating the legendary mountain fighter in expelling the Russian infidels. It was this collective memory of resistance that was reawakened every time the Chechens revolted against the tsars (in all, seventeen times) that kept this sullen mountain people's dreams of independence alive as the Russian Empire tottered around them.

As a people with a deep well of historical grievances and fresh memories of independence lost, the tsarist-era Chechens passed on their sense of victimization, of highlander pride and martial traditions, to a new generation. This generation was to grow up in the Communist successor to the tsarist empire, the Union of Soviet Socialist Republics (USSR), and to experience a horrific fate that surpassed even that of the tsarist conquest in its all-encompassing terror and brutality. While the Soviet heirs to the tsarist throne were to claim to have a humane solution to the "nationality problem" in the multiethnic Communist state, the Soviet leader Josef Stalin's cruel solution to the "Chechen problem" was to more closely resemble Hitler's "Final Solution" to the Jews in Europe.

Genocide

The Jews understand us best.
— Lyoma Usanov, member of a Chechen delegation
  speaking to the Holocaust Memorial Museum in
  Washington, DC, February 2000[1]

Religion is not the key to understanding Chechens;
their painful past is.
— Fred Weir, American journalist[2]

"Comrades" The Chechens in the USSR

With the collapse of the Russian Empire in 1917 and the ensuing years of civil warfare between the Bolshevik Communist "Reds" and the tsarist "Whites," the Chechens, like the other recently conquered mountain peoples, briefly regained their liberty. The memory of their former independence was fresh in the minds of the Chechens, whose elders still sang ballads lionizing the anti-Russian jihad of Imam Shamil. Like the Poles, Finns, and the peoples of the small Baltic states of Estonia, Latvia, and Lithuania, who seized the opportunity afforded by the Soviet Communist overthrow of the Russian Empire in 1917 to regain their liberty when the tsarist "Prison of Nationalities" collapsed, the Chechens took advantage of the collapse of Russian central authority to reclaim their former independence.

While other non-Russian Muslim subjects of the empire, such as the Volga Tatars, had long been subsumed in the multiethnic Russian Empire, the recently conquered Chechens still lived on stories of their old freedoms and cherished the historical memory of their grandfathers' struggle against the Russian tsars. During the course of the Russian Civil War (1917–1923), the Chechens largely remained spectators to the ebb and flow of conflicting Russian-dominated armies, although their forces fought on both sides to maintain their independence. Chechen forces, for example, fought vigorously against the White (pro-tsarist) forces of General Denikin, which sought to destroy their self-proclaimed Mountain Republic and reincorporate it into the Russian Empire.[3] This desperate struggle between the Chechens seeking their independence and tsarist forces aiming to keep the empire together at any cost resulted in tremendous Chechen loses and the destruction of their lowland city of Gudermes.

Ultimately, the tsarist Whites lost the Russian Civil War. The fact that such a large percentage of their forces were involved in suppressing the militarily proficient Caucasian highlanders instead of fighting against their Bolshevik Communist enemies did not help their cause. It should also be noted that on occasion the Chechens fought on different sides during this conflict, with the Russified Chechen lowlanders joining the tsarist Whites and the highlanders supporting the Bolshevik Communists.

By 1921 the Bolshevik Communists finally won the battle for control of the Russian Empire, and the Chechens' homeland once again was forcefully incorporated into a transcontinental state dominated by ethnic Russians, now known as the Union of Soviet Socialist Republics. On this occasion, however, the official role of the ethnic Russians in the new Communist state was to be less pronounced than it had been under the Russian tsars. In the new transethnic Soviet state, a genuine effort was made to create a *union* of nationality-based Soviet Socialist Republics (SSRs). This union of fifteen full Soviet republics was no longer considered to be an empire of, and for, the Russians. Unlike the explicitly *Russian* Empire of the Romanov tsars, the new Union of Soviet Socialist Republics was to make an effort to accommodate and even promote the non-Russian nationalities.

It is often forgotten that there were many Bolshevik Communist idealists in the USSR who genuinely worked to construct a more progressive society for the empire's "uneducated, backward, toiling masses," regardless of their nationality. Not surprisingly, the social revolution resulting from Soviet rule was to lead to vast transformations among the USSR's undeveloped Muslim peoples. During the Soviet period, the conservative, inward-looking Islamic population of the Russian provinces was forcefully modernized, secularized, and Europeanized by their Communist masters.

But the battle to drag the former Russian Empire's "backward" Muslim populations into the new Soviet era was not easy. For the Soviet commissars who arrived in the mountain villages of the Caucasus, the Chechens epitomized the very backwardness that the new Communist state sought to forcefully eradicate in the name of Marxist progress.[4] The "superstitious" Chechen men were members of impenetrable Sufi mystical brotherhoods, the women hid their faces from outsiders and were married off when they were young, the villagers lived in walled *auls* with winding alleys and stone houses that had specially designated women's quarters, and the distrustful mountaineers engaged in such "antiprogressive" activities as blood feuds, pilgrimages to local shrines for cures, and uprisings that were inevitably led by xenophobic mullahs.

It was a generation of bold, idealistic Communist Party activists and commissars who were to carry out a transformation of this region. In the

Caucasus region, the Communist Party activists transformed Chechen society (often at gunpoint) by going into the most inaccessible mountain villages and spreading mass literacy, opening schools, and exiling or executing traditional community leaders who resisted their "infidel" innovations. Instead of attending mosques for traditional religious education, a new generation of Chechen children grew up becoming Soviet Young Pioneers or members of Komsomol (the Leninist Communist Youth League).

In the process of forcing their Marxist worldview on the conservative highlanders, Communist officials also directly confronted obscurantism and stifling local traditions among the Chechens and Dagestanis that kept women from fully participating in society. In addition, Chechen children (including girls) were given a compulsory education in which they studied secular topics instead of the previous religious-based curriculum that had been in Arabic.

A major facet of the Bolsheviks' modernizing policies that aimed to bring the perceived benefits of the Communist revolution to *all* Soviet peoples was their war on religion. Soviet leader Vladimir Lenin considered religion to be a conglomerate of superstitious holdovers from the feudal period or earlier. Like Karl Marx before him, Lenin contemptuously described all religions (but reactionary Islam in particular) as the "opiate of the masses." In their efforts to forcefully secularize the Chechens as a means of "liberating them from the chains of superstition," the Soviet commissars closed their mosques, banned their Islamic celebrations and replaced them with Soviet holidays, and undermined the influence of their village elders and priests.

In the face of these campaigns, the Chechens' two main Sufi religious brotherhoods, known as the Naqshbandi and the Qadiriya orders, went underground to avoid detection. Ironically, even Chechen members of the Communist Party surreptitiously partook in Sufi religious ceremonies during the Soviet period. Good Chechen Communists secretly partook in *zikirs* (chants) and continued to have Muslim burials. As these Muslim Marxists noted, socialism may have offered a "workers' paradise" on earth, but it offered no heaven for the Communist Party faithful after their death.

During their offensive on Islam, the Soviets executed mullahs, replaced the Chechens' Arabic script with the Russian Cyrillic alphabet, and on many levels dragged the Chechens from the era of anti-Russian jihads and *muridism* into the modern, industrial era. As part of this developmental process, the capital of the newly established Chechen-Ingush Autonomous Soviet Socialist Republic (ASSR), Grozny, was developed into a major urban center. Tens of thousands of Soviet Russians were settled in the city. These Russian "big brothers" were utilized in the development of the oil industry in Chechnya. In the process, Grozny eventually was chosen as the site for the construction of one of the Soviet Union's largest oil refineries.

As the simple Chechen farmers and peasants watched in awe, oil wells went up throughout their countryside, Russian factory workers came to work in the new centers of industry in Grozny, new roads were built into the two main mountain valleys of the south, schools were constructed even in the smallest of villages, and the Socialist Revolution began to be felt in the most remote mountain hamlets.

In effect, the Kremlin launched a vast campaign of social engineering in the Caucasus that aimed to do nothing less than transform the highlanders from "backwards, tribal, religious reactionaries" into modern Soviet citizens. The newly envisioned Chechen "Soviet Man" ultimately was to be an "internationalist," whose loyalties and sense of community transcended his narrow attachment to his ethnic origins and linked him to the greater USSR. He also was to be an atheist, speak fluent Russian (the language of international communication), and identify with his fellow Soviet workers in the experiment in state socialism known as the USSR.

Not surprisingly, the Soviet project strongly altered the Islamic culture of the Chechens. In many ways their experiences behind the Iron Curtain accelerated their isolation from the rest of the Muslim world and increased the already dominant role of informal Sufi folk Islam among the common people. During the Soviet atheist period, the average Sovietized Chechen Sufi grew to have even less in common with the typical Arab living in the Gulf states of the Middle East, where strict Islamic practices remained unaltered. With the closure of their mosques, execution of their trained religious leaders, destruction of their holy Qur'ans, Europeanization-secularization of their culture, replacement of their Arabic alphabet with Cyrillic, and so on, the Soviet Chechens' social and religious practices became limited to informal customs and ancient folk beliefs. These local religious traditions had little in common with strict Orthodox Islam officially enforced with such severity in Saudi Arabia by the Wahhabi conservatives and religious police.

In addition to these far-reaching social projects, the Soviet revolutionaries also enacted several important territorial-administrative changes in the Caucasus that were to profoundly affect the Chechens. Most important, the Chechens and the neighboring Ingush people were given their own dual administrative-republic homeland like other nations and ethnic groups in the USSR (including the multiethnic Dagestanis). The Chechen and Ingushes' bureaucratic-territorial unit was known as the Chechen-Ingush Autonomous Soviet Socialist Republic (ASSR). This ASSR was, like the neighboring Dagestan ASSR, included within the administrative framework of the larger Russian Soviet Federated Socialist Republic (the RSFSR). In many ways it was an ethnic "reservation" within the larger ethnic Russian republic.

It is important to emphasize that the tiny Chechen-Ingush Autonomous SSR, like myriad other small ethnoterritorial units or "reservations" that found themselves under the auspices of the vast Russian Republic, *was not a full-fledged Soviet Socialist Republic (*SSR), such as the first-tier Azerbaijan SSR, Georgian SSR, Ukrainian SSR, Kazakh SSR, Armenian SSR, or Russia itself. For this reason, the small Chechen-Ingush territorial autonomy inside of Russia had no officially recognized "right" to secede from the larger USSR or from the Chechens' mother republic, Russia, should the USSR one day collapse.[5] The smaller Chechen-Ingush *Autonomous* SSR was considered to be under the jurisdiction of the larger Russian Soviet Federated Republic and, following the disintegration of the USSR in 1991, found itself (like many other ethnically based autonomous "reservations," such as Tatarstan or Dagestan) forever linked to, and ruled by, the Russian Federal Republic. Because of this historical border construction, the Chechens' microrepublic could not secede from Russia and achieve independence in the same fashion that the fifteen full SSRs did in 1991 when the USSR later collapsed.

Rebels Chechen Anti-Soviet Uprisings, 1921–1944

In spite of the undisputed success the Communists' social and territorial programs had in transforming the conservative highlanders into Soviet citizens, it is important to note that the Chechens, more than any other nation in the multiethnic USSR, actively fought against the Soviets' attempts to remold their society. This response stemmed to a large degree from the Soviet government's ham-fisted social policies, which aimed to forcefully transform this clan-based mountain people into model Soviet citizens overnight. It should not come as a surprise that the Communist commissars who were assigned the task of Sovietizing the Chechen-Ingush autonomous republic had little toleration for the traditional ways of its conservative Muslim people.

For their part, the vast majority of the "counter-revolutionary" Chechens simply saw the Soviet atheist "infidels" as a more intrusive, meddling version of the tsarist administrators who had long vexed them with their alien rules and regulations. Not surprisingly, soon after the introduction of Communist rule, discontent spread among the Muslim highlanders, who found it impossible to identify with the goals of the Communist Revolution. As a result, during the late 1920s and 1930s, the Soviet authorities found that the Chechen highlands were full of "anti-Soviet reactionaries," "saboteurs," and "antiprogressive elements" who actively worked to resist Moscow's authority.

In addition to these new problems, the Soviets had to deal with the perennial issue of the Chechens' tradition of raiding. The following report issued by a People's Commissar of Finance who visited the neighboring multiethnic Autonomous Soviet Socialist Republic of Dagestan in April 1923 clearly indicates that the Chechens continued to make poor neighbors:

> Special attention should be paid to attacks by Chechens. When we spent a night at the railroad station in Chir-Yurt, the neighboring station at Khasavyurt was attacked, two train attendants were killed, a road repairman wounded, and a cargo train plundered. Such attacks are a well-nigh-daily occurrence.
>
> I am enclosing reports by the Avar and Andi [two related Dagestani

ethnic groups] executive committees in which they request the permission to form their own anti-Chechen units and demand Chechnya's disarmament. The sentiments, which I noted in conversations with rural dwellers, were clearly hostile. If Chechen banditry is not put an end to in the immediate future, one cannot exclude that some districts will spontaneously rise against Chechnya.[6]

Like the Russian authorities today, in the 1920s the Soviets were faced with the twofold task of curbing the Chechens' traditional raiding practices and transforming them into law-abiding citizens. As these socioeconomic programs were being forcefully implemented, state-sponsored land policies, such as the collectivization of property and the arrest of large landowners, further destabilized Chechen society.

The Chechen response was as timeless as the mountains themselves. They reacted to the Soviet intrusions by retrieving their hidden weapons and launching a series of uprisings in 1929 that were to last, on and off, right up until the outbreak of World War II. An account of these spontaneous, anti-Soviet revolts paints a picture of determined highlander resistance that differs only in minor ways from the descriptions of desperate last stands in burning villages drawn by the tsarist generals seventy years earlier. In his account of the Chechens' revolt against the Soviet authorities in 1929, the respected Chechen émigré scholar Abdurahman Avtorkhanov, for example, describes the clashes between Chechen insurgents and soldiers belonging to the GPU (State Political Directorate) sent to crush them:

> The whole of Chechnia exploded. It is impossible to describe the nightmarish events which followed, so we will limit ourselves to the main points . . . The GPU detachments completed operations against the [local Chechen] Soviet executives in three days, and on the fourth day, towards one o'clock in the morning, it surrounded the house of the former leader of the insurgents, Shita Istamulov. He was taken by surprise, but in response to an ultimatum to surrender he and his brother Hassan opened fire. At dawn, when help came to Shita, part of his house was ablaze and Hassan was badly wounded. Some hundred Chechen horsemen surrounded the GPU detachment besieging Shita's house, and after an hour of fighting the GPU force of about 150 men was practically

annihilated. Shita Istamulov appealed to all Chechens to join in a holy war for the re-establishment of the imamate of Shamil and the eviction of the "infidels" from the Caucasus.[7]

The following Soviet account of another Red Army campaign that aimed to forcefully disarm the Chechens provides further eyewitness evidence of the true nature of the relations between the rebellious highlanders and the new Soviet government:

> The operation proceeded in the valley on August 25, when Korol's group surrounded the village of Ackchoy. They gathered a meeting of the village population to offer the people to surrender arms within two hours. Since no arms were surrendered at the announced time, 15 shrapnel shells were fired at the village, of which ten were intended to kill. After two Chechen women were wounded, the population began surrendering arms.
>
> On that day in the morning Kozitsky's group approached the village of Keloy where they demanded that arms should be surrendered; only 9 rifles were brought to them. Artillery fire was then opened at the village. Right after the first shells were fired, crying and shouting females rushed to the group's staff. Elders came later to promise that all arms had been surrendered. Yet in between houses men with arms could be seen, and the artillery fire continued. After an hour's shelling, 15 more rifles were surrendered, a search was immediately launched to produce more arms than had been surrendered, and the artillery repression was repeated.
>
> Rebel leader Gotsinsky surrendered on September 5 after four days of artillery fire at the villages of Khimoy and Khakmaloy. The village of Daay was shelled and bombed on August 29; four people were killed, five wounded and 20 houses were destroyed.
>
> The demand was made that the people of Daay should surrender Ansaltinsky [a rebel]. The planes which were supposed to bomb Daay on August 28, dropped bombs on [the village of] Nakchu-Keloy, following which its people decided to voluntarily surrender the arms they had.[8]

While much of the USSR was transformed into "the world's first workers' state" without resistance, the Chechen highlands by contrast remained a "no-go zone" for much of the 1920s and 1930s. Time and again Soviet troops had to engage in pacification campaigns in the Chechens' mountains that resembled those of their tsarist predecessors. If there had been a ranking of ethnic groups within the multiethnic USSR reflecting their level of progress on the road to becoming modern Soviet citizens, the stubborn Chechen highlanders of the 1930s surely would have ranked among the lowest and most resistant.

As these accounts vividly demonstrate, a situation that often bordered on outright war prevailed between Moscow and the Chechens as the Second World War loomed on the horizon. While the Chechens had been Sovietized to a considerable degree, a large segment of this proud people still seethed in the face of the Kremlin's intrusive social policies. While these Chechen malcontents outwardly came to resemble other Soviet citizens on many levels, inside they retained the highlander rebel tradition of their ancestors.

Fortunately for the Soviet authorities, an indigenous Communist leadership had emerged among the Chechens by the mid-1920s led by a developing native intelligentsia. The indigenous Chechen Communist cadres genuinely hoped to bring the material and social benefits of socialist modernism to their undeveloped countrymen. These local Chechen "fellow travelers" on the road to Communism facilitated the introduction of many of the Soviets' more revolutionary policies in Chechnya and acted as something of a shock absorber or bridge between the Kremlin and the mass of the Chechen people.

By the 1930s, however, Stalin had turned on the indigenous Communist Party leaderships of the many ethno-autonomous republics of the USSR. Seeing them not as collaborators, but as cryptonationalists, the Soviet leader unleashed a bloody purge that was to leave these Soviet ethnic territories living in stunned submission right up until the Gorbachev political thaw of the late 1980s. In 1937, Stalin's bloody campaign came to Chechnya, and the Chechen Communists who had decided to work with the Kremlin were slaughtered in droves by the NKVD (pre-KGB secret police).

Rather than humbly submit to the executioner's bullet, many of the Chechen-Ingush Autonomous Republic's top Chechen Communist officials instead followed the path of the nineteenth-century *abreks* and took to the hills to fight back. Anatol Lieven remarks in his account of the rebellion, "The revolt of the Chechens is striking when compared to the passivity of many of the other peoples of the Soviet Union in the face of Stalinist terror."[9] While other republics' local Communist administrations resigned themselves to being purged by the dreaded secret police, the Chechen Communist administration fought back.

By 1940 the Chechen anti-Soviet rebels had found in Hasan Israilov a leader worthy of leading them against their Soviet masters. Israilov, who was also a well-known poet, wrote a manifesto before riding into the hills with his rifle to lead his people in rebellion. His lofty sentiments and naïve belief in the possibility of support from the outside world are as timeless as the unanswered pleas for assistance sent by his modern Chechen successors, who similarly asked for Western assistance in the 1990s. His words capture the false hopes and almost childlike belief in the willingness of the West to support the Chechens' doomed cause. Israilov summed up his people's aspirations as follows:

> For twenty years now, the Soviet authorities have been fighting my people, aiming to destroy them group by group: first the *kulaks* [wealthy peasants], then the *mullahs* and the "bandits," then the bourgeois-nationalists. I am sure now that the real object of this war is the annihilation of our nation as a whole. That is why I have decided to assume the leadership of my people in their struggle for liberation . . .
>
> I understand only too well that Chechenia-Ingushetia—indeed the whole of the Caucasus—will find it difficult to get rid of the yoke of Red imperialism. But a passionate faith in the justice and hope that the freedom-loving people of the Caucasus and of the world will come to our assistance inspires me in this enterprise which you may consider foolhardy and senseless, but which I believe to be the only possible path. The brave Finns [who were involved in a war for independence with the USSR at this time] are proving that this great empire built on slavery is devoid of strength when faced with a small-freedom-loving nation. The Caucasus will be a second Finland and we will be followed by the other oppressed nations.[10]

As Israilov's revolt spread through the collective farms of Chechnya in the spring of 1941, somber news reached the Caucasus that Hitler's Germany had invaded the Soviet Union. Word soon came that the Soviet republics of Belorussia and Ukraine had been completely overrun by the Nazis with a speed no one could have foreseen. The German invaders were said to be fast approaching the Caucasus and the vital oil fields of Baku in Azerbaijan.

As Hitler's seemingly invincible war machine obliterated whole Soviet armies, it appeared as if the Soviet experiment in socialism was doomed. World War II had come to the USSR, and the Chechens living isolated from the world were to be drawn into the global maelstrom with tragic consequences.

Blitzkrieg The German Invasion of the USSR and the "Betrayal" of the Chechens

On June 22, 1941, Adolph Hitler, the Soviet's German partner in the Molotov-Ribbentrop Pact, which had cynically aimed to divide Eastern Europe between the Soviets and the Nazis, betrayed Stalin and invaded the USSR. In that momentous summer, Hitler's fast-moving panzer tank divisions rolled across the western marches of the unprepared USSR, annihilating whole Soviet divisions and capturing tens of thousands of Red Army prisoners (including many hastily mobilized Chechens who fought in the Red Army).

As the Nazis swept over vast stretches of Belorussia and the Ukraine, the Red Army general staff saw only too clearly that the Germans' ultimate objective was the oil fields of the Transcaucasus in Azerbaijan. The Germans' petrol-guzzling tank divisions and Luftwaffe air force aimed to do nothing less than punch through the Russian lines at the city of Stalingrad and move south through coastal Dagestan to the oil fields of Azerbaijan. The Soviet Union was engaged in a life-and-death struggle against the seemingly unstoppable Nazi invaders, and the key to victory lay in preventing the German invaders from reaching the Caucasus.

In response, millions of Soviet citizens of all nationalities were drafted to fight in the Red Army and prevent the Germans from achieving victory at Moscow, Stalingrad, and Leningrad. In the process, 17,413 citizens from the Chechen-Ingush ASSR were commissioned directly into the Red Army, and another 13,363 Chechens joined the Chechen-Ingush ASSR People's Militia to fight the invaders.[11]

Fortunately for the Chechen people, the German war machine was abruptly halted on the northwest frontier of the Chechen-Ingush Autonomous Republic near the city of Mozdok. Their home republic was to be spared the horrors of direct Nazi occupation. For this reason, while some dissatisfied Chechens had defected from the Red Army to the Nazi Wehrmacht during the height of the conflict (or most likely, they had been captured by the swiftly advancing Germans along with Soviet citizens from all nationalities), *the vast majority of Chechens never came into direct contact with the German invaders.*

Very few Chechens even saw the Nazis, and certainly the Chechen civilian population never collaborated with the invaders. Some of the Chechens (and Russians and members of other ethnic groups) who had been captured earlier by the victorious Germans certainly did fight in Nazi units, but Germans considered them nothing more than cannon fodder. One Soviet prisoner-of-war soldier claimed, "The captors simply handed out German uniforms and only the foolhardy refused."[12]

While Soviet intelligence services suspected the Chechen mountain rebels led by Hasan Israilov (who had continued their "subversive anti-Soviet guerilla activities" throughout the period of the German invasion) of having carried out secret negotiations with the Nazi invaders, the Chechen rebels had made it clear that they would not accept Berlin's rule any more than they had Moscow's.

Regardless, the Soviet air force considered Israilov's Chechen mountain guerillas to be a serious enough threat to bomb them on several occasions during the conflict with the Germans. Chechen historian Avtorkhanov sarcastically compared the Soviets' military campaign against their own Chechen citizens with the struggle against the Nazi invaders as follows:

As is well known, in 1941–2 Soviet military aircraft were completely inactive in the front line against the enemy. On the other hand, they bombed their own savagely. In the spring of 1942, there were two Soviet air raids over the Chechen-Ingush Mountains. In some *auls* (the villages of Shanto, Istumkala and Galanchozh) the number of dead was greater than that of the living. While Stalin shelled his own people, not a single German had set foot on Caucasian soil, and when the Germans finally came to the Caucasus in the summer of 1942 they never penetrated into Checheno-Ingush territory.[13]

In considering the issue of Chechen "collaboration" with Hitler, it is only natural that there is some debate on where the Chechens would have fit in the Nazis' racial classification system. Most probably the Chechens fell into the "non-Aryan" category of *Untermenschen* (literally "under-beings," similar to the "mongrel Armenian-trading nation," despised Crimean Tatar-"Mongols," or Semitic Jews) and would not have fared well in the Third Reich had the Germans emerged victorious.[14]

For their part, the Chechen anti-Soviet rebels operating in the mountains seem to have distrusted the Nazis. In June 1942, Israilov's guerrillas issued a decree which declared that the Germans were to be "welcomed and treated as guests" in the Caucasus only if they acknowledged the independence of the Caucasian peoples.[15]

In light of all the above, we can dismiss the absurd Soviet propaganda claims that the Chechen people engaged in "mass betrayal of the Soviet Union with the Hitlerite invaders during the heroic Soviet peoples' defense of the Fatherland." The average Chechen villager in the Caucasus never had the chance to collaborate with the Germans, who were halted beyond the border of his people's lands.

Regardless of the actual facts, the charge of mass treason and collaboration with the Nazis was subsequently leveled against the entire Chechen nation—men, women, and even children and the elderly. It seems that the charges of national treason were simply a pretext for eradicating the historic problem of the turbulent Muslim highlanders of Chechnya and the neighboring regions. In hindsight, it appears that Josef Stalin and NKVD-KGB chief Lavrenti Beria had formulated a frighteningly simple solution to the "Chechen problem" during the Nazi invasion— total ethnic cleansing.[16]

While the removal of the Chechens and other Muslim highlanders was to be a cold, state-sponsored "surgical" operation designed to liquidate a Soviet "traitor nation," it also may have had an undercurrent of ethnic racism. The motives for the deportation of the Chechens may have had a closer resemblance to the racial hatred that drove Serbian paramilitaries to kill off their Bosnian Muslim neighbors in the 1990s. Stalin, who himself was from the Christian mountain republic of Georgia, knew the Caucasus well and most certainly had a historic antipathy toward his people's hereditary foes, the Muslim highlanders. This racist view of the Caucasian *cheorny* (blacks), who were stereotyped for "reproducing like rabbits," their "laziness and criminality," and their "filth, ignorance, and Islamic superstition" was as prevalent in the USSR as the more widely recognized problem of anti-Semitism. In his work on the deportations, Otto Pohl bluntly states:

> Even if one accepts the Stalinist claim that the Chechens and Ingush collaborated with Nazi Germany in disproportionate numbers, a claim since repudiated by the Soviet government under Khrushchev, only ethnic hatred can explain the punishment of the entire population including children . . . Ethnicity rather than political loyalty was the determining factor in the Soviet deportations.[17]

In addition, as the victorious Red Army subsequently poured into Eastern Europe occupying the countries that later were to form the Soviet puppet states of the Warsaw Pact, the Soviet government seriously contemplated continuing the momentum and invading the Republic of Turkey. There may have been a fear that the Chechens, or other historically obstreperous, pro-Turkish mountain peoples, such as the Turkic Karachai and Balkars, could sabotage the Soviets' aggressive war aims in this southward direction. There is also evidence that the NKVD-KGB feared the Chechen Sufi religious orders. They feared that the Sufis would declare a jihad against the Kremlin should the USSR invade Muslim Turkey.[18]

To deal with this potential threat, Stalin and Beria decided to launch a preemptive strike against the traditionally distrusted Muslim peoples in the winter of 1944. The plan to deport the Chechens, known as Operation *Chechevitsa*, would also be facilitated by the fact that the Red Army was already deployed near the region.

All the pieces for the destruction of the highlanders were put in place, and several predominantly Muslim Soviet nations arbitrarily deemed to have been found guilty of "total mass treason" by their government, namely, the Chechens, Ingush, Karachai, Balkars, Meshketian Turks, and the Crimean Tatars were secretly targeted for a level of destruction that not even the nineteenth-century General Yermolov could have envisioned.

February 23, 1944 The "Liquidation" of the Chechens

The wider deportation campaign in the Caucasus against several targeted groups, known as "Operation Mountaineer," began with the surprise roundup and removal of the Turkic Karachai farming-shepherding people, whose homelands lay to the west of the Chechens. The Soviet mechanized deportation brigades then moved against the Buddhist Kalmyk Mongol seminomads to the northeast.

By the winter of 1944 the Chechens' turn had come. The vast majority of Chechens were unaware of their government's intentions because the Soviet police state kept the news of the previous ethnic cleansings hidden. History had taught the Soviets that if they were to engage in something as ambitious as the *likvidatsiia* (liquidation) of the warlike highlanders without stirring up resistance, the targeted peoples could not be forewarned of their fate.

Officially, the Chechens were told that the Red Army brigades were arriving in their republic to carry out war exercises and repair and extend roads in Chechnya in order to establish solid communication networks in the Red Army's rear. Declarations issued at this time by the authorities proclaimed, "Let us make an example of our roads and bridges!" and "Let us help our beloved Red Army in its maneuvers in the mountains!"

In February of 1944, tens of thousands of Red Army troops began to pour into the doomed Chechen-Ingush Republic. All Chechen villages soon had a garrison housed in their vicinity. In all, 83,003 regular Soviet troops and 17,698 NKVD-KGB special operatives arrived in the Chechen and Ingush lands at this time (i.e., roughly the number of US troops deployed in 2003's Operation Iraqi Freedom against Saddam Hussein). In the ultimate betrayal, a large percentage of these Soviet soldiers were subsequently billeted directly in Chechen households.[19] By all accounts the Red Army soldiers encountered the traditional hospitality of the mountaineers, who made them feel welcome. It will be recalled that thousands of Chechen citizens had been drafted into the Soviet army when the Nazis invaded. For this reason many Chechens genuinely identified with the Soviet army conscripts billeted in their homes.

The warm hospitality accorded to the Red Army soldiers by the simple villagers serves as ample testimony that Stalin's efforts to keep the Chechens' fate hidden from them had been successful. While some Soviet soldiers secretly warned their Chechen hosts, this was the exception to the rule, and most Chechens remained oblivious to their fate right to the end.

Having placed his troops in position without having raised suspicion among the doomed Chechens, the NKVD chief, Lavrenti Beria, finally sent a secret telegram to Stalin on February 22, 1944. In this telegram, Beria gleefully described the horror of the remaining loyal Chechen Communist authorities when they heard Beria's deportation orders. Beria informed them that their entire people were to be lulled into gathering in public areas and deported to the far reaches of Asia the following day:

Molayev [a Chechen Communist], who chairs the Council of People's Commissars Government of the Chechen-Ingush Autonomous Soviet Socialist Republic, was informed about the Government's decision to deport the Chechen and Ingush populations, as well as about the relevant motives for such a decision. After hearing my report, Molayev quailed, subsequently regaining his composure and promising to fulfill all orders that will be issued to him in connection with the deportation . . .

The deportation shall commence at dawn on February 23, 1944. It was intended to cordon off local districts for the purpose of preventing the populace from leaving [the] territory of populated localities. The populace shall be invited to attend a rally, with some receiving time for collecting their belongings. The rest shall be disarmed and taken to marshalling areas. As I see it, the deportation of Chechen and Ingush populations will prove to be successful.[20]

Fittingly, the faithful Chechen Communists who collaborated in the deportation of their own people were subsequently betrayed and were deported themselves, despite their loyalty to Moscow. It also should be stated that 132 Chechens who had received the Soviets' highest war medal, Hero of the Soviet Union, were deported as well.[21] This fact alone utterly disproves the notion that the Chechen people were deported because of collaboration with the Nazis.

But it was not just the Chechen Communist officials who were betrayed by NKVD leader Beria. It was the entire Chechen people who offered their hospitality to the very soldiers who betrayed them. One Chechen account bitterly states, "The local inhabitants, with Caucasian hospitality, accepted the soldiers and officers, not suspecting that in several months these very soldiers would kill many of them."[22] Another report states, "The mountaineers accepted the soldiers as their sons, gave them everything, food and clothing, they were not willing to believe the rumors already circulating about the deportation, and they frequently gave hospitality to the soldiers and officers."[23]

From such experiences, the Chechens developed the saying that translates to "lying like the Soviets."[24] This saying, more than any other expression, summarizes the Chechens' collective sentiment toward the Soviet leadership.

As this unforeseen betrayal unfolded, mechanized army divisions and heavily armed NKVD troops quickly fanned out throughout the republic, occupying the countryside and the capital of Grozny. This was done without opposition, since most of Hasan Israilov's mountain rebels had by this time already been suppressed.

As the number of troops in the republic increased to unprecedented levels, unsettling rumors began to spread among the Chechen villagers that the Kalmyk and Karachai peoples had previously been rounded up and deported to the depths of the USSR. Most Chechens, however, refused to believe that such a monstrous fate awaited them since so many of their men were loyally serving in the ranks of the Soviet armed forces.

Such was the situation in Chechnya when the heavily armed soldiers stationed among the Chechens commenced Red Army Day celebrations held annually on February 23, 1944. According to eyewitness accounts, the Soviet troops called on the unsuspecting local people to participate in the festivities, and many came to gather in public places with their children in tow. Most made their way to village squares at the appointed time for music, dances, and bonfires, which had been promised to them by the Red Army officers stationed among them.

As the Chechens gathered in village squares, the armed Red Army soldiers suddenly announced that, as "traitors to the Soviet homeland," the entire Chechen people, men, women, and children, were to be punished with deportation from their homelands to an unspecified destination. Those who were suspected of actively collaborating with the Germans were to be executed on the spot. While some hotheaded Chechen men resisted, most realized that resistance was futile in light of the fact that the Red Army had encircled all Chechen villages and neighborhoods in the capital of Grozny.

As the decree was translated into Chechen for the elderly who did not know the *lingua Sovietica* of Russian, wailing began to spread among the people. From recently declassified KGB documents pertaining to the event, we now know that those who were present at the Red Army celebrations were surrounded by machine gun–carrying soldiers and herded onto American-loaned Studebaker trucks. The panicked population, who feared they were about to be executed, was then transported in hundreds of convoys to the capital of Grozny. Once there, the deportees were boarded onto cold cattle trains to await the arrival of the kin from smaller villages in the outlying countryside and upper mountains.

In less-populated highland areas of the Chechen-Ingush Republic, the NKVD militia troops and Red Army units surrounded Chechen hamlets, burst into houses and dragged out their inhabitants (often their former hosts), and herded the startled population to trans-shipment points. Many deportees had only a few seconds of warning before they were expelled from their homes and herded like cattle onto awaiting trucks.

A Chechen survivor has left the following account of the event, which is typical of the ritualized narratives of "The Deportation":

> Early in the morning of February 23, 1944, on the squares and on the outskirts of the village in the mountains, they were aroused by automatics and machine guns; they announced the order of the State Committee of the District, they searched out and directed everyone to the train station. Then began the second part of the "scenario," soldiers entered all doors, armed with automatics, led by an officer or sergeant who gave them 10–15 minutes to expel the elderly, children and women from the homes, the wounded were tossed out of medical stations. Any who resisted—they shot! Any attempting to escape—they shot! Any who incorrectly understood the order they shot! They had given (the decree of deportation) in Russian and many did not speak Russian . . . In the highlands of Chechnya, in several hours, hundreds of people were gunned down, men, women, children and the elderly.[25]

The transgenerational narratives of the deportation form a powerful means of passing on a sense of victimization to those who did not personally experience the events of 1944, as the following example demonstrates:

> Then many told how on Soviet army day (the symbolism is real is it
> not?) February 23, 1944, the inhabitants in the villages were led to the
> squares—as if for a holiday—and, not being given time to collect their
> things, even time to go to their homes, they were driven by vehicles and
> deposited at the nearest train station. They told how those who were
> unable to walk were killed on the spot. They told how in the village of
> *Khaibek* the sick, among them women and children, were burned alive.
>
> Yes, and they talked about the exile, which is remembered by every
> Chechen, old and young—and even of the Caucasian wars in the last
> century, as if they happened yesterday, and for every Chechen the name
> of General Yermolov [the tsarist general who brutally conquered the
> Chechens] is inseparable from the name of Grachev [the Russian general
> who launched the 1994 invasion of Chechnya].[26]

Among the Chechen survivors of the tragedy of 1944, the bloody events that took place in the above-mentioned highland village of Khaibek hold a special place of horror. An account of the massacre which took place in that village should be given here in light of the anguish and rage that the legend of Khaibek continues to evoke among the post-Soviet Chechens.

According to NKVD accounts, as the Chechens began to arrive in their tens of thousands for transfer onto cattle cars in the Grozny train station, it became apparent that the troops were operating under a tight operating schedule. "Operation Mountaineer" involved tens of thousands of soldiers, one hundred and ninety trains, and most tellingly, an *entire* tank division. This deprived the Red Army of these desperately needed resources for the war front. The forced transfer of approximately half a million Chechen and Ingush mountaineers over thousands of kilometers was a major logistical exercise.

For this reason, NKVD generals in charge of the operation were urged by Stalin to expedite the "removal" of the Chechens. They did this by refusing to allow Chechens the designated fifteen minutes of time to gather the allotted twenty kilos of food, blankets, and extra clothing before being taken from their houses (this seemingly minor point led to starvation and death from exposure for many who were not told where they were going or for how long they would be away).

The NKVD and Red Army soldiers involved in the deportation also confiscated the possessions of the deported people, which varied from household utensils, furniture, and heirlooms to cattle and farming equipment. This gave these military units added incentive to prevent the deportees from bringing their most prized possessions with them to their places of exile.

As the mechanized troops hurried to meet their deadlines, they found other imaginative ways to expedite the transfer of villagers from the isolated mountain hamlets to Grozny. The story of Khaibek reveals the true nature of this expedited ethnic cleansing. By all accounts, on the snowy night of February 23, the NKVD found itself unexpectedly delayed by the difficulties in marching hundreds of Chechens, including the elderly and infants, through the snow from the isolated highland village of Khaibek down to Grozny. In order to meet their deadline and perhaps earn promotions (medals were awarded to the generals in charge of this successful military operation against fellow Soviet citizens), the accompanying Soviet officers hit upon an idea that would speed up the process. Calling for a halt, the soldiers crowded the slow-moving villagers into several nearby storage buildings, doused them with gasoline and simply burnt everyone alive.

Villagers from neighboring hamlets could smell the burning flesh of the tortured inhabitants of Khaibek as they passed nearby and recall witnessing the soldiers' hurried disposal of their victims' blackened bodies. Sadly, the atrocity at Khaibek was not an isolated event, and as many as twelve smaller hamlets experienced a similar sad fate. The NKVD account of the sickening slaughter at Khaibek coldly states, "In view of the impossibility of transportation and the necessity of fulfilling on schedule the goals of 'Operation Mountaineer,' it was necessary to liquidate more than 700 inhabitants of the village of Khaibakh."[27]

A Chechen survivor of this massacre left the following simple account of this atrocity, which compares drastically to the official account:

I was born in 1912 in the village of Motskara, in the Galanchosk region. Now I live in Gekhi-Uch. I confirm that my family, and my relatives, to the number of 19, children, women and the elderly, were shot and burned in Khaibek by soldiers.

My brother Alimkhojaev Salambek, 35 years old, worked as a teacher. He was shot as he walked along the road. His wife is still living, her name is Besiila . . . To this day she preserves the braid of her sister, Partakhi. Partakhi, together with her children, was shot and burned in Khaibek.[28]

Among the Chechens burnt alive in the slaughter at Khaibek were the grandmother, aunt, and two cousins of a young infant named Dzhokhar Dudayev. It was this same Dudayev that was later to lead his people in militarily confronting the Russian Federation in the First Russo-Chechen War of 1994 to 1996.[29]

One does not have to be a psychologist to understand the impact that the telling and retelling of the tale of the slaughter of relatives at Khaibek and elsewhere had on Chechen children such as Dzhokhar Dudayev, who grew up far from their homes in exile. In this respect, the future president Dudayev was no different from his people. All Chechens are either directly or indirectly related to someone who died in the deportation of 1944. Not surprisingly, for the Chechens, the burning of Khaibek's inhabitants by their own country's authorities has become a symbol of Soviet and Russian rule over their homeland.

The following account of an interview with an elderly survivor who recalled the deportation takes the sterile reports by NKVD commissars of "liquidations" of Chechens and puts a human face on this tragedy:

Five of Muradov's children, too sick to travel, were executed on the spot. Calmly, he related how one son, bleeding to death, begged for his help. "I cannot help" replied the father, who was wounded but survived and was then deported himself. His wife and last surviving child vanished in exile.[30]

Another Chechen survivor left the following account which, like the previous eyewitness testimony, brings this hidden atrocity to life more than half a century after the event:

First soldiers came to live in our houses and we put them up like guests. Lots of them came to every house. They ate with us, dumped all their gear everywhere. We had about 30 in our place and they were there for more than a month.

One day, we were told there would be a very important meeting and all the men were taken away. I had three sisters and we were put on a train wagon together. My brother was born on the train. It was so cold. It was a cattle train and there were no windows, just darkness. They never told us a thing, didn't tell us where we were going.

Some people were in other villages at the time, so when we were deported they were split up from their families and it took years and years before they ever found their relatives again. In the train, we would shout from carriage to carriage, trying to see if there were relatives. Oh God, I can't forget this for more than an hour, even today.[31]

The eyewitnesses agree that after the mountain *auls* had been emptied of their inhabitants and all Chechens suspected of rebellion summarily executed, the villages were systematically burnt by NKVD troops. A Russian eyewitness recalled, "For days one could see *auls* burning in the mountains."[32] Today many of these ancient highland villages, with their vandalized stone towers, collapsed stone walls, roofless houses, desecrated cemeteries, and crumbling mosques, remain abandoned. In the absence of their former inhabitants, an ancient way of life that had been sustained and passed on for eons from one generation to the next disappeared forever.

This assault on the Chechens' ancient way of life was not to be limited to the Chechen-Ingush Republic. In addition to the deportation of the Chechens residing in their titular republic, another thirty thousand Chechens who lived across the border from the Chechen-Ingush ASSR in the neighboring regions of Dagestan also were arrested in the NKVD's sweeps and deported as well. The deportation units also began a manhunt for Chechens in the neighboring republics of the Transcaucasus (south side of the Caucasus), and scores of Chechens living far from the battlefront in the Soviet Socialist Republics of Azerbaijan and Georgia were caught up in the NKVD's net and deported. The further the NKVD's net was spread from Chechnya, however, the flimsier Stalin's pretext for deporting the widely dispersed Chechen "Nazi collaborators" became.

Knowing the Chechens' proud character, it should not come as a surprise that small bands of desperate Chechens in the mountains were able to avoid the deportation and to carry out anti-Soviet hit-and-run attacks for years after the event. According to a Russian source, "It took almost half a century to bring about calm and order in the region and the physical extermination of the prominent *abreks* and the liquidation of their reserves of weapons in the mountains."[33]

For the most part, however, there was no escape for the members of this doomed nationality.[34] Even the small numbers of die-hard Chechen fighters left behind in the peaks of their empty native mountains were eventually tracked down by Soviet troops and executed.

When the traumatized Chechen people had, by various means, finally been herded to a central trans-shipment point in Grozny, an NKVD report triumphantly proclaimed, "The operation proceeded in an organized fashion, with no serious incidents of resistance or other incidents. There were only isolated cases of attempted flights."[35]

From these newly declassified NKVD-KGB documents, we know that some 387,229 Chechens, and 91,250 Ingush who shared the Chechen-Ingush Autonomous Soviet Socialist Republic with the Chechens, were herded onto cattle cars known as "echelons" for deportation from their homeland to the depths of Soviet Asia. This population was shipped like livestock from their homeland at the rate of 80,000 per day.

In their absence, the streets of their once-bustling villages were filled with burning embers and an eerie silence. Plows lay abandoned in their fields, cattle roamed aimlessly until they were collected and slaughtered by the Red Army troops, once-bustling schoolrooms were empty, and ancestral homes that had been built from stone over the centuries lay abandoned and looted as Soviet soldiers dragged off prized family treasures, household articles, and furniture.

In less than a week the Chechens' ancient way of life had been utterly destroyed, and they were about to embark on a terrifying journey toward an unknown fate. The "problem" of the Chechens apparently had been solved once and for all. In the process, a people who had tilled the lands of their forefathers since biblical times were seemingly destined to disappear forever from the pages of history.

"Crematoria on Wheels" The Journey to Exile

Once crammed into the fetid cattle cars, the Chechens commenced the second part of their punishment and began the terrifying journey from the homeland most had never left to the distant deserts and plains lying far to the east in the wastes of Soviet Central Asia. While they did not know it at the time, the vast majority of them were being transported hundreds of miles from their mountain home in Europe to the Central Asian Soviet republics of Kazakhstan and Kyrgyzstan.

In the ensuing journey, survivors recall that many train carts were so tightly packed that there was no room to sit, and many deportees died from suffocation. The deportees realized that the only modification for humans was a pipe placed in the floor for a toilet. The vast majority of cattle cars, however, lacked even this "facility." Mark Taplin writes of these train cars, "The cattle cars set aside for Beria's ugly errand had already been used for his earlier deportations; they were caked in old feces, and smeared in dried blood and urine. With practice the NKVD had perfected these sinister operations to a ruthless science."[36]

And ruthless the deportation was. The Chechen deportees, who were dehumanized in Soviet bureaucratese by the term "special contingent," recall that the troops who deported them were delighted to discover such a high percentage of children among the "traitors." The presence of so many children facilitated the process of squeezing a greater number of deportees into the cattle carriages. An official report from the period advised that, "The compression of the cargo of the special contingent from forty to forty five persons in a carriage, taking into account 40–50 percent children, is completely expedient."[37]

The Chechens were locked into the guarded carts for two to three weeks as the trains made their way across the wintry heart of the Soviet Union to the distant Soviet republics of Kazakhstan, Kyrgyzstan, and the Russian province of Siberia. All Chechen families have tales of losses suffered on the trains to the places of exile.

From information gleaned from declassified NKVD reports and the eyewitness accounts of survivors, it can be ascertained that the trains carrying the stricken deportees made their way from the Caucasus Mountains, along the north shores of the Caspian Sea, through the emptied plains of the Kalmyks, who had been previously deported, and deep into the heart of landlocked Central Asia. While the journey was to take less than a month, for the horrified survivors these were to be the longest weeks of their lives.

Scores of Chechens died in transit to their unrevealed places of exile, and witnesses spoke of seeing the pitiful bundles of rotting Caucasian corpses left along the rail tracks. The heavy death toll resulting from the deportation would indicate that the Soviet regime's calculated neglect during the journey and resettlement led to a loss of life on a scale that was genocidal. The eyewitness accounts, such as the following report, make this abundantly clear. "From cold and the dirt they began to fall ill. The people were mowed down by typhus, they were not able to bury those who died. On the rare stops on the empty steppes, soldiers walked through the wagon taking off bodies."[38]

Another survivor of the terrible journey to Central Asia recalled, "The train again halted at a half station on the steppe, the door was opened. From the neighboring car a screech reached us. Who had died? It turned out to be a pregnant woman, but the baby died."[39] Another account states:

> I have talked to some of the survivors and they said that they had to stand up in the wagons packed like sardines with the windows of the trains boarded up and with no stops for food and hygiene. Many people suffocated and died and their bodies stayed in vertical positions until the train stopped at its predetermined intervals and then and only then were the bodies taken out and dumped on the side of the railway with no permission to bury any of the dead.

Other narratives claim that the deportees in some carts were able to cut holes in their guarded carriages to slide dead loved ones through the floor and thus prevent the outbreak of diseases resulting from rotting corpses. While the dead could thus escape the heavily guarded trains that have been described as "crematoria on wheels," there was to be no escape for the living. Anyone who tried to flee from the trains at rare stops was instantly gunned down by the armed guards.

As pious Sufi Muslims, some of the mountaineers were loath to dispose of their dead loved ones by tossing them from the train. They considered it to be a supreme desecration of their loved ones' bodies. As the following account of the journey to Central Asia left by a deported mountaineer makes clear, the highlanders' traditions placed supreme importance on providing a proper Islamic burial for their departed kin:

> We were put into goods wagons at the train station. It was cold and pitch black dark and everybody was shouting and crying because they couldn't see or find a place to sit. We didn't know where we were going, we had no idea. There was a Russian woman who had married a Karachai and she was also thrown in with us. She was the one who told us—"Don't worry, we're going to Central Asia. It's a good place, we'll be all right." That was the first time I'd heard of it.
>
> This went on for 20 days. Near my corner, there were an old man and [a] boy. They both died from the cold and we kept them secretly among us so that the guards wouldn't just throw them out of the train. They were throwing bodies out like rubbish. We wanted to keep them and bury them later.[40]

As this ancient custom of burial broke down during the deportation, it added to the deportees' misery. Death plays a highly important ceremonial role among the highlanders, and the Chechen dead are blessed and then wrapped in ritually purified white sheets. A cleric then reads the *fatiha* (the first chapter of the holy Qur'an) in the ear of the deceased, and the family honors their departed loved one with ritualized dirges and prayers. Then he or she is placed, facing Mecca, in the sacred soil of their ancestral graveyards, which have been lovingly tended for centuries.

The importance of properly commemorating death to the Chechens is demonstrated in the fact that many of the Chechens' cherished graveyards predate the arrival of Islam in their land. These sacred spots play a vital in role in this people's life rituals and celebrations. The graves of deceased loved ones are visited during Islamic festivals. The dead are also honored by their living descendants in prayers and during holidays, thus preserving a very real bond between generations that have passed away and those yet to come.

Among the Chechens, honoring the dead is also a way of paying respect to one's elders, acknowledging the divine nature of God, and reaffirming one's links to one's family, clan, and people. Even today Chechens rise in their cars or bus seats when they pass graveyards on autobuses, and they gather with their families to celebrate Islamic festivals in the sacred confines of their clan graveyards (although this latter tradition is much criticized by Wahhabi fundamentalists from Saudi Arabia, who consider it to be a pagan superstition).

In light of these hallowed traditions, it is not surprising that the Chechen deportees spoke in tones of horror after seeing the NKVD train guards casually toss the bodies of their loved ones onto the side of the railroad tracks like trash. The Chechens' fear was that the bodies would "be consumed by dogs or be profaned by rotting far from their ancestral homes." The psychological toll that such indignities took on this people, who proudly maintained their Islamic culture throughout the Soviet period, can only be imagined.

In addition to retelling the terrible story of the profaning impact of the deportation on Chechen burial customs, the transgenerational Chechen deportation narratives place special emphasis on the debasing nature of this inhumane experience. While the desire to provide a proper burial to those who passed away was of primary concern to the Chechen deportees, this proud mountain people also struggled to maintain their sense of dignity and pride in other ways.

This task was, however, made difficult by the circumstances on the packed, unsanitary train carts. Social taboos and traditional Islamic customs of defecation and separation of the sexes, for example, broke down completely during the train journey to Central Asia. In an interview with an elderly group of survivors of the deportation, Yo'av Karny, for example, recorded the following sad story: "One [survivor] told me of seventy-two hours spent aboard a cattle car without food or water, and the humiliation of being ordered, at one train station, to relieve themselves in public, men and women together. One old man insisted on doing so behind the car. A Soviet soldier immediately shot him dead without warning."[41]

According to the Chechen deportation narratives (and corroborating NKVD-KGB accounts), the guarded railcars transporting the Chechens made their way in a completely disorganized fashion to their various destinations deep in the heart of the Soviet Union. The deportees report that there was complete chaos in the routing process, and some deportees from the same family or village ended up being deposited thousands of kilometers away from one another. The most horrifying stories, however, are of cattle cars that could not be opened en route for various reasons. These arrived at their destination with all their occupants dead from dehydration and starvation.

Those mountaineers who survived the transportation process to their places of resettlement subsequently suffered from pneumonia, dysentery, malnutrition, dehydration, and typhus. They also suffered from the more subtle effects of the psychological trauma resulting from the unexpected destruction of their families, homes, and way of life. The psychological trauma was compounded by the fact that the Chechen people had to resign themselves to accepting the fact that their own government was trying to destroy them. With no hope of recourse or expectations of acquittal from the patently false charges of "mass treason," the Chechen people had only one thought — to survive their resettlement in their strange places of exile and live through the winter.

Survival The Chechens in Exile

After three weeks, the weakened survivors arrived in the frozen wastes of Siberia and the vast, open Soviet republics of Central Asia and quickly found that their troubles were far from over. Some Chechens were exiled to the Soviet republic of Tajikistan or the Yakut ASSR in Siberia, but the vast majority of the Chechen deportees were funneled through Alma Ata (Almaty), the capital of the Kazakh Soviet Socialist Republic. In all, 239,768 Chechens were directed to this republic and settled in the vast and foreboding wastes of Kazakhstan.

The transition from the sheltered mountains and hills of Chechnya to the empty plains of Eurasia could not have been greater. Even today one flies over the undulating steppe lands of Kazakhstan and looks in vain for signs of inhabitation. In the 1940s this open plain was even more barren than the prospect offered today. In the late war period, Kazakhstan was a largely undeveloped monotonous plain resembling the plains of North Dakota. It was considered suitable only for the tough Kazakh nomads, whose herds of sheep and hardy steppe ponies wandered over its open expanses.

Most of Kazakhstan consists of a vast steppe land known for its harsh winds, which blow unimpeded from the north Siberian forests in the winter, bringing blizzards and deep snowfall. In the summer the winds blow from the desert republics to the south, bringing a dry continental heat, which can be stifling for those unused to such blistering conditions. Considering the dramatic change in climate and conditions, it is not surprising that thousands of the Chechen highlanders died in the first months and years of their exile.

Following their expulsion from the cattle trains onto the outskirts of villages or small settlements dispersed across the Kazakh plains, many of the Chechen deportees died from malnutrition, typhus, dystrophy, and intestinal problems. Others died from exposure resulting from their poor housing, which usually consisted of primitive dugouts constructed from sod. Such "homes" could not sufficiently keep out the snow and freezing weather. A Chechen survivor of the deportation recalled, "In the driving snow storms and snowy blizzards, in the 40 degree frost, on the endless steppe, the Chechens and Ingush fell. The 'special settlers' had been directed to a special regime of settlement. In the first months alone more than 70,000 people died."[42] According to eyewitness testimonies, those who perished in the first deadly winter could not be buried in the frozen ground and were placed in trees until the ground thawed. Only when spring came were the bodies given proper Muslim burials in the alien soil of their new "home."

The deportees' tremendous economic and psychological problems in adjusting to life in Kazakhstan were magnified by the fact that the NKVD's agents had been active among the local Kazakh herders and farmers. The NKVD warned them in advance that dangerous "traitors to the Soviet Union" would be arriving in their midst. Although they were Sufi Muslims like the Chechens, the local Kazakh villagers were both frightened by the arrival of the strange deportees and unwilling to mix with these people for fear of incurring the wrath of the Soviet secret police. There seems to have been a genuine belief among the parochial shepherds and peasants of Kazakhstan that the foreigners deposited in their midst from lands beyond their plain were "cannibals" or "traitors" to the Red Army in which so many of their own men were serving. This sort of rumor was directly propagated by the local Soviet officials. One Chechen deportee recounted an encounter with the local Kazakhs as follows:

The situation was desperate: our men had to steal livestock from the Kazakhs, mainly their sheep. Father told me once that a group of Kazakhs riding on horseback had caught up with him as he was driving their sheep away. He drew a circle around himself with his knife and said, "Don't cross the line. I'm starving and I'll fight to the death." They thought about it for a while and rode off.[43]

On a more practical level, there was also the very real threat of diseases, such as typhus, spreading from the sickly deported populations to the surrounding peoples. Consequently, little effort was made initially on the part of the local Central Asian population to assist the desperate deportees. The Chechens were truly on their own in their new world, and the odds of this scattered people's survival as a distinct ethnic group seemed slim.

For their part, the deportees from among the Chechens and other targeted nations, such as the Ingush, Kalmyks, Karachai, Balkars, Volga Germans, Crimean Tatars, and Meshketian Turks, found this cold welcome to be deadly. It effectively deprived them of a source of much-needed local assistance in surviving their first winter. A deportee, for example, left the following sad account of his people's arrival in Central Asia. In many ways this testimony captures the real horror hidden by the Soviet term "removal" and serves as a lament for all those victims of Stalin's barbarity:

My niece, Menube Seyhislamova, with ten children, was deported with us. Her husband who had been in the Soviet Army from the first day of the war had been killed. And the family of this fallen soldier perished from hunger in exile in Uzbekistan. Only one little girl, Pera, remained alive, but she became a cripple as a result of the horror she had experienced and of hunger.

Our men folk were at the front and there was no one to bury the dead. Corpses would lie for several days among the living. Adshigulsim Adzhimambetova's husband had been captured by the Fascists. Three children, a little girl and two boys, remained with her. This family was also starving just as we were. No one gave either material or moral help. As a result, first of all, the little girl died of hunger, then in one day, both the boys. Their mother could not move from starvation. Then the owner of the house threw the two children's bodies onto the street, onto the side of the irrigation canal. Then some children, the Crimean Tatars, dug little graves and buried the poor little boys.

Can one really tell it all? I have such a weight on my heart that it is difficult to remember it all. Tell me why did they allow such horrors to happen?[44]

Those who survived the first horrible winter in their places of exile in Kazakhstan continued the struggle to survive. From all accounts, the portion of the Chechen population that was exiled to the mountainous Soviet republic of Kyrgyzstan (in all, 70,997, the second-largest concentration of Chechen deportees) fared slightly better than their kin who found themselves in Kazakhstan.

It was in the years after the first harsh winter that the stricken Chechens gradually began to come to grips with the enormity of the calamity that had befallen their community. It quickly became obvious that their people had not died off in the thousands . . . *but in the tens of thousands.* Clearly Stalin intended that that portion of the Chechen nation that survived the deportation would lose its ethnic cohesion and disappear as a distinct ethnic group. For ethnologists, archeologists, historians, linguists, and anyone with respect for human rights, the disappearance of these indigenous groups with their traditions from bygone eras was to be both a humanitarian tragedy and a well-hidden genocide.

While the Soviets could have physically destroyed the deported populations in their entirety, the loss of such significant proportions of the exiled nations and the dispersal of their remainder was seen as sufficient to ensure that these ethnic communities would never again exist as viable nations. Instead, the scattered and weakened survivors were to be utilized as a class of helots to engage in manual labor in their places of exile.

And this is exactly what happened. Once in exile, the Chechens and other targeted nations were quickly put to work doing the sort of manual labor that the surrounding populations dreaded. The Chechens, for example, were forced to engage in hard physical labor building roads and rail lines across the frozen wastes of Kazakhstan. Others were forced to work in dangerous mines and perform menial tasks in factories. All of these unhealthy and physically demanding activities ensured that the death toll among the deported farmers and peasants of Chechnya, who had little experience with such labor activities or immunities to local diseases, would continue to rise.

It was this death toll that has led many to label the Chechen deportation genocide. In dealing with the death toll among the deportees, Otto Pohl has used newly declassified NKVD documents to clearly demonstrate that approximately 104,903 of the 387,229 deported Chechens (over one in four) had perished by the year 1949, sufficiently proving that the deportation amounted to genocide.[45] The United Nations General Assembly defines genocide as:

> [A]ny of the following acts committed with the intent to destroy, in whole or in part, a national, ethnical, racial or religious group, such as:
>   a. Killing members of a group
>   b. Causing serious bodily or mental harm to members of a group
>   c. Deliberately inflicting on the group conditions of life calculated to bring about its physical destruction in whole or in part

While the NKVD reports serve a purpose in providing us with a clear picture of the tremendous scale of losses suffered by this micronation during the deportation and exile *in numerical terms*, they also run the risk of anesthetizing us to the very real nature of this people's losses *in personal terms*. A non-Chechen is hard put to imagine the long-term impact that the loss of so many loved ones had on an individual basis among this people. In addition, it is certainly hard for Westerners, who live in countries long known for their civil society, to imagine the capricious nature of a regime that would try to eradicate its own citizens in such a systematic fashion.

Hunger and famine stalked the Chechens right up until 1949, when the hardened survivors began to complete simple huts, grow their own crops, and acclimatize to their new homeland. It was only at this time that the death rate among the exiles tapered off and some form of demographic stability returned.

Having survived the trauma of forced displacement in physical terms, the Chechen survivors finally began to rebuild their shattered lives under the watchful eyes of the state and to confront the more subtle psychological effects of their experience. While no psychological study was ever conducted on the deportees by the Soviet authorities, there can be little doubt that the Chechen children in particular were scarred by the experience of being ripped from the security of their homes and forced to witness the deaths of so many family members. It should not come as a surprise that it was this generation which grew up in exile that was to lead the Chechen people in their bloody military confrontations with the Russian Federation for independence in the 1990s.

In the twelve years following the deportation, the Soviet regime kept both the young Chechen "traitors" (many of whom were born *after* their supposed crime of "mass treason") and the elderly from returning to their homeland by confining them to special settlements run by state *kommandanty* (commanders). The Chechens speak with revulsion of their humiliating years spent in the *spetskomandantskii* (special commandant) regime in their places of exile. During this period, they were brutalized by camp guards and utilized as slave labor in their regions of resettlement.

To complicate matters, the deportees were forbidden from going beyond a three-kilometer region around their camps to try to search out family members. Those who did so were arrested and shipped off to the GULAG (State Prison Camp system) to do twenty-five years of hard labor in Siberia. The harsh conditions in the GULAG lumber camps of Siberia, where hard-core Chechen malefactors worked in lumber and gas camps in freezing conditions, led to a high mortality rate among those sent to this region. A sentence of hard labor in Siberia was seen as a death sentence.

Ironically, the Chechens' situation improved somewhat when some of their men who had been serving on the front in the Soviet army finally were demobilized and sent to rejoin their families in exile after the war. But the joy from these reunions was short lived. For Chechen men, the humiliations encountered in the special settlement camps were endless. Many suffered from the anguish of being unable to support their families, and a general listlessness and sense of fatalism appears to have initially prevailed among the Chechen males, who take pride in protecting their loved ones.

The humiliation of being unable to provide for their families was exacerbated by the harsh policies of the deportation regime. This strict regime required that the head of each exiled Chechen household report the deaths in the family and work progress on a weekly basis to the tyrannical commandants. Chechens speak of the degradation of having to report on the loss of a loved child, spouse, sibling, or parent to the camp commanders, who considered the losses of the "special resettlers" to be mere statistics.

But the Chechens, a proud mountain people with a strong martial tradition, did not take this abuse lying down as the other deported nations did. The Chechens were known for being the most uncooperative workers in their places of exile. Few hid their hostility to, and contempt for, the authorities. While other deported groups, such as the Soviet Germans, were known for "devoting themselves to socialist labor" or for their stunned submission, the Chechens quickly became known for their defiance of the authorities.

This defiant attitude was expressed in the theft of state property, refusal to send children to school, disobedience during corvée labor, sabotage of construction projects, "anti-Soviet religious activities," and on occasion, the murder of particularly oppressive government officials. In her work on the first Chechen War, Vanora Bennett quotes a Chechen survivor of the deportation proudly recalling, "Sometimes they [the authorities] would try to split up families or take away our rights . . . but then they'd be found dead on the highway . . . and after a while they learned to treat us with respect."[46] While the Chechens appear to have eventually established a hospitable rapport with the local Muslim Kazakh and Kyrgyz populations in Central Asia, they never ceased to display hostility toward the Soviet authorities.[47]

In his account of the exiled nations and peoples of the notorious GULAG (State Prison System), Alexander Solzhenitsyn further corroborates the picture of the Chechens as prone to resistance, stubborn and unbendable. After himself spending time in the state prison network, he wrote of his experience, "Only one nation refused to accept the psychology of submission," and this applied "not to individual insurgents, but to the nation as a whole . . . no Chechen ever tried to be of service or to please the authorities. Their attitude towards them was proud and even hostile." Solzhenitsyn was also to state: "No one could stop them from living as they did. The regime which ruled the land for thirty years could not force them to respect its laws."[48] While most of the stricken deported nations accepted their exile with resignation, the Chechens resisted the all-powerful Soviet authorities with increasing vigor by the 1950s. The following account of a Chechen uprising in the GULAG is typical of their unusual resistance:

> In the concentration camps there were over 4,000 arrested Chechens. When they heard that their compatriots in the transit prison had rebelled, they did the same, killed the camp administrators, burnt down camps Nos. 3 and 4, broke into the internal guard house, where they killed the camp controller who kept a list of internees, and seized machine guns and ammunition. With the help of these arms, the Chechens killed the sentries in the guard towers and, firing back at the guards as they ran, escaped into the taiga.

The Chechen deportees also found more subtle ways to defy the authorities. While their clan system had been disrupted during the deportation by the breakup of villages and clans linked to ancient territories, the Chechens discovered new means of maintaining inner spirituality and resistance in the face of daily oppression. Unity and opposition to the authorities were expressed as never before through a built-in network of underground spirituality that had linked all Chechens in the face of outside oppression for decades, namely their Sufi mystic brotherhoods. Far from diminishing the influence of the religious orders, the death of such a large proportion of the Chechen nation during the exile years appears to have increased their awareness of their mortality and belief in the afterlife. While the Soviets aimed at creating a transnational, atheist *Homo Sovieticus*, the exile experience, ironically enough, appears to have actually deepened the Chechens' sense of Sufi religiosity and Chechen ethnicity.

Throughout the plains of Kazakhstan, the Chechen exiles continued to gather to chant Allah's name in *zikirs* as a means of defiance, to visit Sufi holy men in search of blessings and miracles, to bury their dead with full Islamic rites, and to pass on their secret religious traditions to their children, even as the atheist Soviet regime attempted to eradicate their "mountain superstitions."

Interestingly, many strict Muslim purists in the Middle East, in particular Wahhabi fundamentalists in Saudi Arabia, are prone to offering criticisms of the Chechens' popular Sufi mysticism (which is seen as being an "un-Islamic divergence" from the true path of strict Orthodox Islam). But few critics of the Chechens' Sufi Islam can doubt that it was these very Islamic folk customs which enabled the Chechen deportees to preserve their sense of solidarity, collective identity, and unity of purpose during the harsh exile years. The Chechens' Sufi orders also helped preserve their language (which was no longer taught in schools or found in newspapers or books in their places of exile), their links to their former homeland, and their sense of community as they found themselves dispersed across strange lands.

Most important, the Chechens' Sufi brotherhoods instilled in them a collective urge to return their people to the sacred soil of their ancestors. It was in the cherished hills and home villages of the Caucasus that the graves of their ancestors and the holy sites of saints' tombs were to be found. While the exiles' prayers were directed toward Mecca, their deeper spirituality linked them to the holy soil of their forefathers in the Caucasus Mountains.

In addition, the Chechens' anti-Soviet Sufi orders kept this exiled people from intermarrying with non-Chechens and instilled in them a distrust of outsiders in general, and Russians in particular. This helped prevent the breakdown of the Chechen nation through assimilation or intermarriage, an option that might have proven attractive for the numerous Chechen widows/widowers or those who sought to avoid passing on the stigma of "traitor to the Soviet nation" to their children. While there were cases of intermarriage between Chechens and outsiders during this period, these outsiders were only accepted by the endogamous Chechens if they "became Chechen" by accepting their beliefs, customs, and language.

Intertwined with the Chechens' Sufi beliefs were the patriarchal traditions of the Caucasus that were maintained in exile, such as the veneration of family elders, traditional cuisine, customs dictating modesty for women, the importance of providing hospitality to guests, and the proclivity to seek revenge for insults real or imagined. By sustaining these and other markers of identity, the Chechens demonstrated their collective defiance of the Soviet system that had attempted to destroy them.

71

Perhaps the most interesting method the Chechens used to defy their Soviet masters and sustain their collective identity, however, was demonstrated in this people's mass effort to rebuild the nation in demographic terms. After the initial trauma of deportation and the loss of over one in four Chechens, the Chechens demonstrated a collective will to demographically rebuild their people through increased rates of reproduction. By the time of Stalin's death in 1953, a Soviet census among the deported Chechens showed that an astounding 42 percent of this exiled people were under the age of seventeen, demonstrating a remarkably high rate of birth considering the unpropitious surroundings the exiles found themselves in over the previous nine years.[49]

As many other communities that have experienced natural or man-made calamities have done throughout history, the devastated Chechen families appear to have instinctively compensated for the loss of such a high proportion of their nation by inaugurating a baby boom. This increase in the birthrate strengthened the nation in numerical terms. Remarkably, the number of Chechens who returned to their homeland after their release from exile in the years 1956 and 1957 was almost as high as the number deported, this despite the massive losses sustained in the deportation and resettlement process.

But it was not easy being a Chechen child in the 1940s and 1950s. As children living in the "special settler camps" in Central Asia, young Chechens were taunted and often beaten by the locals in the nearby schools for their tattered clothes, lack of school supplies, inability to speak fluent Russian, and reputation as "traitors to the Soviet state." Experiences of this sort led many young Chechens to see the Soviet system as one that was diametrically opposed to their people.

For their part, the exiled parents suffered from the indignity of being forced to engage in menial jobs that were loathed by the local populations. They also suffered from the tremendous strain of trying to protect and provide for their traditionally large families in occupations that were alien to them. The task of providing food and shelter was made all the more difficult by the constant harassment that the exiles received at the hands of the local police and NKVD officials, who made it abundantly clear to the deportees that the "punished nations" had no rights as Soviet citizens.

During this grim period, the Chechens' holy men continued to preach eventual return to the sacral homeland of their ancestors as a means of overcoming the burdens of life in exile. It was at this time that disturbing rumors reached the deportees of desecrations that had taken place in their home villages during their forced absence. Word came that, in the Chechen and Ingushes' absence, their autonomous republic had been liquidated and demoted from an Autonomous Soviet Socialist Republic into a simple Russian province known as the Grozny Oblast (Territory).

If this were not enough, much of the territory in the southern regions of the disbanded Chechen-Ingush ASSR had been sliced off and granted to Georgia, the home republic of their oppressor, Josef Stalin. Other sections of the Chechen and Ingush territory were granted to the Russian province known as the Stavropol Territory, the neighboring Dagestan ASSR, and to the small autonomous republic of North Ossetia (this latter land was never given back to the Ingush, who clashed with the Ossetians to regain it when the USSR fell).

It also began to appear that tens of thousands of Russians and smaller numbers of Ossetians (a neighboring Caucasian people who are Christian animists) and some Avars and Dargins (Muslim groups living in the Dagestan ASSR) had been settled in the Chechens' abandoned villages and very homes in their absence. That the ancient stone houses built to house generations of Chechen families had been taken over by Russian Christians was insult enough, but this affront was compounded by the fact that many of the new settlers in the Chechens' homes attempted to erase any memory of the previous inhabitants in order to legitimize their own claims to their houses and lands. Moss-covered gravestones were toppled, hallowed mosques desecrated, and the Chechens' distinctive walled compounds subdivided to house smaller Russian families.

In addition to these random acts of individual vandalism, the Soviets used the vast resources at their disposal to systematically cleanse the Chechens' former territory of many traces of their eons-long inhabitation of the region. Ancient village mosques were demolished, the rich literature in the Chechen language was burned, street signs in Chechen were replaced with Russian signs, and most important, the revered graveyards that had been tended by Chechens for generations were plowed over and their sacred stones used for paving roads. This latter act of impiety more than any other caused feelings of revulsion and outrage among the Chechen exiles. The smaller number of Muslims from the neighboring autonomous republic of Dagestan who were forced to settle in the Chechens' former lands, on the other hand, appear to have respected the Chechens' graveyards and to have felt strong guilt for settling in their lands.

For all intents and purposes the Chechens, like the other deported Soviet peoples, such as the Ingush, Kalmyks, Meshketian Turks, Crimean Tatars, Volga Germans, Karachays, and Balkars, had been eradicated from the USSR's ethnic map in every sense, and this Orwellian "erasure" extended to the most minor of details.[50] The expunging of the memory of the Chechens extended to town and topographical names. In a calculated insult, the lowland Chechen market town of Urus Martan, for example, was renamed to honor the very Soviet troops that had deported the Chechens and henceforth became known as Krasnoarmeiskii (in Russian, "Red Army"). Similarly, Achkoi Martan, a village that was to become the focus of many battles in the post-Soviet Russo-Chechen wars, became Novosel'skii (in Russian, "New Village"), Shalin became Mezhdurechenskii ("Between the Rivers"), and so forth. All the powers of the totalitarian state that had once been deployed to modernize and Sovietize the Chechens were now being devoted to eradicating their very memory.

In the process, much of the progress the Bolsheviks previously had made in increasing literacy and identification with the Soviet state was dissipated. At this time the Chechens fell behind the rest of the USSR's peoples in terms of education, career advancement, and cultural development and became a disenfranchised nation of menial workers.

For thirteen long years the Chechens and other exiled nations suffered and endured in their places of exile, always dreaming of their lost homeland and living with the hidden rage that came with the knowledge that they had been unjustly punished. From 1944 to 1953 the Chechens, who were later to play such a conspicuous role in news headlines from post-Communist Eurasia, had quite simply disappeared. Few in the West or the Muslim world knew or cared of their suffering behind the Iron Curtain. In their places of exile the deportees waited impatiently for the death of Stalin, for many Chechens felt that with the death of the feared dictator they could reunite and force their way back to their cherished Caucasian homeland.

Finally, the good news arrived in the scattered "special settlement" camps of Kazakhstan, Uzbekistan, Kyrgyzstan, Tajikistan, and Siberia, where hundreds of thousands of members of the deported nations languished in exile. On March 5, 1953, the citizens of the USSR were told that their beloved *Vozhd* (leader) had died. As millions of Soviet citizens publicly mourned the death of Stalin, a hidden current of excitement passed through the "special settlement" camps of the Chechens and other exiles. While many deported nations, such as the Crimean Tatars, sent mass petitions stressing their loyalty to the Soviet state and hopes of receiving permission to return to their homelands at this time, the Chechens secretly prepared themselves to force their way back to their ancestral lands. Clan and Sufi leaders appear to have used bribery to send word throughout the Chechens' places of exile mobilizing the people for a mass surge to the homeland. With the death of the hated Stalin, the Chechens felt the time was finally ripe to challenge the Soviet system. In an almost primordial fashion, the snowcapped mountains of the Chechens' ancient homeland beckoned to this people, who prepared to return to their lost homes at any cost. It was time for the Chechens to return to the Russian-occupied farms and towns of Chechnya to rebuild their shattered nation in their beloved mountains.

The First Russian-Chechen War

We will beat the Chechens to a pulp, so that the present generation will be too terrified to fight Russia again.
— General Anatolii Kvashin, commander of
    Russian forces in Chechnya[1]

It's not just gangs which are fighting in Chechnya. It's the Chechen people. The men have taken up arms. They are fighting for their homes and for their land and for the graves of their forefathers.
— Russian Deputy Defense Minister Georgy
    Kondratyev, speaking of the Chechens' surprisingly
    spirited resistance to Russian Federal Forces[2]

The Final Years of Soviet Rule

With the death of Soviet leader Josef Stalin in 1953 and the subsequent reversal of many of his harsh policies by his more liberal successor, Nikita Khrushchev, the exiled Chechens and Ingush sensed that their moment to return to their homeland had come.[3] They perceived a 1956 decree by Khrushchev, which cleared them of the false charges of collective treason, as a green light to return to the distant Caucasus Mountains. As many as four hundred thousand Chechens and Ingush began a mass, uncontrollable surge back to the Caucasus in that year.

Although the exiled Chechens and Ingush initially were forbidden to return to their native homeland from their exile camps, they ignored this restriction. By 1957, through sheer numbers, they had begun to overrun the local (predominantly Russian) authorities in their former homeland, who were attempting to prevent their return. The head of the newly created Grozny Oblast (District), A. I. Iakovlev, appears to have exerted considerable effort to stop returning Chechen exiles from entering the region, but he and the local police were simply overwhelmed by the huge volume of returnees.

As the Chechens poured back into their homeland on buses and trains, fellow travelers complained about the stench caused by the Chechens' dead as they transported the disinterred bones of loved ones who had died in exile back to Chechnya. For their part, the Chechens relished the chance to inter the remains of their loved ones in their home soil, even if their ancestral graveyards had been desecrated in their absence.

This desecration was seen by the exiles as a supreme act of sacrilege and exacerbated relations between the returning Chechen-Ingush and the new Russian settlers living in their former homes and villages. One Chechen reported:

> When we came back in 1958, all the villages were Russian-occupied . . .
> In the old cemetery, there was a small shrine, the mausoleum of a saint.
> The new settlers destroyed it looking for treasure. They destroyed all
> the graves . . . The Russians began to leave as soon as we came back.
> They seemed to be afraid of us, and perhaps they even had a bad
> conscience.[4]

There were many clashes between the incoming Chechen-Ingush and the Russians who had been living in their homes and villages for twelve years. At the time, local Russian officials passed a law calling for the expulsion of Chechens and Ingush from the region, and there was a real fear among the former exiles that they would be redeported. The joy at returning to their homeland was tempered by the fear that they could once again be expelled from it.

After a few years, however, the Chechens became accepted and gradually began to rebuild their war-torn nation on its ancestral soil. There were no more efforts to expel them, and in 1957 the Chechen-Ingush Republic was reestablished. But tensions with the Russians remained just beneath the surface, as witnessed by the efforts of Chechens to bomb the statue of their nineteenth-century conqueror General Yermolov, which stood in the center of downtown Grozny. In the 1950s Soviet reports also spoke of numerous trials of Chechens for "banditry" and for retaining membership in Sufi brotherhoods, which were banned in the atheist Soviet Union.

Clearly the Chechens continued to feel a sense of collective discrimination, even in their own ethnic republic. This stemmed in part from the fact that the official policy was that the head of the Chechen-Ingush Republic (the First Party secretary), the head of the local KGB, the local police chief, and the top administrators in the oil industry all had to be ethnic Russians.[5] Further, it has been reported that "Russians or Slavs saturated the key appointments in the party apparatus at most levels in Checheno-Ingushestia."[6] In addition, few Chechens attended higher institutes of learning because of discrimination.[7] According to Russian scholar Valery Tishkov, "The Chechen and Ingush people nursed a sense of wounded pride. They had limited rights and opportunities compared to the Russian-speaking members of the republic's population."[8]

By the late 1960s, the relationship between the Chechens and the Soviet government and Russians living in their republic had, nonetheless, gradually stabilized, at least outwardly. In fact, Chechnya became a center for the refining of oil and natural gas in this period (although ethnic Russians dominated the industry). A new generation of Chechens grew up in the Soviet system in succeeding years and became Young Communist Pioneers in elementary school and Komsomol (Communist

Youth League) members as they grew older. But when they returned to their homes, the memory of the attempted genocide of their people that took loved ones from every family continued to be perpetuated, as did their links to Sufi folk Islam. Thus the Chechens lived in two worlds, one Soviet-Communist-atheist and the other Chechen mountaineer.

No one better defines this dichotomy than Dzhokhar Dudayev, the young Chechen who spent his youth in the exile camps in Central Asia and then went on to become the highest-ranking Chechen in the Soviet military before leading his people into rebellion against the post-Soviet Russian Federation as Chechnya's president. Dudayev was born on February 15, 1944, barely a week before the deportation of his people to Central Asia on February 23 of that year. Soon after his birth, Dudayev was, like the rest of his nation, arbitrarily declared a "traitor to the Soviet Union" and deported on the freezing cattle trains to Central Asia, a journey that many newborns did not survive.

Dudayev's family was deported to the harsh plains of Kazakhstan, and it was there that Dudayev spent the first thirteen years of his life. Chechen children such as Dudayev often experienced an educational gap from not being allowed to attend school during those years. Many remember being taunted as "traitors" and living in extreme poverty on the fringes of society during the exile years. They all grew up with stories of the calamity that had befallen their people and vicariously partook in the collective trauma of the *deportatsiia*.

In 1957, however, the young teenager Dudayev joined his family and the rest of his nation in their migration back to their homeland. Upon his return to Chechnya, Dudayev attended evening school and eventually qualified as an electrician. Then, just as the stigma of being a Chechen began to wear off, in 1962 Dudayev entered the Tambov Higher Military Aviation School and graduated in 1966.

Two years later Dudayev joined the Communist Party and continued his remarkable climb in the Soviet system by entering the prestigious Gagarin Air Force Academy in Moscow. At the time of his graduation in 1974, the Russian-speaking Dudayev appeared to be well on his way to becoming the ultimate Soviet Man that had been cultivated by the Kremlin for decades. His Russian, the language of interethnic communication, was said to be better than his Chechen; he did not practice Islam; and he even married a Russian woman named Alevtina "Alla" Kulikova, the daughter of a fellow Soviet military officer.

Never was Dudayev's seeming dedication to the concept of *Homo Sovieticus* more on display than when he loyally fought in the Soviet Air Force during the Soviets' war in Afghanistan in the 1980s. Like thousands of other young Chechen conscripts in the Soviet Army, Dudayev fought on behalf of Communism *against* the jihad of the Islamist Afghan mujahideen (holy warrior rebels). He did so in the ranks of the Soviet's Fortieth Limited Contingent, which occupied Muslim Afghanistan from December 25, 1979, to February 15, 1989.

While many people who discovered the Chechens only in the post-9/11 context came to misconstrue them as a race of Al Qaeda operatives, it must be stated that during the 1980s the Chechens did not fight in Afghanistan in the ranks of bin Laden's small Arab volunteer mujahideen unit. The only Chechens in Afghanistan during the 1980s "Mother of All Jihads" fought, like Dudayev (who was a pilot bombing the mujahideen Muslim rebels in fulfillment of his "Internationalist Duty"), as Soviet soldiers. According to one Russian account of the Soviet counterjihad in Afghanistan, "The Chechens were the best soldiers in the Soviet army at the time."[9]

Having served the Soviet Union faithfully in the war in Afghanistan (and having earned the Order of the Red Star and the Order of the Red Banner medals), in 1987 Dudayev was promoted to general and appointed to command the strategic 326th Ternopil heavy bomber squadron stationed in Tartu, the capital of the Estonian SSR. There he was in charge of a squadron of Tu-22 "Backfire" nuclear bombers, a significant accomplishment for a man from a race that had been officially denied ranks above colonel before his promotion. His appointment came after much lobbying to allow a token member of the Chechen race to be given a high-profile position.

By this time, the liberalizing period of President Mikhail Gorbachev's glasnost (openness) and perestroika (reconstructing) policies had begun to roll back some of the harsher policies of the Soviet police state. It was in this period that the Soviet Union officially repudiated the charges of treason against the Chechens and Ingush and other deported "traitor nations." It was on November 24, 1989, that the Soviet Union's two leading, state-owned newspapers, *Izvestiia* and *Pravda*, published articles that called the brutal deportations "a barbaric act of the Stalinist regime."[10] Then, in June 1990, the Russian historian Nikolai Bugai published an article in the prestigious journal *Voprosy Istorii* (Questions of History) which used Soviet documents to demonstrate that thousands of Chechens and Ingush had loyally served in the Soviet Army against the Nazis and that many of them had received medals and high ranks. It called the deportations a perversion of Leninist nationality policies.[11]

This was also a time of nationalist revival across the multiethnic Soviet Union as many repressed nations took advantage of the new, relaxed climate to agitate for greater national freedom. From Georgia in the south to the tiny Baltic republics of Latvia, Lithuania, and Estonia in the north that had been brutally conquered and annexed to the USSR during World War II, repressed ethnic groups began to demand more national rights. Local national fronts demanded greater autonomy and in some cases outright independence from Moscow.

Interestingly, as the head of the Soviet garrison in the Estonian capital of Tartu, General Dudayev was ordered to lead in the suppression of the Estonian nationalist protestors, but refused to do so. Instead, he flew the Estonian national flag above his base, showing his sympathy with the protesting Estonians, an act that forever won him the gratitude of that nation, which considers him a hero to this day.[12] As a member of a repressed Soviet ethnic minority, it seems Dudayev, ever loyal to the Kremlin, had finally found a line he could not cross. For all his efforts to be the perfect Soviet, Dudayev's conscience would not allow him to suppress Estonians, who were marching in the streets for something his people also craved, freedom.

The Buildup for War

Dudayev subsequently resigned from the Soviet army and ended his career as a soldier. It was at this time (May 1991) that the Chechen National Congress, which was agitating for independence from the Soviet Union (even though the Chechen-Ingush ASSR was not a full Soviet republic like Ukraine, Georgia, Kazakhstan, or Estonia), invited Dudayev to return to his homeland. There, Dudayev seems to have reconnected with his Chechen roots after decades of living away from home and striving to be the perfect Soviet man. In July of 1991 Dudayev was elected leader of the National Congress of the Chechen People. At this time the congress led demonstrations for independence, with many Chechen elders coming to Grozny's main square to perform *zikir* Sufi warrior dances, wearing their traditional folk costumes and brandishing *kinjal* swords. Their chant was "nothing was forgotten, nothing will be forgotten!" in reference to the deportation.

In September of 1991 Dudayev's followers took things even further and forcibly seized the buildings in Grozny that housed the government of Chechnya, in the aftermath of the failed Communist hard-liner coup attempt against Soviet leader President Mikhail Gorbachev in August. Then, on October 27, 1991, Dudayev was elected president of Chechnya. He quickly followed this up on November 1 when he issued a decree declaring the sovereignty of Chechnya (at roughly this time the Ingush part of the Chechen-Ingush Republic seceded and decided to remain a part of the Russian Federation).

Still wearing his Soviet military outfit and his trademark pencil mustache, Dudayev cut a dashing figure, and he was seen by many Chechens as a local boy who had made it big and returned to lead his own people to independence from the weakening USSR. The fact that he was a general gave him a certain clout in Chechen society, which respected martial culture. Many began to believe that he could make their dream of freedom from the Russian Federation/USSR come true.

But it must be clearly stated that the independent nation that the Sovietized Dudayev was working to create had nothing to do with the sort of harsh shariah-based theocracy that would later emerge in distant Afghanistan under the fanatical Taliban fundamentalist tribesmen. The Chechen leaders who gathered around Dudayev tended to be motivated by secular nationalism, not strict Islamic fundamentalism of the sort that was traditionally alien to their society. They were products of a Soviet system that had trained them to define themselves by their *natsional'nost* (officially recognized national identity), not their long-repressed, nonpoliticized Sufi faith. Russian scholar Valeriy Tishkov clearly states:

> The young and middle-aged elements of the population became atheists [under the Soviets]; they no longer read the Qur'an (since it could not be

reprinted or sold), said daily prayers, or observed regular religious rites. By the beginning of perestroika, in all of Chechnya, only thirteen mosques and one Muslim school remained.[13]

This source was also to state emphatically:

Religion played little part in the forming of the new Chechen identity during perestroika (i.e., before the first Chechen war). Apart from some ritual mentions of Islam, the Chechens did not identity themselves as an "Islamic people." I agree with G. Derluguian that "there is no ground for using the Islamic religion to explain the extremely strong and painful national conscience among the Chechens." Furthermore, the religious factor bore little connection to the original Chechen "national revolution." Collective suffering, rather than religion, culture, or language, cemented Chechen identity.[14]

It was thus the collective memory of the deportation, rather than any concept of "jihad" with the Russian "infidel," that drove the secularized Chechen leadership into a secessionist war with the Russians for national independence. Chechen historian Abdurakhman Avtorkhanov summed up the reasons for the "Chechen revolution" as follows:

What is happening now in Chechen-Ingushetia is, in my opinion, a revolt by the children to revenge the deaths of their fathers and mothers in the hellish conditions of the deportation in distant, cold and hungry Kazakhstan and Kirghizia. It is a protest by the whole people.[15]

With Soviet central power collapsing in late 1991 as the Russian Federation president Boris Yeltsin clashed with the Soviet Union head Mikhail Gorbachev, Yeltsin told various Soviet republic leaders to "seize as much sovereignty as you can swallow!" The Chechen secessionists were only too willing to oblige to escape their historic enemy.

Then, on December 26, 1991, the Soviet Union was formally dissolved. It was a day of rejoicing across the former Soviet space as the fifteen full Soviet Socialist Republics (i.e., the Russian Federation, Ukraine, Belorussia, Moldova, Estonia, Latvia, Lithuania, Armenia, Azerbaijan, Georgia, Kazakhstan, Kyrgyzstan, Turkmenistan, Tajikistan, and Uzbekistan) declared their sovereignty. Chechnya was, however, the only Autonomous Soviet Socialist Republic located inside the post-Soviet

Russian Federation to demand full independence from the rump Russian state. (Tatarstan played a game of brinkmanship with Moscow to gain more rights and autonomy, before finally agreeing to remain in the Russian Federation.) While there were many other small autonomous, ethnic-based republics in the transcontinental Russian Federation, especially in the north Caucasus, only Chechnya chose the path of outright confrontation with Moscow.

The Chechen secessionists did not limit themselves to words. In February 1992, Dudayev's armed followers surrounded a former Soviet base on Chechen soil, the 173rd Training Center for the North Caucasus Military District in Grozny. Leading them was a charismatic Chechen soldier of fortune named Shamil Basayev, who had already made a name for himself fighting as a mercenary in the breakaway region of Abkhazia in Georgia. One of the Russian generals from the surrounded base later recalled, "Shamil Basayev sat constantly in my office, a real bandit who kept asking me to give him a machine gun."[16] This Basayev would later go on to become one of the most effective of all the Chechen commanders in the upcoming war with Russia.

After ordering the Russian Federal troops out of Chechnya, Dudayev had his followers seize the weapons in the various bases left on Chechen soil. Their seizure amounted to 40,000 automatic weapons and machine guns, 153 cannons and mortars, 42 tanks, 18 Grad multiple rocket launchers, 55 armored personnel carriers, and 130,000 hand grenades.[17] The Chechen leadership also purchased weapons from neighboring regions, making the Chechens one of the most heavily armed people in the former Soviet Union.

At this time, Dudayev and his followers, who were described as religious "nonbelievers," wrote up a constitution for the new state.[18] It is important once again to note that it had little to do with shariah Islamic law. Valery Tishkov states:

Local intellectuals prepared a constitution for the Chechen Republic (Ichkeria) imbued with the spirit of representative democracy and secular law. Islam was relegated to a minor ritual role; the constitution made no mention of Islam or Allah, and religious liberty was recognized for all citizens. The constitution placed no restrictions on its citizenry on the basis of ethnicity or religion.[19]

In his superb book on the Chechen Wars, *Allah's Mountains*, Sebastian Smith, who spent considerable time with Dudayev's fighters, wrote of the Chechen president, "He had served in Afghanistan, taking part in the merciless bombing of civilians and was by his own admission, a somewhat lapsed Moslem."[20] Dudayev once warned "Where any religion prevails over the secular constitutional organization of the state, either the Spanish Inquisition or Islamic fundamentalism will emerge."[21]

Similarly, Anatol Lieven, who lived with the Chechen rebels during the first war reported:

> The Chechen struggle of the 1990s has been overwhelmingly a national or nationalistic one. In so far as it has taken on a religious coloring, this was mainly because Islam is seen, even by irreligious Chechens, as an integral part of national tradition and of the nation's past struggles against Russian domination. As Soviet officers, neither General Dudayev nor Colonel Maskhadov can previously have been practicing Muslims; even Shamil Basayev, while always a convinced Muslim, did not give me the impression before the war of being a particularly strict one. Islam seems less of a motive force in itself than something which has been adopted both by the Dudayev regime and individual Chechen fighters as spiritual clothing for their national struggle.[22]

Thomas de Waal, who also spent considerable time with the Chechen fighters during this period, similarly stated:

> Proclaiming independence from Moscow in 1991, Chechnya's first rebel president, Jokhar Dudayev, declared a secular state. Dudayev, a former Soviet general, was so ignorant about Islam that he once famously advised his citizens that, as good Muslims, they should pray three—and not five [as Muslims are required]—times a day.
>
> Dudayev's cause was a nationalist one—freeing Chechnya, as he put it, from "two hundred years of persecution" by the Russian state. For him, the key date in Chechen history was Stalin's mass deportation of the Chechen people to Central Asia in 1944. Dudayev frequently said he was

ready to have close economic and political ties with Russia, so long as "historical justice" was restored to his people.[23]

If there were any doubts about the secular origins of Dudayev's Chechen state, Lorenzo Vidino further stated:

The first Chechen War represented a quintessential nationalist conflict where an Islamic dimension was almost nonexistent . . . Dudayev, the undisputed leader of the first war, was a former Soviet general whose knowledge of Islam was minimal. His aim was to build a state preserving Chechnya's social structure and Islamic identity within a rigidly secular state framed by a modern constitution with freedom of religion and the preservation of rights for both Chechens and Russians.[24]

For all these reasons, James Hughes has written, "It was difficult to tar Dudayev with the brush of Islamic radicalism"; while Emma Gilligan has written, "Dudayev's ultimate aim was a constitutional secular state for Chechnya."[25]

But for all the fact that the new Chechen constitution made no restrictions based on ethnicity or religion and was "an almost entirely secular affair" with "no significant Islamic content," it was clear to all that Chechnya was to be for Chechens, not Russians who had been settled in the republic by the Russian and Soviet authorities.[26] At this time, thousands of Russians who had played a key role in the republic's oil industry emigrated voluntarily or were forced out from the breakaway republic. This had a devastating effect on the oil industry. Unemployment, which already had been high in the Soviet period, soared in Chechnya. The secessionist republic was filled with young armed men who did not have jobs, but were committed to the "Chechen revolution." Criminality, especially counterfeiting, surged in the republic at this time.

For its part, Moscow kept the Chechen secessionists at arm's length. It was clear that Chechen President Dudayev wanted to meet personally with Russian Federation President Boris Yeltsin to discuss the issue of Chechen independence, but Yeltsin refused to meet with him. In response Dudayev sent a personal letter to Yeltsin in March 1993, which stated:

Dear Mr. President! I express my deep respects, I wish you health and good fortune to you and your family, peace and prosperity to the people of the Russian state. I appeal to you in the name of all the Chechen people on a question that has fateful significance for mutual relations between our two states. I appeal to you to discuss the question of the recognition by the Russian Federation of the sovereign Chechen Republic. Resolution of this question would remove all barriers in the path to overcoming the many problems in the mutual relations of our states. The Russian Federation would acquire in the Chechen Republic a reliable partner and a guarantee of political stability in the entire Caucasus.[27]

By this time (1993), however, an opposition to Dudayev had grown in Chechnya, and Yeltsin was loath to further legitimize the seemingly eccentric Dudayev in his quixotic quest for independence from the Russian Federation. For this reason, Russian scholar Tishkov reports, "Throughout the crisis not a single top [Russian Federation] government leader contacted President Dudayev directly to listen to his position and propose a way of solving the conflict."[28]

It was at this time that the idea of invading the secessionist statelet in a so-called "Small Victorious War," similar to President Bill Clinton's September 1994 intervention in Haiti which had led to the overthrow of that country's president, Raoul Cedras, began to be seriously discussed in Moscow. President Yeltsin had already tried once to overthrow Dudayev with a relatively small unit of Interior Ministry troops, but this attempt had failed when Dudayev's own fighters surrounded Yeltsin's troops and forced them to withdraw in humiliation.

In October 1994, Moscow sent troops to support Chechen opposition forces who were trying to overthrow the increasingly eccentric and authoritarian Dudayev, but this attempt also had failed. In an embarrassment for Yeltsin, as many as seventy Russian troops were captured in the failed operation and paraded before cameras by a defiant Dudayev before being released.

There were fears at this time that Chechnya might be the first domino to fall in a parade of secessions of small ethnic republics in the north Caucasus, but these fears were overblown, and no other ethnic republic in the Russian Federation appeared willing to confront Moscow. But this perception, and the increasing anarchy in Chechnya, which was still considered by Yeltsin to be a part of the Russian Federation, led to the fateful decision to invade Chechnya and overthrow its secessionist government. As the war clouds appeared on the horizon, a concerned Dudayev told the Kremlin that "if only Yeltsin calls" he would make terms. But by then the Russians let it be known that it was "too late," war had been decided upon.[29]

The Siege of Grozny

On November 29, 1994, Yeltsin ordered the Russian Federal army to "restore constitutional order" in Chechnya, and on December 1, Russian Federation bombers began bombarding targets across Chechnya. It was to be Moscow's largest military operation since Afghanistan, and thousands would die in the bombings that destroyed villages and neighborhoods in Grozny. The transcontinental Russian Federation was at war with Vermont-sized Chechnya in what was expected to be a short war that would boost Yeltsin's ratings in Russia.

Dudayev and his small "National Guard" of several thousand followers were seen as an unworthy opponent of the mighty Russian Federation. The Russian General Staff seem to have entertained the notion that they could launch a bombing blitz, then march into Grozny and quickly restore order. In the process, they would overthrow the rebellious Dudayev government, much as the Soviets had previously done in Budapest, Hungary, in 1956 and Prague, Czechoslovakia, in 1968. The Russian military, including Interior Ministry troops, numbered some 2.4 million, while the entire ethnic Chechen population in Chechnya came to just 900,000.[30] The general tasked with overthrowing the Chechen president and his regime, Pavel Grachev, famously stated he could carry out the operation in "a bloodless blitzkrieg that would not last any longer than December 20th."[31]

It was now time to brutally put an end to the Chechens' quixotic rebellion. On December 11 the Russian Federal troops launched a three-pronged invasion of the Chechen Republic. But one of the columns was momentarily stopped by civilians blocking the road in the neighboring republic of Ingushetia, and the commander of the main column resigned in disgust at being told to shoot civilians. Another Russian column was also blocked as it tried to invade from the Russian republic of Dagestan to the east.

Morale remained low among the Russian conscripts, who made up the bulk of soldiers invading the breakaway republic. As the Russians proceeded across the open plains of the north, one account stated: "Russian commanders seemed to have been unwilling to directly attack Chechen positions, probably in the reckoning that, man for man, the Chechens would be able to defeat the conscript forces which made up the bulk of the Russian armed forces. Instead they relied on artillery and air bombardment."[32]

But clumsy Russian bombardments caused civilian casualties and drove thousands of Chechens to create their own ad hoc citizen defense militias to fight the invaders. One account of this informal process described the mobilization of village defense units as follows: "When the war began the lads in our village got together. 'What shall we do?' We decided to fight. 'Who will be our commander?' We agreed, 'He'll do it.' And off we went."[33]

While Dudayev was not uniformly popular, the senseless killing of Chechens by invading Russian Federal forces drove many villagers to support his rebellion. For example, Chechen militiamen repelled Russian forces in the village of Dolinskoye and caused considerable losses for the enemy, who seem to have expected that a show of force might cause the defenders to lose heart. This area was not, however, a stronghold of support for Dudayev.

But the larger Russian force of roughly forty thousand troops nonetheless was able to take the Grozny airport at Khankala by mid-December. Moving inexorably through the flat plains of northern Chechnya, the Russian forces converged on Grozny and began to bombard the civilian-packed city with Grad (Hail) and Uragan (Hurricane) missiles and aircraft. The Russian bombardment was indiscriminate and began to fill Grozny's morgues and hospitals with dead and maimed civilians. Sebastian Smith, who was one of the rare Western journalists in the encircled city, recorded the unfolding tragedy as follows: "Under President Yeltsin's bombs Grozny, founded in 1818 by a Russian general, disintegrated. The population, once 400,000, began to vanish. Columns of refugees poured out through the unblockaded south, taking only what they could carry or stuff into cars, their children sitting on top of each other in the back seats, serious-faced."[34]

Refugees who fled the city often fared no better than those who stayed. Thousands of fleeing Chechens were arrested as "bandits" and sent to so-called "filtration camps," where abuse and torture were rampant. The most notorious filtration center was PAP-1 on the outskirts of Grozny. Other fleeing Chechens were killed on the spot, as in the case of a group of refugees whose cars were shot at by Russian troops and then crushed by their armored personnel carriers. The Associated Press reported that the Russians "chased and killed the wounded, then dragged them away."[35]

The few intrepid Western journalists covering the conflict said the brutal Russian bombardment of Grozny dwarfed that of the much-publicized Serbian bombardment of the Bosnian city of Sarajevo in the early 1990s Bosnian conflict (which led to US-NATO interventions to save lives).[36] Tens of thousands of Grozny's residents who had been trapped in the city cowered in their basements hoping the bombs would not find them. Anatol Lieven, who was reporting from Grozny at the time, described the bombardment as "a large part of the artillery of the former Soviet colossus pouring its fire into an area of a few square miles."[37] Robert Seely wrote, "To force the rebels from the city centre, rules of engagement designed to avoid large scale civilian casualties were de facto ignored."[38] This source also stated: "The destruction of Grozny was both an act of punishment for Chechen resistance and a show of determination that they would defeat Dudayev regardless of the cost."[39]

One eyewitness to the stupendous destruction wrote, "The destruction of Grozny was apocalyptic . . . I saw a lot of deaths. I saw people who got wounded by shrapnel from mortar fire and they were dying very slow deaths. But it was very difficult to go and help them because the next target could be you."[40] A Chechen was to bemoan the destruction of Grozny as follows: "It was the most beautiful city in the world. But my beautiful city was destroyed by Russia and together with it, all Chechnya and the people living there."[41]

Russian journalists also reported large numbers of civilian casualties in the city of Grozny.[42] One BBC report stated: "Western journalists, including BBC correspondents, reported that the Russian artillery was indiscriminately targeting civilian apartment blocks as the capital was rocked by the sheer power of the attack."[43] Germany's Chancellor Helmut Kohl described the destruction from Russian bombardments as "sheer madness," while observers from the OSCE (Organization for Security and Cooperation in Europe) described it as an "unimaginable catastrophe."[44] Among other targets destroyed in what human rights groups described as a crime against humanity was an orphanage in Grozny.[45]

As the Russians began to systematically demolish the Chechen capital in an effort to overwhelm her outnumbered defenders, however, something unexpected happened. Hundreds of average Chechen volunteer fighters chose not to flee the inferno, but to pour into Grozny to defend their capital. Most of those Chechens streaming into the capital did so on an ad hoc basis and were not under the control of President Dudayev, who many frankly disliked for his eccentric ways. Smith points out that the Chechen fighters were inspired not by politics but by "their national mythology of the warrior and defense of freedom," and most were fighting "for freedom" and their "families," in their own words.[46] As they had done for centuries, the Chechens were spontaneously coming together to defend their *ka'am*, their nation. War correspondents witnessing this spontaneous movement observed, "It was if something ancient was happening among the Chechens."[47] Sebastian Smith wrote:

> The Chechens fought in mobile, self sufficient groups and their sense of mission was so high that most of them seemed genuinely to have lost any fear of death. Wearing home-made smocks of white sheets and wrapping white ribbons around their weapons to hide in the snow, the Chechens operated in groups of between five and 20, rarely more. A well armed group might have one machine-gun, one or two anti-tank rocket propelled grenade launchers (RPG) and automatic rifle for each man . . . The ironic effect of President Yeltsin's war, particularly the savage aerial bombardment, was that Dudayev's tawdry rebellion had become a people's uprising.[48]

It was these Chechen militiamen who were to turn the killing streets of Grozny into an urban forest and to wreak havoc on the army of Russian conscripts sent in with poor morale, training, and leadership. The rebel fighters' or *boyeviks'* weapon of choice was the RPG-7 or RPG-18 Mukha, which could be fired down from buildings and destroy tanks with its armor-piercing round. The rebels referred to this rocket grenade launcher as the "Chechen Atom Bomb." Lester Grau and Timothy

Thomas, American analysts at Fort Leavenworth, wrote of the Chechen *boyeviks'* use of RPGs and other light weapons against the Russians:

> The proliferation of rocket-propelled grenade launchers surprised the Russians, as well as the diversity of uses to which they were put. RPGS were shot at everything that moved. They were fired at high angle over low buildings as mortars, and were also used as area weapons against advancing infantry, antitank weapons and, on occasion, as air defense weapons. They were sometimes fired in very disciplined volleys and were the weapon of choice for the Chechens, along with the sniper rifle. Not only were the Russians faced with well-trained, well-equipped Chechen military snipers, there were also large numbers of designated marksmen who were very good shots using standard military rifles. These were very hard to deal with and usually required massive fire power to overcome. The Chechen standard hunter-killer team consisted of an RPG gunner, machine gunner and sniper . . .
>
> [Chechen] Ambushes were common. Sometimes they actually had three tiers. Chechens would be underground, on the ground floor, and on the roof. The ambushers would concentrate fire against targets when possible. Multiple RPG rounds flying from different heights and directions limit a vehicle commander's ability to respond. Escape routes were always predetermined.
>
> Chechens weren't afraid of tanks and BMPs (armored personnel carriers). They assigned groups of RPG gunners to fire volleys at the lead and trail vehicles. Once they were destroyed, the others were picked off one-by-one. The Russian forces lost 20 of 26 tanks, 102 of 120 BMPS, and 6 of 6 ZSU-23s in the first three day's fighting. Chechens chose firing positions high enough or low enough to stay out of the fields of fire of tank and BMP weapons. Russian conscript infantry simply refused to dismount and often died in their BMP without ever firing a shot.[49]

The Chechen hunter-killer teams would "hug" (sneak up on) Russian columns, fire on them at close range taking out tanks, then flee to escape the inevitable overwhelming retaliatory Russian bombardment. The Chechen *boyeviks* had to fire and move fast. Dudayev described their tactics as "strike and withdraw, strike and withdraw, exhaust them until they [the Russians] die of fear and horror."[50] It was a deadly cat-and-mouse game, and the rebels became the ultimate urban guerillas playing it. As the Russians continued to flatten Grozny around them, the Chechens made them pay a high price for any advance into the city. Lieven wrote in glowing terms of the Chechen fighters' courage he witnessed as follows:

> The stamina of the Chechen fighters under this pressure (as much of a pressure on the nerves as a physical danger), for weeks on end, was deeply impressive; as for the defenders of Bamut, in the Caucasian foothills, who defended the village for fifteen months in the face of a bombardment to which they could not reply, their performance places them in the ranks of the great epic defenders of history, alongside the men of Verdun and Masada.[51]

Carlotta Gall and Thomas de Waal also spent time with the Chechen fighters and compared them favorably to their Russian counterparts:

> The Chechens, by comparison [to the Russians], were fearless and often merciless. Natural marksmen who learn to handle guns as small boys, they picked off fleeing soldiers easily. Hundreds of volunteers ran in to grab weapons from dead Russian soldiers, especially seeking the prized sniper rifles with night-sights, the more experienced hacking off the big machine-guns from the armoured vehicles.[52]

There were some experienced fighters among the Chechens, most notably the five-hundred-man National Guard led by the charismatic Shamil Basayev, who had previously led a unit of Chechen volunteers fighting in the breakaway Georgian province of Abkhazia. There also was the unit led by Aslan Maskhadov, the "chief of staff" of the Chechen "army," who was a former artillery colonel in the Soviet army. But most Chechens learned the art of war in hands-on combat. Their unique martial culture, which stressed bravery and the warrior ethic, their history of deportation and conquest, and their deep desire for independence drove them to fight against the odds.

Journalists who were there at the time stress that the "nonpracticing" Muslim Chechens, few of whom were reported to have much knowledge of Islam outside of their Sufi cultural traditions, did not see their struggle as a jihad.[53] As the First Russia-Chechen War went on, religion would begin to provide the rebels with a greater sense of unity, higher purpose for their sacrifices, and sense of mission, but it remained a subtext to the conflict for both sides. It was the quote of "never again," referring to the deportation, not the concept of holy war that inspired the *boyeviks*.[54]

The core of the Chechen force numbered little more than three thousand men at the height of the war, although this small force was bolstered for larger offenses by part-time militiamen.[55] The Russian defense minister, Pavel Grachev, however, made the preposterous claim that there were six thousand "foreign mercenaries" who had somehow made their way into Russian-surrounded Chechnya to defend the Chechens and twelve hundred "dangerous criminals."[56] Yeltsin upped the ante and claimed there were "10,000 foreign mercenaries," but these wild claims belied the truth.[57] The truth was that a Russian Federation force of forty thousand bolstered by tanks, heavy artillery, and an air force was beginning to be stymied by small bands of some three thousand lightly armed Chechen fighters defending their homeland and people.

The Russians were soon to discover how badly they had underestimated the Chechens, whom they disparaged as "bandits." On December 31, 1994, the Russians launched a full-scale New Year's Eve assault on Grozny from two sides, timed to celebrate the birthday of the overall commander Russian General Pavel Grachev. They did not, however, totally surround the city, which allowed the Chechens to receive supplies and reinforcements from the south and east, and this proved costly. The first day of the assault was a complete disaster for the Russian Federal troops. The Russians stayed in their armored vehicles without providing flanking infantry for them, so the Chechen defenders simply lobbed RPG rounds and grenades down on the tanks and APCs (armored personnel carriers) from the surrounding nine-story buildings and destroyed the Russians, whom they labeled "cowards."[58] One account of the Chechen destruction of the Russian probe on New Year's Eve states the following:

> From point-blank range, Chechen fighters opened fire from different directions and trajectories, destroying the leading and rear tanks, then picking off armour in between. The Chechens managed to "kill" so high a number of Russian tanks and APCs due to their ability to fire at very close range and fire several volleys at their given targets. Many tanks received not one, but multiple hits from anti-tank grenades. Disoriented and

petrified, the Russian conscripts panicked. The early hours of 1 January turned into a slaughter of several hundred Russian teenagers as Chechen fighters methodically incinerated dozens of troops inside their vehicles and shot down those who managed to flee the burning armour.[59]

A Chechen fighter recalled seeing a Russian column of tanks and APCs "moving like a herd," which was then attacked with Chechen rocket-propelled grenades. In the Chechen's words, the column was "sliced up and burned to the devil."[60] A Russian source called the Russian soldiers going up against the Chechens "cannon fodder going to the slaughter."[61] One analyst called the subsequent ambush in Grozny's Freedom Square a "turkey shoot," as the Chechens allowed the Russians into the city center, then surrounded and ambushed them, killing hundreds of Russians who appeared to be lost.[62]

The invading Russian force was almost obliterated and lost dozens of T-72 tanks before managing to regroup and break out of the deadly ambush. As the Russians retreated it became obvious that their losses had been catastrophic. The first unit to spearhead the invasion, the thousand-man 131st "Maikop" Brigade, for example, had lost nearly 800 men, 20 of its 26 tanks, and 102 of its 120 armored vehicles.[63] Eyewitnesses report that Freedom Square had turned into "a horrific inferno of burning tanks and dead bodies."[64] The Russians lost more tanks in the battle than in the battle for Berlin in 1945.[65]

Scores of frightened Russian conscripts also were captured by the Chechens in the conflict. In response, many of their mothers traveled at great risk to Grozny, where they met with the Chechen leadership and asked that their sons be released. President Dudayev, in a goodwill gesture, agreed to release them after extracting "a promise of eternal indebtedness to their brave mothers."[66] One brave Russian mother made her way to Shamil Basayev's professional unit to free her son. After freeing the son, Basayev told him, "Do you understand what a heroic mother you have?"[67] Basayev began the policy of releasing his prisoners only to their mothers after he had previously released thirty soldiers to the Russian army. He had forced them, however, to promise they would not serve again in Chechnya, only to hear that they all had been returned to the front lines that very night.[68]

At this time, the differences between the Chechen defenders and the Russian invaders became even more obvious. The cobbled-together Russian army was made up of demoralized conscript troops who often did not believe in their mission, which was to crush the independence drive of a small nation. For this reason the Russians tended to be rather casualty-phobic and prone to avoid conflict when possible.

By contrast, the Chechens seem to have rallied to the defense of their nation and were willing to die for it. One Chechen captured the differences in the fighting motivations between the Russians and his people by stating: "They're not fighting for anything, we're fighting for our homeland — we're not afraid to die."[69] Another stated: "We're just defending our land. They have planes, helicopters, multiple rockets, mortars and we have no weapons except our spirit . . . We know what happened in 1944 and about the 19th century. All our history we've fought with the Russians and we just don't want them here."[70] Unlike the Russian conscripts, the Chechens fervently believed in their cause. One Chechen fighter claimed, "You could say the whole population here is involved in the defense. Every street has provided several groups of four or five volunteers."[71]

The highly motivated Chechens of Grozny were said to "dance around" the Russians as they took advantage of their knowledge of the their home city to move through sewers, back alleys, and destroyed buildings to attack them. The best among them was the elite commando unit led by Shamil Basayev. One eyewitness claimed of Basayev's men, "As soon as they went in all hell would let loose, the fight would suddenly escalate."[72] As for Basayev himself, one eyewitness stated in awe: "He was crazy. There would be fire coming from everywhere, rooftops, cars, everything, and he would just walk out in the middle of the street firing like mad at them."[73]

While many Russians had expected to win the war through a display of force, they seem to have underestimated the Chechens' willingness to stand their ground and fight for their homes, nation, and independence. For all these reasons, General Pavel Grachev began to change tactics. Having been badly burnt for trying to probe the city with troops, the Russian Federal forces began to rely even more on long-distance artillery and aerial bombardments to blast the Chechens out of their positions and force them to give up their symbolic defense of the Presidential Palace in the center of Grozny. At one point the Russians were raining four thousand artillery rounds a minute onto Grozny in the largest bombardment since World War II.[74]

As the bombs and missiles destroyed the city center around them, the Chechens tenaciously defended the symbolic Presidential Palace, which previously had been the old Communist Headquarters, until January 19, 1995. The final stroke was when a "bunker buster" penetration bomb broke through nine floors and entered the cellar of the Presidential Palace, forcing the Chechen commander Colonel Aslan Maskhadov to finally abandon it. On the following day, the Russians triumphantly raised their flag above the blackened hulk of the Presidential Palace.

Having taken the Presidential Palace, the Russians announced that the "military phase in operations in Chechnya is over" and switched the "normalization" process over from the Ministry of Defense to the Ministry of Interior. But the Kremlin's pronouncement was premature, and Chechen rebels continued to ambush and snipe at Russian troops in southern Grozny. Chechen Chief of Staff Aslan Maskhadov continued to lead troops from a fallback headquarters in a hospital, and Russian troops continued to die. It would take another month before the Russians succeeded in encircling the city with an army that had swollen to almost fifty-five thousand (outnumbering the Chechens by more than ten times) and cutting off the rebels' southern supply routes.[75]

As the net closed in on them, the last Chechen fighting unit, Shamil Basayev's experienced Abkhaz Battalion, broke through Russian lines and escaped to the south on the symbolic day of February 23, the date of their people's deportation in 1944. While the Russians proclaimed that Grozny was theirs, it had come at a high price of as many as four thousand of their soldiers' lives.[76] Russian sources claim that as many as twenty-seven thousand people died in Grozny itself during the siege. Ironically enough, many of these were ethnic Russians who had lived in the city but had been unable to escape to the Chechen villages of the south because they had no roots in them.[77]

The Second Stage of the War

Having abandoned the ruins of what had previously been one of the finest cities in the Caucasus, Chechen military leader Aslan Maskhadov then began to fight the Russians in the open plains between the city and the Caucasus Mountains to the south. Despite the odds against him, Maskhadov was determined to fight the Russians "position versus position" in defense of a series of towns in the plains. This conventional, frontline battle was meant to show the world that the Chechens were a nation with an army defending their homeland, not mere "bandits."

This decision to fight frontally in the spring of 1995 proved costly, however, as the Russians' artillery, tanks, and air force gave them an advantage over the small Chechen "army." After a three-month siege, the small town of Argun fell on March 23 followed by the "Fortress Town" of Bamut, which had fought tenaciously. But progress had been much slower than the Russians anticipated because of the Chechens' almost suicidal determination to resist and defend small hamlets against much larger forces.

At this time the Russians made an example out of a typical plains town known as Samaskhi, which seemed to be a repeat of the nineteenth-century tsarist Russian "pacification" tactics. On April 7, 1995, the Russians surrounded the doomed hamlet and refused to let any of its inhabitants leave. Then they shelled it mercilessly and poured into it and began to systematically massacre its civilian inhabitants. The Russian human rights group Memorial claimed that more than one hundred Chechen civilians were killed in the "mopping-up operation," many of them women, children, and the elderly.[78] Locals raised the number to three hundred killed.[79] Most of those Chechens who were killed in Samashki were burnt alive or blown to pieces. The oldest victim of the massacre was ninety-six years old.[80]

When the rampage was over, the village had been reduced to smoldering houses with burnt bodies inside them. It was state-sponsored terrorism and a microcosm of what had been happening on a larger scale in Grozny. The irony of the slaughter was that there were few Chechen fighters left in the village to defend it, as the elders had convinced them to leave before the Russians arrived so as to avoid conflict.[81] Shamil Basayev and other *boyeviks* who would later resort to terrorism against the Russians would cite the deliberate slaughter of dozens of civilians in Samaskhi as the inspiration for their own terror campaign against Russian civilians. The United Nations subsequently issued a scathing report of what became known as the Samaskhi Massacre, which stated:

It is reported that a massacre of over 100 people, mainly civilians, occurred between 7 and 8 April 1995 in the village of Samashki, in the west of Chechnya. According to the accounts of 128 eye-witnesses, Federal soldiers deliberately and arbitrarily attacked civilians and civilian dwellings in Samashki by shooting residents and burning houses with flamethrowers. The majority of the witnesses reported that many OMON troops were drunk or under the influence of drugs. They wantonly opened fire or threw grenades into basements where residents, mostly women, elderly persons and children, had been hiding.

Russian human rights NGOs carried out an investigation into the incident and concluded, *inter alia*, that: (a) Federal troops had conducted a "cleanup" operation, including extensive house-to-house searches, during which they killed civilians, mistreated detainees and committed arson; (b) at least 103 civilians, most of whom did not participate in the armed clashes were killed; (c) owing to the blockade of the village by Federal troops, the wounded did not have access until 10 April 1995 to qualified medical assistance, as a result of which many of them died; (d) indiscriminate arbitrary detention of the male population of the village was carried out, during which torture, beatings, mistreatment and summary executions were reported.[82]

Despite the global condemnation, the Russian Federation did not prosecute any of those involved in the bloody massacre, thus losing much of its already tattered moral high ground.

By May 1995, the Russians had brutally conquered the Chechen capital and the plains, while the Chechen *boyeviks* and thousands of fleeing civilians had retreated up two southern mountain valleys, the Argun and the Khulkhulau. It was in these river valleys that the rebels' only towns remained. They were Shatoy in the Khulkhulau and Vedeno in the Argun. Vedeno, which became the Chechen government's fallback capital, was a town replete with history. It was dominated by an ancient fortress that had once been Imam Shamil's capital in his battle against the Russians in the nineteenth century. It was also the home of the rebels' most effective field commander, Shamil Basayev.

While the Chechens appeared to be determined to fight to the death to maintain their mountain redoubt at Vedeno, they faced considerable

problems. They were running low on ammunition and cut off from supplies and reinforcements. The Chechens' fighting spirit also seemed to
be flagging as they soberly assessed the odds of victory against the much
larger Russian Federal force.

The Russians sent a personal message to Basayev at this time, when
they targeted his house for a bombing that killed eleven of his relatives,
most of them women.[83] The youngest victim was a nine-month-old baby.
Among the other victims were Basayev's wife, child, and sister, a fact
that seemed to further embitter the Chechens' most dangerous leader.[84]
An enraged Basayev subsequently would tell Anatol Lieven, "You talk
about terrorism forfeiting our moral superiority before world opinion.
Who cares about our moral position? Who from abroad has helped us,
while Russia has brutally ignored every moral position? If they can use
such weapons and threats so can we."[85] After the bombing, Basayev
claimed, "At that moment I swore I would kill Russian pilots wherever
I found them," a threat he would fulfill in just two weeks.[86] One analyst
later would write, "To some extent the Russians bear at least some responsibility for Basayev's ruthless career."[87]

To compound matters, on June 4 the Russians launched a surprise attack on Vedeno, their only truly effective operation of the war, and were
able to capture Basayev's hometown from the outgunned rebels. On June
13 the Russians then took the Chechens' last remaining mountain town,
Shatoy. At this point the *boyeviks'* fortunes plunged to their lowest point,
and for all their determined resistance, their battle for independence appeared to be lost.

It was at this time, less than two weeks after the destruction of his
house, that the unpredictable Basayev was to turn the tables and do the
unexpected. He told a group of one hundred and twenty of his best men,
"I'm going to take the war to Russia. Who wants to come with me?"[88]
Basayev would launch a daring *nabeg* (an old-fashioned highlander
raid) seventy miles into Russia that was to take the horrors of war-torn
Chechnya into the peaceful heartland of the enemy for the first time.

It all began on the following day, June 14, 1995, when a unit of Basayev's followers numbering approximately 119 *smertniks* ("suicide" fighters) commandeered several Russian military trucks and bribed their way
through notoriously corrupt Russian checkpoints deep into the neighbor-

ing Russian province of Stavropol. The Russian-speaking Chechens wearing Russian uniforms pretended to be a convoy bringing Russian bodies back to Russia for burial until they were stopped by policemen outside the city of Budyonnovsk 70 miles (110 kilometers) north of Chechnya.

Budyonnovsk was a sleepy town of sixty thousand people, whose closest ties to the war were that the much-hated Russian Hind helicopters flying raids into Chechnya were based there. When Basayev and his men finally were stopped, they realized their secret mission to drive deeper into Russia and "stop the war or die" had been exposed, and they gunned down the policemen and barreled into the city with guns blazing. The inhabitants realized the danger only when dozens of battle-hardened mountain *boyeviks* poured into their city and attacked the police station with RPGs, machine guns, and assault rifles. The Chechen raiders then raised their green-and-white wolf flag over the city hall. The horrors of Chechnya had now come to Russia with a vengeance.

As Russian reinforcements raced into the city, Basayev and his men began to pour through the streets collecting hundreds of hostages and herding them toward the city's main hospital. Once there, the Chechens captured the entire hospital and all of its staff and patients (including women with newborns in the maternity ward) and held them hostage in what was perhaps the largest and most brazen hostage taking in history. Estimates vary as to how many hostages were taken, with the numbers ranging from two thousand to five thousand.

The Chechens then planted land mines in the lower floors of the hospital and positioned snipers and machine gunners in key defensive locations. Basayev made an ultimatum: his demands were that the Russians end their war against his people and that the Russian media be allowed to interview him and his fighters/terrorists. It was the ultimate embarrassment for Russian President Boris Yeltsin, who had tried to downplay to his people the horrors of the increasingly unpopular war in Chechnya.

The Russians vowed not to negotiate with "bandits" and told Basayev that they had arrested two thousand Chechens and would shoot them if he and his men did not surrender.[89] Unmoved by the threat, Basayev demonstrated a new sense of ruthlessness when he had five captured Russian pilots from the nearby helicopter base taken outside and executed in cold blood, as earlier he had promised to do following the bombing of his house. Basayev's men chose to execute the helicopter pilots because of his deep hatred for their role in strafing and attacking civilians in the Chechen homeland.

At this time, Basayev also pointedly refused a Russian offer of a plane, money, and safe passage abroad. He vowed to stay in the hospital until Russia met his demands for a negotiated end to the war in Chechnya. Basayev declared, "For seven months we've had fighting in our land. Every bullet hits a Chechen or part of Chechnya. We've had enough and now we'll continue to fight, but on Russian land, so that the bullets hit Russia, not Chechnya."[90] He claimed to have launched the raid to make Russians feel "the real horror of the war that the Russians have unleashed on his people."[91]

Basayev also declared to journalists, "We hope at least one of you will tell the truth. We are not bandits. We are a country at war with another state. They have taken our families, our land and our freedom."[92]

President Yeltsin, however, refused to negotiate with Basayev and, to the horror of his people who watched the tragedy unfold live on television, ordered his elite Alpha commandos and *spetsnaz* special forces to storm the booby-trapped hospital, which was guarded by 119 heavily armed, desperate *smertniks* surrounded by thousands of hostages. It seemed that the Russians were more intent on killing the hostage takers and not giving in to their demands than on saving the hostages. One account of the incident would state: "The [Russian] security services behaved along the lines of traditional Soviet practice, which held that everyone including the hostages and hostage-takers must die and thereby destroy any full record of the incident."[93]

The result was a bloody fiasco. As Russian tanks shelled the hospital and set it on fire, APCs and attack helicopters sprayed it with cannon fire. The carnage only stopped when screaming hostages were filmed on Russian television standing in the shattered windows of the hospital waving white sheets, some with blood on them, and begging for their lives. One Russian commentator stated of the fiasco: "Saturday, June 17th will go down in the annals of the struggle against terrorism as a day of folly, unprofessionalism of the military and the complete idiocy of their superiors."[94] Another stated, "Everyone is asking who gave the order for this crazy assault—but no one knows."[95]

At this point Basayev did show some compassion and released some patients, mainly women and children. But the rule that it is not safe to be a hostage in Russia for the simple fact that the Russian security forces might kill you was vividly proven and would be proven over and over again in the future.[96]

Basayev, however, did not surrender and promised that he and his men would hold their hostages until the bombing in Chechnya ended. But no sooner had the first attack stopped than the Russians launched a second bloody assault, which ended up being repelled with massive loss of the hostage and Russian attackers' lives. The carnage was broadcast on television and highlighted the ineptitude and callousness of the Russian authorities. To compound matters, President Yeltsin was in Halifax, Canada, for a "Group of Seven" industrial nations' meeting at the time, and the hostage crisis demonstrated to the world and his people how uninvolved he was in the running of the Chechen conflict. It was at this time that the Russian prime minister, Viktor Chernomyrdin, stepped onto the stage and did the previously unthinkable. He directly negotiated via telephone with Shamil Basayev, the most wanted man in Russia. Russians were treated to the surreal televised images of their prime minister pleading with Basayev, "a dirty bearded terrorist," not to harm the hostages.

After a total of six harrowing days, an agreement finally was reached whereby a ceasefire would be declared and Basayev and his men would be allowed to return home to Chechnya. In response, Basayev released all but 120 to 150 hostages, some of whom volunteered to stay with him and his men to protect them as they returned to the mountains of Chechnya.

On June 21 the ceasefire took effect, and the war in the southern mountains came to a sudden and unexpected halt. For the first time in months, the skies above Chechnya's burning hamlets were clear of bombers and the rumble of artillery ceased. It was a godsend for the hard-pressed Chechen rebels, and Basayev and his *smertniks* were hailed as heroes throughout Chechnya. Against all odds Basayev's desperate gamble had paid off, and the *boyeviks* had been granted a much-needed reprieve. After a long journey back through Dagestan, where locals came out to greet the Chechens as heroes, Basayev's convoy, which included a refrigerated truck carrying the bodies of sixteen slain rebels, reached the Chechen mountains. There Basayev and his men quickly scattered into the countryside to celebrate their improbable victory, which had given the rebels a much-needed morale boost and proved to the Russian people that the war was far from contained.

For the Russians the whole episode had been a debacle, and many residents of Budyonnovsk blamed the Russian authorities as much as the Chechen hostage takers. They claimed the Chechen terrorists had had more concern for their safety than the Russian forces who had attacked them with tanks, rockets, and machine guns.[97] News sources reported that "the [Russian] troops were blamed for killing more hostages and bystanders than rebels."[98] One hostage reported, "They [the Chechens] demonstrated what was happening in their land. They didn't abuse us."[99] Another stated, "They treated us well, even gave us some chocolate. They tried to calm us down every day. But during the storming, it was horrible — bullets and glass and plaster flying everywhere."[100] One freed hostage said, "They shot at us, our own troops shot at us. The Chechens were good to us."[101]

Not all hostages were as forgiving, and one stated, "For so many years they [the Chechens] have been raping our girls and killing our men. They have done only harm to this land."[102] In total approximately 120 to 150 hostages and bystanders were killed during the raid, the majority shot dead by their own country's security forces during the failed storming of the hospital. Robert Schaefer states, "According to the hostages' own accounts, most of the casualties were from Russian artillery and direct fire attacks."[103]

For his part, Basayev was unrepentant and declared, "The Russians have taken the war to our homeland, so why shouldn't we take the war to Russia? I wanted the Russian people to know exactly what war feels like. I wanted them to feel our pain. They needed to know that this war is not an abstract notion. I wanted to wake them up."[104]

Meanwhile, talks between the Russians and the Chechens under the auspices of the OSCE (Organization for Security and Cooperation in Europe) took place. Finally, on July 31, 1995, a deal was reached for a permanent ceasefire and simultaneous disarmament of the Chechens and withdrawal of the Russians from Chechnya. To celebrate the peace deal, the Basayev family invited the local Russian colonel to their house for a traditional Chechen feast of vats of mutton. Both sides were represented in the peace talks by moderates who seemed to want to end the war: on the Russian side, Lieutenant General Anatoly Romanov, and on the Chechen side, Chief of Staff Aslan Maskhadov.

But there were hawks on both sides who were unhappy with the treaty. Some Russian forces recommenced the bombardment of lowland towns in August, while one hotheaded Chechen commander attacked the Russian-occupied town of Argun.

The peace remained tentative throughout the fall of 1995 and began to fall apart when the Russians staged an election among the small pro-Moscow group of handpicked Chechens for the post of president of Chechnya in December. This action provoked a Chechen response, and in that month a son-in-law of President Dudayev, named Salman Raduyev, led an attack on the Russian headquarters in the town of Gudermes. The Chechens managed to surround the Russians and trap them in their base for ten days. The Russians responded by unleashing helicopters and artillery on the town and killing nearly three hundred civilians, but by then the rebels already had escaped.[105] Clearly distrust remained on both sides, and as events would show, the Chechens seemed to have regrouped and rearmed for a renewed struggle with the Russians, who did not appear to be following the accords of the OSCE peace treaty.

Counterattack

Having gained fame for his attack on Gudermes, Salman Raduyev's "Lone Wolf" force then carried out another *nabeg*-style raid into the neighboring Russian province of Dagestan on January 9, 1996. The target of the raid on this occasion was the nearby town of Kizilyar (population sixty thousand) located ten miles from the Chechen border. Kizilyar was a site of both symbolic significance, since it was home to one of imperial Russia's oldest forts in the region, and strategic importance, since it housed an airbase for the much-hated Russian helicopter gunships. The attack began when Raduyev's raiding party of over two hundred *boyeviks* assaulted the Kizilyar airbase, destroyed two helicopters, and killed approximately thirty-three soldiers.[106]

But the Russians considerably outnumbered the Chechens and fought back. Then Raduyev's deputy, Khunkar Pasha Israpilov, an experienced member of Basayev's Abkhaz Battalion, took over and directed a large hostage taking. From the airbase the rebels followed in the footsteps of Basayev and took approximately three thousand people hostage in the town's hospital. The first thing the rebels did was force their hostages to the windows with bed sheets in a reprise of the Budyonnovsk hostage taking.

It was a repeat nightmare for the Russians, who had once again allowed a band of rebels, this time a larger group of 250, to slip into Russian territory and embarrass the government and military by taking hostages. Yeltsin was faced with two bad options: storm the hospital again, as in Budyonnovsk, or let the hostage takers go free.

Predictably, the Russians first tried storming the hospital and fired grenades into it killing several hostages. Israpilov then responded by executing a captured Russian policeman and said that more executions would come if the Russians did not call off the attack.

Leery of the public relations fallout from another clumsy storming operation, the Russians reluctantly agreed to let the rebels/terrorists go if they released most of their hostages. Raduyev and Israpilov agreed to the terms, and eleven buses were brought to take the rebels and the remaining 160 hostages back to Chechnya.

But the Russians were not going to let the hostage takers get away again, and they had secretly flown in 150 paratroopers to attack them when they crossed a border checkpoint into Chechnya.[107] Just as the convoy, which was being escorted by Dagestani police cars, crossed the border, a Russian helicopter gunship attacked it and accidentally destroyed one of the police cars. Israpilov understood instantly that the convoy was in an open field and about to be destroyed regardless of the loss of hostage lives, so he ordered it to hastily reverse back to the border checkpoint they had just passed through. Within seconds the rebels had stormed the checkpoint and disarmed the thirty-seven policemen at the border checkpoint and had taken them hostage.

With the Russians in hot pursuit, the Chechen hostage takers then roared into the nearby Dagestani village of Pervomaskoye and took its population of five hundred hostage as well. The Russians then surrounded the village as the rebels and their hostages furiously dug trenches in order to survive the inevitable Russian assault. It took the Russians five days to prepare their onslaught.

During this period the rebels, who included several women and five Arab mujahideen volunteer fighters from the Middle East, interacted amicably with the local population.[108] One local resident said, "The Chechens shared everything they had with us from the last piece of bread to all the news they received on their radio."[109]

On January 15 the Russians opened fire on the village with artillery, tanks, and indiscriminate air assaults that once again proved the maxim that in Russia a hostage was more likely to die at the hands of the Russian security forces than the hostage takers. As the Russians poured imprecise Grad missiles into the small hamlet and strafed it with Hind gunships, the village's houses, school, and mosque caught on fire.

When the Russian bombardment created an outcry among the Russian public, who feared for the hostages' lives, Aleksander Mikhailov, the chief spokesman for the FSB (the Russian Federation's successor to the KGB) tried to legitimize the imprecise attack by saying, "We believe all the hostages are dead. They have executed the hostages."[110] But journalists soon proved this a lie, as did some hostages who were released, and Mikhailov was fired. The Russian media subsequently reported that the Russian attack on Pervomaiskoye was "not about freeing the hostages, but wiping out the terrorists."[111] In an effort to salvage the situation, crack Alpha and SOBR (Rapid Reaction) troops were sent into the village only to be repulsed at great cost in attackers' lives by the entrenched Chechen defenders. Then, on January 17 the Chechens heard the Russians on their radios discussing withdrawing their troops for a particularly massive bombardment. This time the Russians vowed they would not be humiliated by letting the hostage takers escape; they would wipe out the hostage takers even if it meant killing hundreds of hostages.

In response, Israpilov formed a desperate plan for a breakout. Communicating with the head of Chechen forces back in Chechnya, Aslan Maskhadov, he asked for a diversionary raid from Chechnya. Maskhadov and Basayev responded with a four-hundred-man cross-border surprise attack on the besieging Russian forces. As Maskhadov and Basayev's forces launched a diversionary attack on the Russians, the hostage takers in Pervomaiskoye broke out in groups of fifty. When the rebels and hostages fled at night into Chechnya, the Russians strafed them with helicopters, killing many. But they failed to prevent the groups from escaping. Once again the Russians had been humiliated and had lost the high ground by killing many hostages in their brutal assault.

The next morning journalists found that the smoldering remains of the village and fields on the Chechen border were strewn with the bodies of hostages and smaller numbers of Chechen fighters. One of the former hostages who was released in Chechnya summed up his fury at the Russians, saying, "I feel they betrayed me, my own armed forces betrayed me."[112]

The truce initiated by the Budyonnovsk hostage seizure had come unraveled, and fighting continued in the lowlands of Chechnya. There the number two under Basayev, Commander Ruslan Gelayev, defended the village of Goiskoye for several weeks from a Russian bombardment. He and his men were expelled from the village only when the Russians bombed it with FAEs (fuel-air explosives), otherwise known as vacuum bombs. But it was clear that the rebels had used the break in fighting caused by the truce to rest, recuperate, regroup, and rearm for combat. They claimed to have recovered from the setbacks of the year before, thanks to Basayev's actions in Budyonnovsk, and were raring to continue their lonely battle with the Russians.

However, by this time, the Chechen rebels were not entirely on their own. The previous year a small band of approximately eighty Arab jihadi "brothers," led by a globe-trotting professional holy warrior named Amir (Commander) Khattab, had traveled to the country via Dagestan.[113] The charismatic Khattab, a Saudi citizen whose real name was Thamir Saleh Abdullah Al-Suwailem, had previously fought volunteer jihad in eastern Afghanistan on behalf of the Afghan mujahideen rebels in the late 1980s. When that war was over, the jihadi paladin had traveled to neighboring Tajikistan to wage war alongside Islamist fighters who were trying to overthrow the post-Soviet Communist regime in that country in the early 1990s.

These events took place at a time when another Saudi citizen, Osama bin Laden, created a *separate* terrorist group known as Al Qaeda al Jihad (based in Sudan from 1992 to 1996), which was dedicated not to fighting Russians or Communists frontally, but to the expulsion of US forces from the Arabian peninsula. While bin Laden later asked Khattab to join his nihilist terrorist group in its war against America, the famous warrior rejected bin Laden's request. Khattab chose to continue his own frontline struggle against his traditional foes from Afghanistan and Tajikistan, the Russians. Terrorism expert Fawaz Gerges has analyzed the Arabic language correspondence between these two distinct Saudi jihadi leaders and has concluded:

> Khattab not only competed on an equal footing with bin Laden, but assembled a more powerful contingent of jihadis than the latter. In the 1990s the two Saudi jihadis communicated with each other and tried to pull each other into their own battle plans, but Khattab and bin Laden had defined the enemy differently and both were too ambitious to accept a subordinate role.[114]

Despite such findings by one of the world's foremost scholars on Al Qaeda, analysts who do not speak Arabic have tried to use the presence of Khattab's small unit to show that bin Laden controlled not only the foreign fighters in Chechnya, *but the entire Chechen rebellion from his base in the distant African nation of Sudan, where he was based at this time.*

In the United States in particular, many nonexperts on the Chechens discovered this ancient Caucasian highlander enemy of Russia only *after* bin Laden's 9/11 attacks. They were quick to see all Muslims with weapons or engaged in rebellions or terrorism, from Palestine, to Bosnia, to Kosovo to the ex-Soviet Caucasus as being "Al Qaeda" or "Taliban," or both. This was a misunderstanding the Russians were only too happy to propagate to convince the West that their ancient mountain enemies were actually the West's enemies as well.

The reality is that Khattab was not part of bin Laden's anti-American terrorist organization known as Al Qaeda, and the existence of his small volunteer fighting force certainly is not proof that the entire Chechen secessionist rebellion was "Al Qaeda." As has been systematically demonstrated over the previous chapters, the secularized, Sufi Chechens had been fighting Russia for hundreds of years before bin Laden commenced his terroristic jihad on the United States in 1998 (that is, two years after the First Russo-Chechen War ended). The Chechen secessionists' goal was not to spread anti-American jihadism across the globe or expel US troops from Arabia (as was the case with bin Laden the Saudi Wahhabi) but to achieve the sort of independence from Russia that full Soviet Socialist Republics such as Lithuania and Ukraine had achieved.

Khattab's separate odyssey from that of Al Qaeda began in 1995, when he saw a televised news report of Chechens fighting Russians for independence. In Khattab's Manichean-Wahhabi version of the world, this battle was defined not as a struggle for national independence, but as a black-and-white "holy war" against Christian aggressors. He decided to lead a small band of twelve Arab "brothers" in fighting alongside the Chechens in their "jihad" against the Russian "infidels."

When Khattab's bearded Arab holy warriors arrived in the mountains of Chechnya via Dagestan with their Arabic language, head scarves, devotion to borderless jihad, and strict Wahhabi-Salafi Islam, the Sovietized Chechens found them to be something of an oddity. But then, on April 16, 1996, the Saudi jihadi commander led a unit of his Arab fighters, and some Chechens who had joined him, in an Afghan-style mountain ambush on a Russian column near the village of Yarysh Mardy in the Argun Gorge. The ambushers killed as many as one hundred Russians and destroyed the entire column before escaping into the forested hills.[115]

While Shamil Basayev and Ruslan Gelayev had previously launched similar deadly ambushes in the mountains, what made this one unique was that the media-savvy Khattab filmed his men carrying out the attack. Graphic videos of the deadly ambush were soon being distributed throughout Chechnya and were eagerly bought up by Chechens, who came to see Khattab as an ally and a hero. At this time several dozen Chechens joined Khattab's "International Islamic Battalion," grew Wahhabi-style beards, and began to wear green headbands with *Allahu Akbar* (God is [the] greatest) written on them in Arabic, this despite the fact that the Chechens could not read Arabic.

Khattab's charisma and willingness to shed his blood fighting on behalf of the Chechens, at a time when the much-admired US and European democracies had resigned Chechnya to its fate, impressed the Chechens' most effective and flamboyant field commander, Shamil Basayev. Basayev subsequently called Khattab his "brother" and allowed him to stay at his father Salman's house in Vedeno.

At this time, Khattab and his Arab fighters began to preach the notion of jihad to the Chechen fighters and to convert some of these Sufi, ex-Soviet citizens to their austere Saudi strain of Wahhabi-Salafi Islam. This began the process of converting many of the *boyeviks* to a more radical version of Islam than the moderate Sufi Islam that the vast majority of Chechens had traditionally adhered to. But one must not make the mistake of assuming that the entire country of Chechnya became radicalized by a few dozen Arab jihad missionaries. Thomas de Waal has written of his wartime experience with the Chechens and Khattab as follows:

> In fact, most Chechens remained very suspicious of the incoming Middle East zealots, like Khattab, known as "Wahhabis" because of their allegiance to a particularly austere form of Sunni Islam. Most Chechen Muslims by contrast are adherents of the mystical Sufi form of Islam and pray at home rather than in the mosques. They visit shrines and say prayers at the tombs of their ancestors. The women do not wear veils. Local traditions tend to be stronger than Muslim observance. Even in the 1840s and 1850s, when the Islamic chieftain Imam Shamil led resistance to the Russian tsar's armies in the region, he said that the Chechens were good warriors, but bad Muslims. He was unable to stop them smoking, playing music and dancing.[116]

It should be said that the radicalization of small numbers of Chechen fighters was not condoned by the secular Chechen president Dzhokhar Dudayev, or his moderate Chief of Staff Aslan Maskhadov, or the mufti (chief religious official), Akhmad Kadyrov. Akhmad Kadyrov in particular would come out strongly against the foreign Wahhabi missionaries/fighters, who were intolerant of the Chechens' Sufi-secular traditions. He and his Sufi followers were to lead a battle against the foreign Wahhabis and their alien ways. The Russians would later exploit the tension between Kadyrov and the foreign *Vakhabity* (Wahhabis) to create divisions among the Chechens.

Regardless, the secular Dudayev had inadvertently unleashed the genie of jihad among the hardened *boyeviks,* and his secular influence would begin to wane with his death just five days after Khattab's famous ambush. President Dudayev's death came after he had begun to negotiate with the Russians to end Boris Yeltsin's increasingly unpopular war in the spring of 1996. President Yeltsin was up for reelection at that time, and his advisors strongly urged him to end the quagmire in the Caucasus to improve his ratings among Russian voters.

For this reason, the Russians finally had given in to Dudayev's request for a face-to-face meeting to solve the crisis. They were setting it up when Dudayev came out of hiding to speak to a Russian representative near a mountain village called Gekhi Chu. But while Dudayev was on the phone speaking to a Russian member of parliament, a Russian aircraft tracked his signal and killed him with a precision-guided missile. Chechens across the country held *tesirs* (mourning ceremonies) in Dudayev's honor, and he was buried in a secret location known not even to his Russian wife. The vice president, Zelimkhan Yandarbiyev, was then chosen to replace Dudayev as president, and all the Chechen commanders swore loyalty to him.

Interestingly enough, Dudayev's death increased the prospects of peace. Yelstin could now claim to have decapitated the "bandit rebellion." The Russians could now declare "victory" and pull their troops out of the endless quagmire in Chechnya. This would help Yeltsin win votes among voters who were choosing between him and the revived Communist Party.

It was with this goal in mind that Yeltsin and the new Chechen president, Zelimkhan Yandarbiyev, met in Moscow and declared a truce on May 27, 1996. Afterward Yeltsin visited a secure Russian base near Grozny and in a televised speech told Russian soldiers there that they had won the war and could now come home. It was all meant to assure Russian voters that Yeltsin had ended the conflict in Chechnya, and it worked. Subsequently Yeltsin was reelected based on his promise to bring the war to an end.

But on the very next day after the election victory, Russian troops across Chechnya broke the truce and opened up massive aerial and artillery bombardments on Chechen targets. The fury of the Russian assault caught the Chechens, who had believed in the truce, by surprise. The whole ceasefire had been nothing more than a ploy by Yeltsin to win votes among war-fatigued Russian voters. Now that the election was over, the Russian side recommenced the war.

But the Chechen commander Shamil Basayev had a humiliating "election present" of his own for Yeltsin. On August 6, the day of Yeltsin's inauguration, fifteen hundred Chechen rebels launched their biggest and boldest offensive of the war, infiltrating Grozny, Chechnya's second-largest city, Gudermes, and Argun. Once in the cities, the rebels besieged the much larger Russian forces, which outnumbered them three to one but were afraid to sally out of their bases to fight.[117] Any Russian unit that attempted to break out was attacked and wiped out. Russian checkpoints and bases across Grozny were brazenly assaulted by Chechen rebels, who effectively pinned down much larger units with sniper and mortar fire.

On this occasion, the Russians could not bombard Grozny to expel the Chechens, since their own men were trapped inside the city with Chechens corralling them into pockets. Russian reporters who were trapped with the Russian forces broadcast panicked reports of the Chechen assault throughout Russia, showing the lie behind Yeltsin's previous claims to having won the war.

The whole surprise attack was a public relations coup for the Chechens and a disaster for Yeltsin and the army. The Chechens proudly proclaimed that they had the ability to put the larger Russian force of twelve thousand under siege. By this time the Chechen rebel force had risen to three thousand, one of the largest Chechen operations of the war.[118] It was the greatest gathering of *boyeviks* since the initial defense of Grozny, and it was remarkable that so many Chechens had been able to infiltrate the city without the Russians getting wind of it.

In response, the Russians repeatedly sent relief columns into the city, but these were ambushed and destroyed by the Chechen rebels at great cost in Russian lives. As in the clumsy New Year's Eve assault on Grozny of 1995, once again burning Russian tanks and APCs with soldiers' bodies in them filled the streets of Grozny. The Chechens succeeded in killing almost 500 Russian soldiers and wounding 1,407 in Russia's second-greatest defeat of the conflict.[119] It also was a total humiliation for Yeltsin and the army. It showed that the resilient Chechens could continue to wage the war indefinitely. The Chechens had trapped the Russians and achieved a spectacular checkmate.

Faced with an unpopular and endless conflict in Chechnya, Yeltsin finally decided to wash his hands of the war, after calling it the worse decision of his presidency.[120] Yeltsin subsequently would turn responsibility for it over to the head of the National Security Council, ex-Soviet general Alexander Lebed. The straight-talking Lebed had deep respect among both the Russian people and the Chechen leadership, whom he met in person in the mountains of Chechnya and the Dagestani town of Khasavyurt to discuss peace. In Lebed the Chechens found someone who was not afraid to tell the Russians how bad the situation was in Chechnya and a bold leader who truly wanted to end the war.

On August 21 a deal was signed to end the war, and Russian troops began to withdraw back to their bases and the Chechens to their positions. Aslan Maskhadov firmly ordered his *boyeviks* not to attack the retreating Russians, and the peace held. By August 31, 1996, the last Russian troops had withdrawn from Grozny. On November 23 a formal peace deal was signed calling for the total withdrawal of all Russian troops from the Republic of Chechnya. The Khasavyurt Accord was titled "Joint Relations between the Russian Federation and the Chechen Republic." Chechnya was now a de facto state, although its de jure legal status would be put off until December 31, 2001. On May 12, 1997, President Yeltsin and Aslan Maskhadov met in Moscow and signed the final version of the agreement, known as the Russian Chechen Peace Treaty. The Russians and Chechens agreed to reject war "forever" and to build relations between the Russian Federation and the Chechen Republic of Ichkeria "on the generally recognized principles and norms of international law." Following the loss of tens of thousands of lives and the destruction of most towns in Chechnya, the Chechens were, after an unimaginably brutal war, free of Russian rule for the first time since the nineteenth-century defeat of Imam Shamil and his *murids*.

It was a time of public celebration, as the Chechens dreamed of doing what the breakaway Serbian province of Kosovo would later do and achieve recognition as a sovereign nation. As the Chechens raised their green-and-white wolf flag over Grozny's war-blackened buildings and celebrated the withdrawal of the last Russian Federation troops, many imagined a bright future.

In a sign of their hopes for peace with Russia, the Chechen people overwhelmingly voted for the moderate military commander Aslan Maskhadov to be their new president in the 1997 elections, which were designed to choose the slain Dudayev's successor as president. They did not vote in large numbers for Shamil Basayev, who ran against him (but was seen as a terrorist by the Russians and too extreme in his anti-Russian stance by most Chechens), or for interim president Zelimkhan Yandarbiyev, who ran on an Islamist platform that did not conform with the Chechens' secular aspirations. Across Chechnya this resourceful people began to dig away the rubble from their bombed-out homes to rebuild their devastated homeland. It was to be a difficult task, for as many as 35,000 people had been killed in the war and another 400,000, or almost half of the micronation, made refugees.[121]

But for all the Chechen people's hopes for peace, independence, and stability, there were factors operating in both Chechnya and Russia that ultimately were to see this people's dreams crushed. Most important, the Russian military could not forgive the Chechens for the humiliation that had seen them lose approximately seventy-five hundred soldiers in just two years (the United States by contrast lost less than seven thousand troops in its war in Texas-sized Afghanistan *and* California-sized Iraq *over twelve years*).[122] Even as the tentative peace took hold, the Russians began preparations to reinvade Chechnya.

Some commanders in Chechnya, such as Shamil Basayev, Khattab, and Salman Raduyev, continued to see the Russians as the enemy. As Basayev became closer to the Arab jihadi Khattab, who dreamed of spreading the so-called "jihad" from secessionist Chechnya to the Muslim republic of Dagestan and beyond, the seeds of the Second Russo-Chechen War began to be planted in Chechnya.

War plans also were nurtured by the Russian generals in the Kremlin who considered the Khasavyurt Accord to be an act of "treason." All it would take was a spark to reignite the inferno in Chechnya and send the Chechens down the path to war with the mighty Russian Federation, which would subsequently be ruled by a new leader named Vladimir Putin.

Chaosistan

The war with Russia will continue.
— Shamil Basayev, rogue Chechen warlord[1]

The story of independent Chechnya from 1996 to 1999 is a tragic one of a small state, the first and last independent state on Russian Federation territory, whose implosion at the hands of radical warlords led Russia into reinvading what the Kremlin claimed was an unstable "bandit-terrorist republic." It need not have turned out that way, and indeed, in the beginning, there were tremendous grounds for hope. This hope was manifested in the presidential elections held in January 1997, soon after the initial withdrawal of Russian troops from Chechnya. In these elections, Aslan Maskhadov, the chief of staff of the Chechen military forces and the man, along with Shamil Basayev, most credited with defeating the Russians, was elected president by approximately 60 percent of the electorate. The election was declared fair by observers from numerous countries, who observed it under the aegis of the OSCE (Organization for Security and Cooperation in Europe).

Maskhadov was popular among average Chechens, who had suffered terribly during the war and continued to suffer from the consequences of the conflict (for example, unemployment was at around 80 percent; pensions, salaries, and funds for education were no longer coming from Russia; 60 to 70 percent of the people had lost their homes and apartments in Russian bombardments; approximately 50 percent of the Chechen population was displaced; the country's factories and infrastructure had been destroyed; many people were traumatized and had lost loved ones, and so on).[2] Maskhadov, who as seen as a moderate, promised to work with the Russian Federation, which surrounded the tiny, economically unviable state of Chechnya on three sides, to gain funds to rebuild the republic and reestablish economic and diplomatic ties with Russia and the world. According to Russian writers Alexei Malashenko and Dimitri Trenin, "The elections demonstrated that most Chechens wanted to avoid a new confrontation with Russia and favored dialogue."[3]

The BBC would report that Maskhadov's "quiet pragmatism won the respect of Russian negotiators," who saw him as someone they could work with to end the state of hostility between their two countries.[4] Maskhadov, who was known for his "readiness to compromise," actually traveled to Moscow and met Russian president Boris Yeltsin and famously shook his hand.[5] In response, the Russians provided Maskhadov with some initial funds to establish his authority in Chechnya. The Chechen parliament was also filled with newly elected, moderate representatives, who wanted to reestablish friendly ties with the mighty Russian Federation and rebuild their country.

In spite of the Chechen people's desire for peace, democracy, and independence, there were, however, numerous forces operating in the republic that would ultimately destroy their aspirations. It all began with the 1997 presidential election, which seemingly established Chechnya as a model, Western-leaning, secular democracy of the sort the slain president Dudayev and newly elected president Maskhadov had fought to create. Maskhadov, the overwhelming victor in the elections, believed that "the proclamation of *Shariah* as the supreme law (the distinctive feature of an Islamic state) would propel the republic back into the Middle Ages."[6] His dream, and that of the majority of Chechens, was to create a moderate, parliamentary democracy with friendly ties to Russia. But, as it transpired, not everyone was satisfied with Maskhadov's election to the presidency or his critical views of shariah Islamic law.

Basayev and Khattab The Jihadi Warlords

Maskhadov's first problem was Shamil Basayev, the hero of the Chechen War in the eyes of many of the *boyevik* fighters. The charismatic Basayev had taken off his military fatigues when the war was over and donned a suit and *papakha* (a traditional wool hat). He had told reporters that he wanted to return to a quiet life of raising bees in his hometown of Vedeno in the mountains. But clearly he was a man of action who relished the idea of wielding power. It seems to have frustrated him tremendously when he only received 22 percent of the vote in the 1997 presidential election. Many Chechen civilians admired Basayev for his role as a warrior, but now that peace was declared did not want him antagonizing Russia. Inflammatory comments such as his declaration, "The war with Russia will continue. For Russia has behaved in a brutal, inhuman manner in Chechnya. Russian troops have killed 100,000 people, they wrecked everything and then left," frightened many war-weary Chechen civilians.[7]

Initially, Shamil Basayev accepted his election loss gracefully, despite the fact that some of his followers wanted to launch a coup, and he actually traveled to meet the victor, President Maskhadov. At Maskhadov's home he swore on a holy Qur'an that he would support him.[8] Taking his former comrade-in-arms at his word, Maskhadov decided to win over this flamboyant figure and his followers and offered him a position in his government. In April 1997, Shamil Basayev was appointed deputy prime minister. According to Ilyas Akhmadov, who later served as the Chechen foreign minister, "Maskhadov needed Shamil to neutralize the criticism of the government (that was coming from unruly elements) and to impose order."[9] President Maskhadov also gave Shamil Basayev's younger brother, Shirvani, the post of the head of the State Committee for Energy Resources.[10] But Shamil Basayev subsequently resigned from the government four months later after having an argument with President Maskhadov over a political appointee.[11]

Desperate to bring this influential commander back under his tent, President Maskhadov convinced Shamil Basayev to rejoin his government for about six months in 1998. On this occasion, Basayev served as acting prime minister. But once again he resigned in frustration after failing to destroy the mounting scourge of kidnapping for cash (to be discussed later) and following another confrontation with Maskhadov over an appointment to a government post.

The loss of Basayev was to be crucial and was to lead Chechnya down the slippery slope of a second war with Russia. As will be demonstrated, the impetuous Basayev quickly became an outspoken opponent of Maskhadov and began calling for him to resign for having "sold out Chechnya" by working too closely with the Russians. Ultimately, Basayev was to join the radical Chechen foreign minister Movladi Udugov, also a critic of Maskhadov, in creating a military-political party called the Congress of the Peoples of Chechnya and Dagestan. As this party's name hinted, its goal was to "liberate" Dagestan's people (the vast majority of whom were actually quite content under the Russians) from Moscow's "infidel" rule.

In furtherance of this goal, Basayev would subsequently travel to the south to four jihad camps known as the Kavkaz (Caucasus) Complex to undergo a transformation from nationalist freedom fighter into an Islamic Che Guevara. These training facilities near the Chechen village of Serzhen Yurt, known by the Arabic names of Alos Abudzhafar, Yakub, Abubakar, and Davlat, were built in former Komsomol and Young Pioneer camps from the Soviet era and were run by the roaming Arab jihadi paladin, Amir Khattab.[12] During the war Khattab had been awarded the medal of *Koman Siy* (Honor of the Nation) and the rank of general by the Islamist successor to the slain Dudayev, President Zelimkhan Yandarbiyev. Khattab subsequently had been allowed to stay on in Chechnya with his Arab jihadi volunteer followers.[13] A Chechen noted of these wealthy foreigners, "They were bearded, wore green or black shirts and long robes over their pants, and were armed with expensive pistols. They went to the market and paid with dollars. There was no [political] power here, there was disorder everywhere, and their influence was very strong."[14]

The spread of Arab jihadist influence was to have disastrous consequences as Khattab began training Chechens, Dagestanis, Turks, Arabs, and Central Asians (Kazakhs and Uzbeks for the most part) in forty-five-day-long classes on *dawa* (religious indoctrination in the strict Wahhabi-Salafite tradition that rejected Chechnya's traditional relaxed Sufism) and in jihadi warfare. Participants learned to carry out ambushes, plant land mines, shoot a variety of light infantry weapons (such as the AK-47 Kalashnikov assault rifle, the RPG-7 grenade launcher, the Dragunov sniper rifle, and the PK-40 machine gun), and to wage guerilla jihad against the Russian "infidels." Many young Chechen fighters who could not find work in their shattered homeland joined Khattab, who also offered them cash stipends. This money came from charities in the Arab Gulf States, such as the Al Haramein Foundation, which considered the funding of jihadi conflicts across the globe to be a religious obligation.

While Khattab did not involve himself directly in the increasing internal conflict between the growing gangs of Chechen Wahhabi converts and the majority of Chechen Sufis (to be discussed shortly), he clearly saw his job in the Caucasus as unfinished business in his never-ending jihad. Most important, Khattab, who learned Russian, dreamed of spreading his borderless jihad from his base into the multiethnic province of Dagestan to free his "Muslim brothers and sisters."

There was a basis for Khattab's ambitious plan that caught the restless Basayev's imagination. As it transpired, in the late 1980s, Arab missionaries had imported Saudi-style Wahhabism to neighboring Dagestan, and some disenfranchised young men were drawn to its austere tenets. These devout followers caused tension in the 1990s as they began to clash with the ruling Sufi majority and authorities.

Then in late 1997, a prominent Dagestani Wahhabi from the Avar tribe, named Bagauddin Magomedov, fled to Chechnya with as many as two hundred families to find sanctuary from the pro-Russian Dagestani authorities. He called on Khattab to help him in returning to his homeland to liberate Dagestan from "infidel" rule. He and his followers then joined up with Khattab and began to create an "Islamic legion" in the Chechen city of Gudermes to liberate the Russian province of Dagestan from Moscow's rule.

Most important, Khattab also had contacts with Wahhabi-Salafites still inside Dagestan. There were Wahhabi militants in the neighboring regions of Dagestan that had declared their villages of Kadar, Chaban-makhi, and Karamakhi (the so-called "Kadar Zone"), a shariah Islamic law "republic." To an extent, the Wahhabi Kadar Zone was created as a protest against corruption, criminality, and nepotism among Dagestan's ruling "neo-Communist" clans, but it gradually began to assume a more sinister aspect. In 1996 the Kadar Wahhabi militants killed the Dagestani government-appointed administrator of their region and began to engage in bloody clashes with local Sufi moderates, whom they considered to be "bad Muslims." The Kadar Zone militants also beat local police and stole their weapons. If this were not inflammatory enough, they encouraged Wahhabis from throughout Dagestan to travel to their "republic" to study "pure Islam" and work to overthrow the "infidel" Dagestani authorities. The Wahhabis could be spotted by their long beards (with shaven mustaches in the Saudi Wahhabi tradition), and the women wore black *chadors* or *burqas* (veils), which were alien to the region.

In the Kadar Zone, the militants heavily enforced strict Islamic law, and dug trenches around their villages and placed armed guards around them to keep outsiders away. Their military leader, Jarullah, went on to declare the zone independent of the Russian province of Dagestan and said Russian laws no longer applied in the "*Jamaat* of Dagestan" (a *ja-maat* traditionally meant a local ethnic or village community, but in the postwar context increasingly came to mean a Wahhabi enclave or armed fighting or terror unit). The Wahhabi militants even assumed control of roads passing through their territory, which threatened communication and transport in their region of Dagestan.

When the moderate Sufi mufti (chief religious official) of Dagestan spoke out against the creeping threat of the Wahhabis, he was assassinated by a remote-control land mine, and the Wahhabis were blamed.[15] There were several other bombings and terror attacks in Dagestan that the Sufi moderate majority blamed on the Wahhabi radicals, who were at war with the Russian-appointed authorities and their secular ways. The Dagestani government responded by passing a law titled, "On the Fight against Islamic Fundamentalism." It also sent troops to retake the secessionist Kadar Zone radical villages that were located to the southwest of the Dagestani capital of Makhachkala. The government forces were, however, repulsed by the heavily armed Wahhabi militants, who were led by a firebrand and karate champion named Nadirshah Khachilaev.

In response to these events, Russian Federation Interior Minister Sergei Stepashin (later prime minister) decided to travel to the Kadar Zone and meet with the Wahhabis personally to try to defuse matters. There he agreed to leave the Kadar Zone Wahhabis alone and essentially conceded to their demands to be independent, much to the frustration of local Dagestani authorities. This was seen as a victory for the radicals in the enclave, who, for their part, promised not to try to proselytize or challenge the central authorities.

But this truce did not stop the Wahhabis in the western highland district of Tsumadi-Botlkhk (the so-called Avaristan region), which was populated by ethnic Avars and Dargins, from also declaring their zone an "Islamic republic" and overthrowing secular Russian-Dagestani law. Thus there were two secessionist Wahhabi enclaves in western Dagestan, one in the Kadar zone and one in Avaristan, that sought to break away from the republic's authority and create shariah enclaves.

For Khattab, who had been watching the events closely, this turn of events signaled the beginning of the overthrow of the Dagestani government. He began to dream of using the Kadar Zone and Avaristan regions as a springboard for "liberating" Dagestan from Russian rule. His neverending jihad, which he had begun against the Russians in Afghanistan back in the 1980s, would continue *within* Russia and lead to the liberation of all her "imprisoned" Muslim peoples in the Caucasus.

To show his approval of these developments and to cement relations with fellow Wahhabis, Khattab married Madina, the fifteen-year-old daughter of a prominent Wahhabi from the Kadar Zone (an ethnic Dargin from the village of Karamakhi).[16] Khattab and his wife subsequently had three children. Several of Khattab's Arab lieutenants also married women from the three Wahhabi villages in Dagestan.

At approximately this time (December 22, 1997), Amir Khattab led a major raid by 115 Arab, Chechen, and Dagestani mujahideen against a Russian army base in the town of Buynaksk, which is located about fifty miles across the border inside Dagestan (i.e., in Russia). The unprovoked raid was on the 136th Armored Brigade, which had previously gained notoriety for its harsh tactics fighting in the Chechen War. In the raid, Khattab claimed to have destroyed several Russian tanks, although he lost his close friend Abu Bakr Aqeedah, an Afghan-Arab veteran, in the attack.[17] His unit was ambushed by Russians on its return, but received help from Raduyev's forces and managed to make its way back to Chechnya with only minor losses.

By the end of 1997, a situation that bordered on anarchy existed in western Dagestan as Khattab's bands of Chechen, Dagestani, and Arab jihadis shot at Russian army and MVD (Interior Ministry) units and launched more than eighty attacks on Russian border posts.[18] The Russians estimated that as many as twenty-five hundred jihadists were trained at Khattab's camps, which were run by Arab military instructors and preachers.[19] Armed attacks on Dagestani border guards and checkpoints seem to have been a graduating rite of passage for jihadis trained in Khattab's camps. Alumni from his training camps also smuggled weapons to Nadirshah Khachilaev's Wahhabi secessionists in the Dagestani Kadar Zone and to the Avaristan Wahhabi enclave just across the border.

At roughly this time, reporter Sanobar Shermatova managed to carry out an extraordinary interview with Khattab in his house near Serzhen Yurt, which provides considerable insight into his worldview:

Shermatova: In Russia you are considered a world class mercenary but in Chechnya you are considered a hero. How do you see yourself?
Khattab: I am neither a mercenary, terrorist nor hero. I am a Muslim, a simple Mujahid who fights for the glory of Allah. Russia oppressed the

Muslims, therefore I came in order to help my brothers free themselves
from Russia. They fought against Muslims in Bosnia, Tajikistan, and
Afghanistan. I help my brothers.

Shermatova: Here in Chechnya there is now [1998] peace. What are you
doing here now?

[Khattab:] There is no war here, but Russia fights with economic methods.
I direct a training centre where young men are taught to use weapons.

Shermatova: I see you have decorated your walls with cartridge belts.

Khattab: I am relaxed when they are at hand. One can only have peace
when a weapon is nearby.

Shermatova: Have you had military training?

[Khattab:] No, for me school was Afghanistan.

Shermatova: During the war they say you personally tortured captured
Russian soldiers. Is this true?

Khattab: No, this is propaganda. In my brigade we did not touch one
captive. I myself personally gave five soldiers to their mothers.

Shermatova: What sort of family do you come from, do you have a peace-
time profession?

Khattab: My family is moderately prosperous, perhaps wealthy. I am a
soldier of Allah, I know no other profession.[20]

Clearly Khattab, the self-proclaimed "soldier of Allah," had his eyes set
on overthrowing the pro-Russian rulers of Dagestan, and with Basayev by
his side, he had a powerful local war leader to protect him and his men
from Maskhadov. By the summer of 1999, there were few in Chechnya or
Dagestan who did not know that Khattab and Basayev were planning on
attacking the Russian republic of Dagestan. A Dagestani general would
state: "That the rebels would be coming into Dagestan was known to everyone before the events. That there would be a war in August was spoken
of as early as the spring of [1999] — beginning with operational workers
from the power structures and ending with women in the bazaars."[21]

While President Maskhadov was to call on Khattab to be expelled
from Chechnya on several occasions, feeling it would be calamitous if
the Arab jihadis caused another war with Russia, his power was limited.
He did not want to start a civil war with the increasing number of armed
Wahhabi gangs in the country, or with Basayev, who was not himself a

Wahhabi convert (Basayev was a Sufi of the Qadiriya brotherhood). Thus Khattab and Basayev plotted to drag the war-weary Chechen people and those of Dagestan into another bloody conflict with Russia, even as the weak Chechen president and the vast majority of his people tried in vain to bring peace to their war-torn land.

The Wahhabi Warlords

Khattab and Basayev were not the only rogue warlords whom the moderate president of Chechnya had to deal with. Most notably, President Maskhadov was troubled by the son-in-law of the former president Dzhokhar Dudayev, Salman Raduyev, and his thousand-man "General Dudayev's Army." This dangerous force, like most ad hoc fighting units, had failed to lay down its arms after the war was over. Raduyev, it will be recalled, was the commander who led the "Lone Wolf" hostage raid on Kizil Yar and Pervomaskoye, Dagestan, during the war. He subsequently had been shot in the face either by a disgruntled Chechen comrade or by a Russian sniper and had traveled to Germany to have reconstructive surgery. His opponents, who nicknamed him "Michael Jackson" as a result of his facial reconstruction, claimed his injuries made him insane. Raduyev was nonetheless an eloquent spokesman for disgruntled elements seeking the overthrow of President Maskhadov.

Raduyev declared Maskhadov a traitor for making peace with Russia and led a months-long protest rally in central Grozny calling for his overthrow. This rally ultimately led to the shooting death of the Chechen security chief Lechi Khultygov, a key Maskhadov ally. In response, Maskhadov stripped Raduyev of his rank of brigadier general and demoted him to private. He was ordered to be arrested, but this order was never fulfilled for fear of starting a war with his intensely loyal fighters. Raduyev also gave his support to the various Wahhabi *jamaats* in Dagestan, even though he was not himself a Wahhabi (Raduyev actually had been the head of the Chechen-Ingush Republic's Komsomol during the late Soviet period and opposed the Wahhabis' influence inside Chechnya itself).

The spread of Saudi-style, radical Wahhabism (or Salafism) among many Chechen fighters began during the war and accelerated during the subsequent years. This was in part because of the extreme poverty that afflicted postwar Chechnya. Prior to the war, Chechnya had ranked as the second-poorest republic in Russia (after Dagestan, which was ranked eighty-ninth in the federation), and the war had exacerbated this problem. Few Chechen men could find jobs in the aftermath of the war, so those who were fighters tended to remain in their armed units in the hopes of receiving salaries and maintaining their influence and power. In a process that can best be called the "Kalashnikovization" of Chechen culture, these personal armies then took control of districts throughout Chechnya and ran them as fiefdoms. Ultimately, there were said to be 160 armed groups ruling tiny Chechnya and controlling its economy.[22]

At this time, Arab missionaries, who had arrived during the war, began to pay fighting units and even some local religious leaders to cast aside their traditional Sufi beliefs and convert to Saudi-style Wahhabism. The Arab Wahhabi *takfiris* (those who label other Muslims "infidels") hated traditional Chechen Sufi Islam and even killed some local Sufi imams, including the imam of Grozny, and tried destroying ancient local Sufi mystic shrines known as *ziyarets*. The Arab fundamentalists openly proclaimed that, having defeated the Russian "infidels," they were going to defeat moderate Sufi Islam. In this sense, the wealthy Arabs had influence far beyond their small numbers in Chechnya, which led to the radicalization of many unemployed armed men. The average Chechen, however, found the Arabs and their alien form of Islam to be repugnant.

Regardless, these Arab-Chechen Wahhabi units then began to enforce shariah law throughout their territories. They would stop couples from holding hands, enforce the head scarf on previously free Chechen women who grew up in the Soviet system, force women to sit at the back of buses, publicly whip people for drinking alcohol, and in essence declare war on Chechnya's easygoing Sovietized Sufi culture. The vast majority of Chechnya's moderate population, who had voted for Maskhadov precisely because he was opposed to the Islamic platform of interim president Zelimkhan Yandarbiyev (who received only 10 percent of the vote) and the outspoken Islamist Movladi Udugov (a candidate who received less than 1 percent of the vote), were upset by this usurping of the president's authority. Among them was a humble surgeon from the village of Alkhan Kala, located in the foothills of the Caucasus, named Khassan Baiev. Baiev, a local doctor who would later play an important role in the Second Russo-Chechen War of 1999 to 2009 (he would operate on both Basayev and Raduyev), recorded his intense dislike of the foreign Arab Wahhabis who came into his hospital as follows:

> The so-called Wahhabis were beginning to cause problems in Chechnya. They claimed our ancient traditions contradicted the Koran. We insist our children show respect to their elders by standing up when they enter the room and yielding their place. They asserted this respect was misplaced; only Allah deserved such reverence. We welcomed the humanitarian aid we received from the Middle Eastern countries, but we did not like being told that our Islam was not true Islam . . .
>
> I had been told that the Wahhabis offered young men what we considered large sums—$100 to $200 a month—to join their movement, which distressed the elders, who ordered them out of the villages. Many young men joined solely to support their families.[23]

Dr. Baiev was not alone in his distaste for the fanatical Arab Wahhabis. The most outspoken opponent of the Wahhabis was the mufti of Chechnya, Akhmad Kadyrov, who had been appointed chief religious official by President Dudayev. Kadyrov called for the outlawing of Wahhabism as a "poisonous" threat to Chechnya's traditional Islam.

To compound matters, one of the Arab Wahhabi preachers issued a *fatwa* (decree) legitimizing the kidnapping of "infidels" for profit. Soon Wahhabis and criminals were kidnapping people from neighboring provinces, including Russians, Dagestanis, and other north Caucasians, and holding them hostage for ransom payments. This became a major business for Chechen criminal Wahhabi gangs, who captured hundreds of non-Chechens and held them for ransom to supplement their meager incomes. The hostage takers could be brutal and made their hostages work as slaves, beat them, or cut off body parts to send to relatives as threats. The hostage-taking crisis turned many Dagestanis, who had previously been sympathetic to the Chechens, against them.

No Chechen kidnapper was more notorious than Arbi Barayev, also known as the "Terminator" for his skill in martial arts (many young Chechen men were drawn to various martial arts, a trend the Tsarnaev brothers would follow in Boston). After the war, Barayev transformed his Special Purpose Islamic Regiment into a Wahhabi criminal gang, which ran a lucrative hostage-taking business from the western town of Urus Martan. He became notorious internationally after his men kidnapped four members of a British telecom company known as Granger, who were working with the Melkhi *teyip* (clan) to set up a cell phone company. When the Melkhis responded by arming themselves and kidnapping three of his men, an infuriated Barayev had the four British telecom workers beheaded and their heads left by the side of the road as a warning.[24] Barayev also was implicated in the murder of six international Red Cross workers who were running a hospital in the town of Novye Atagi. The attackers broke into the hospital at night and systematically murdered the nurses and one male employee in cold blood. Most international aid organizations pulled out of Chechnya shortly thereafter, and this undermined President Maskhadov's prestige.

In response to these outrages, especially the murder of the British workers that occurred while he was on a trip to Britain, President Maskhadov ordered his Chechen interior minister, Nasrudi Bazhiyev, and Shadid Bargishev, head of the newly formed antiabduction service, to arrest Barayev. But Arbi Barayev had these officials killed and tried killing President Maskhadov himself in a bombing assassination attempt.

Barayev joined with other Wahhabi radicals and began moving to overthrow Maskhadov. Chechnya's fighting men thus became divided between those who supported the Wahhabi minority's plans for a Saudi-style shariah Islamic state, and those who supported Maskhadov and Mufti Akhmad Kadyrov's moderate path, which called for peace with Russia. The Wahhabi radicals claimed only to recognize "Allah's supremacy" and were at war with Chechnya's secular government. To compound matters, many of the highland clans had fighters who joined the radicals, while the lowland clans remained loyal to the secular-Sufi traditions.

Things came to a head in June 1998 in the town of Gudermes, Chechnya's second-largest city. It was there that Baguddin Mogamedov and his Dagestani exiles from the Avaristan region had set up an Islamic institute that paid young men to study Wahhabi Islam. Much to the chagrin of the surrounding Sufi population, these Islamic students then created morality patrols that terrorized the common people. Chief among the enforcers was Arbi Barayev and his Special Purpose Islamic Regiment. Their main rivals were the moderate Chechen mufti Akhmad Kadyrov and his armed supporters, the Yamadayev brothers (i.e., a military clan led by Sulim Ya-madayev and his brothers).

The mounting tension led to outright conflict between the moderate majority and the radical Wahhabi minority when some of Barayev's "religious police" tried arresting a former fighter for buying alcohol. When he resisted, they killed him. In retaliation, the Yamadayev brothers and their militia, who were no saints themselves and had been in the kidnapping business, killed two of Barayev's men. This led to an armed battle in the streets of Gudermes between the Wahhabis and the secular Sufis led by the Yamadayev brothers and several Sufi clans and *virds* (brotherhoods). The Wahhabis got the worst of it, and as many as a hundred of them may have been killed in six days of violence between as many as one thousand men. President Maskhadov reacted to these events by officially disbanding Barayev's notorious Special Purpose Islamic Regiment and disbanding its shariah courts of law.

The defeated Chechen and Arab Wahhabis then fled to the town of Urus Martan, Chechnya's third-largest town, to plot their overthrow of Maskhadov and the imposition of shariah law. There, a Jordanian missionary named Sheikh Fathi had set up a seminary and orphanage, which indoctrinated Chechens to be Wahhabis. But the fundamentalists were clearly up against a general population that did not like them. Julie Wilhelmsen has written:

In general, the Wahhabis' influence on Chechen society was limited. Attempts at introducing strict Islamic customs in the interwar period failed . . . Most Chechens disliked the Wahhabis . . . The majority of Chechens are Sufis [who] belong to either the Naqshbandiya or Qadiriya tariqat [brotherhoods or orders], and have little in common with the type of fundamentalist Islam preached by the Wahhabis. Many of the customs that the Wahhabis wanted to introduce—such as a ban on music, on traditional feasts and weddings, special ways of dressing for men and women—directly contradicted the strong traditions that regulate Chechen society. The introduction of extreme corporal punishment, such as cutting off fingers for drinking alcohol, was quickly abandoned and substituted by fines. And despite the introduction of shari'ah courts, secular courts continued to operate.[25]

Sensing that the people were behind him in his struggle with the Wahhabis after the events in Guderemes, Maskhadov lashed out at the Arab missionaries who were "splitting Chechen society and bringing the republic to the edge of civil war."[26] After accusing them of trying to "poison" his people and turn them into "Taliban," Maskhadov announced on television, "We are Naqshbandi and Qadari Sufis. There is no place for any other Islamic sects in Chechnya."[27] Maskhadov then went on to attack Wahhabism directly for the first time stating:

> The worst thing about it is the fact that it seeks to divide us according to our faith. And this happens in every place that Islamism wins over. They divide us according to faith, which subsequently leads to civil war. They say that only they are Allah's chosen ones that only they are walking along the true path. And everyone else is their enemy. We have always been proud of the fact that we are Chechens. And now they are telling us: Do not say that you are the Chechen nation. They want to deprive us of the faith of our fathers, our sheikhs and ustadhs (Sufi masters). They want to rob us of our customs and traditions and adats (pre-Islamic customs).
>
> They are not even content with the fact that we call Chechnya an Islamic state. They say that the president, the parliament, and the grand mufti are meaningless. Everything is to be in the hands of the Emir [Khattab]. The Emir who, I must add, came here from God knows what country and who furthermore is not even Chechen. They take the Koran in and find words in it that claim it is permissible to abduct people that they can use them as a source of income. Their calls [are] for the immediate start of a war in Dagestan and aim to pit Chechnya and Dagestan against one another.[28]

Lecha Khultygov, the director of Maskhadov's Chechen National Security Service, warned Chechens "not to let the [Wahhabi] camel get into our place."[29] For his part, the moderate Sufi religious leader Mufti Akhmad Kadyrov, who was described as a "dauntless anti-Wahhabi," called for the seizure of Wahhabi "literature which teaches radical Islam."[30]

At the same time (July 1998), the Sufi Congress of Muslims of the Caucasus demanded that "Wahhabism, a movement new to our region, be banned through legislation; that the literature they distribute be confiscated; and that Chechen youth be protected form theological propaganda which teaches radicalization."[31] President Maskhadov then banned all Wahhabi military units, political parties, newspapers, and television. He also ordered Khattab to close his jihad camps and leave the country.[32] Maskhadov then ordered the Dagestani Wahhabi exiles out of the country and announced:

> We are no longer going to tolerate in our land foreign nationals who are trying to enforce their rules. All Arabs, Tajiks, Pakistanis, and others arrived in Chechnya not to promote the law of Allah in the republic, but rather to split Chechen society into different groups, movements and parties so as to prevent the building of an independent Chechen state. They will be expelled from the territory of Chechnya. We will not have a replay of the Afghan or Tajik scenario here.[33]

President Maskhadov had the full support of the Sufi Chechen mufti, Akhmad Kadyrov, the Chechen Parliament, the Yamadayev brothers of Gudermes, a successful commander from the war named Ruslan "Khamzet" Gelayev, and the majority of the population. But the president and his supporters desperately needed *Russian* support to build their strength vis-à-vis the radical Wahhabi warlords and bring stability to their shattered nation.

Unfortunately, Moscow did not see fit to support Maskhadov, who had put himself out on a limb in extending the hand of friendship to the Russians with the aim of acquiring desperately needed reconstruction aid. Russia's goals increasingly came to focus on isolating Maskhadov and working for the collapse of the Chechen state he was desperately trying to stabilize. In essence, Russia enacted an economic blockade against tiny Chechnya that led to exactly the sort of impoverishment and tensions that created the Wahhabi-criminal threat to Maskhadov (and ultimately, to the Russian province of Dagestan). Russia quarantined Chechnya behind a wall of block posts, trenches, and troops, and this further damaged its economy. This all served to undermine Maskhadov's credibility among his people, who had hoped that his accommodating approach toward Russia would assist them in rebuilding their lives. Clearly Russia had come to discount the moderate Maskhadov as a negotiating partner and began to label all Chechens "bandits" and "kidnappers," despite Maskhadov's efforts to arrest those guilty of participating in the hostage trade.

In the end, Maskhadov was unable to force the expulsion of the Arab and Dagestani Wahhabis from Chechnya, and they continued to mobilize against him and against peace. Having been resoundingly beaten in the presidential elections by Maskhadov and pushed out of Gudermes by the anti-Wahhabi Yamadayev brothers, the radical Wahhabi opposition began to clamor for the introduction of shariah law in Chechnya. They began to call Maskhadov a "traitor to Islam" for having a secular law system, and they prepared for a civil war.

On February 3, 1999, President Maskhadov gave in to their pressure in order to avoid a civil war (and also to co-opt the Wahhabi movement) and reluctantly declared shariah law and disbanded parliament. Maskhadov hoped that the introduction of shariah law (something that would have horrified the secular President Dudayev and was certainly opposed by most Chechens) would mollify the Wahhabi extremists, but it only empowered them further. Having attained their goal of turning Chechnya into an Islamic theocracy, they began to plan the overthrow of the "infidel" pro-Russian government in neighboring Dagestan.

At this time the Islamist Chechen politician Movladi Udugov, who had received less than 1 percent of the vote in the 1997 presidential election, declared the formation of the notorious "Congress of the Peoples of Chechnya and Dagestan," which was composed of Arabs and Chechen and Dagestani Wahhabis. Its stated goal was the "unification of the Caucasian peoples on the basis of the laws of Allah," which would begin with the "decolonization" of Dagestan. To President Maskhadov's horror, Shamil Basayev (now back in his camouflage fatigues) was then declared the Congress's emir (Arabic military commander).

Chechnya's moderate foreign minister, Ilyas Akhmadov, strongly disagreed with this alarming development and claimed, "Shamil [Basayev] was gradually stepping into the role of the informal protector of believers in Dagestan. They were trying to suggest to him that he might be a modern-day Imam Shamil, which of course flattered his ego."[34] Akhmadov then offered a psychological analysis that goes a long way toward helping to explain Basayev's motives, stating: "He had already been a war hero and national leader, but he was a failure as a Presidential candidate, a failure as Prime Minister, and he could not accept that his political career was finished."[35] Udugov's "Congress" gave the restless Basayev a new path toward glory, fame, and power. This seems to have been a cynical ploy by Shamil Basayev to circumvent President Maskhadov and the Chechen electorate and put himself in charge of a united "imamate" of Chechnya and Dagestan. Robert Schaefer has written:

If Basayev did not convert to radical Islam, then at least he adopted the rhetoric and trappings in order to manipulate those symbols for his own benefit—taking the title "Emir Abadallah Shamil Abu Idris" starting in 2003. Basayev knew that religion could be used as an ideology, and personal beliefs, however strong, would have been secondary to what the situation demanded at the time.[36]

At around this time, the rhetoric of Basayev and the Wahhabis he had aligned himself with began to refer to the Muslim fighters as mujahideen (holy warriors) or *shaheeds* (martyrs of the faith), fighting jihad against *munafiqs* (traitors of the faith) and *shirk* (paganism) to establish "Allah's will" and defeat the *kafirs* (infidels). This Arabic jihadist jargon would have been completely alien to most post-Soviet Chechens, who had never dreamed of establishing a harsh shariah law theocracy or "imamate" of the sort based in Sudan (the model for the Wahhabis), but of national independence of the sort achieved by Estonia (which incidentally gave Chechnya the model for its secular constitution).

As part of this process of radicalization/Islamification, Basayev, Raduyev, Israpilov, and Udugov demanded that Maskhadov resign and claimed he had "traded freedom for cabbage soup from Moscow."[37] The militia commanders who were in opposition to President Maskhadov, the so-called Commander's Council, then created a parallel government known as the Shura Council (an Arabic term), which aimed to overthrow Maskhadov. This group held rallies of thousands of fighters in Grozny calling for the removal of the "un-Islamic" Maskhadov. Paul Murphy was to write of this process, "In the spring of 1999 Shamil Basayev was the most powerful leader in Chechnya."[38] As for President Maskhadov, he worried about Basayev and impending war, stating:

After the war I was tired, I was dreaming about rest, as was the rest of the Chechen nation. But even then it looked like war was imminent. With dismay I listened to speeches of a variety of politicians and

133

commanders. These calls for holy war, the liberation of the Caucasus, flying Islamic green flags over the Kremlin! I knew everything was heading towards war.[39]

Basayev also threatened the pro-Russian authorities in Dagestan and promised that if the Russians ever tried to retake the Wahhabi enclaves in the Kadar Zone or Avaristan he would intervene to protect his Dagestani "brothers and sisters." By the summer of 1999, members of Basayev and Khattab's fighting force had once again taken to raiding Dagestan, and Russian aircraft had targeted their bases in Chechnya in response.

As hundreds of exiled Dagestanis and a lesser number of Arabs and Chechen Wahhabis trained for jihad in Urus Martan and Khattab's camps, there were few in Chechnya who did not know that the radicals would invade Dagestan soon. A worried Maskhadov even warned the Russians that the Wahhabis were planning an attack. Among other things he told the Russian prime minister, "I think that the independent Chechnya should exist in its present boundaries, but Basayev thinks differently. He would like to try the Chechen experiment in other bordering territories, first of all in Dagestan, through which he can seek access to the two seas, the Black Sea and the Caspian."[40] But the embattled Chechen president's warnings were not heeded by the Russians, who had essentially written him off as an ally.

Having been defeated in the 1997 elections, Basayev, Zelimkhan Yandarbiyev, and Udugov had teamed up with the Dagestani Wahhabis to circumvent Maskhadov's authority and create a larger "imamate," "caliphate," or "emirate" that encompassed both Dagestan and Chechnya. Khattab and Basayev seemed to have been convinced by the exiled Dagestani Wahhabi leaders that the people of Dagestan were restless under Russian rule and craved "liberation." As tensions heated up in the late summer of 1999 in the dry mountains along the Dagestani-Chechen border, the pieces for the Second Russo-Chechen War began to be put in place by a band of no more than two thousand extremists who dreamed of recreating the nineteenth-century theocracy of Imam Shamil.

The Wahhabi Invasion of Dagestan

The unsanctioned August 1999 Wahhabi invasion of Dagestan from Chechnya actually began when one of the Dagestani leaders of the Chechnya-based "Congress of the Peoples of Chechnya and Dagestan" was lured back into the Tsumadi-Avaristan Wahhabi enclave of Dagestan by local authorities on August 2, 1999. Once there, the Dagestani police besieged his enclave and tried to arrest him and his followers. The Dagestani authorities then began to attempt to reestablish administrative authority in the surrounding Wahhabi region.[41] This gave Basayev, Khattab, and Bagauddin Magomedev (the exiled Dagestani leader) the excuse they were looking for to launch their grandiose invasion of the Russian province of Dagestan with the aim of "liberating" it.[42]

On August 7, 1999, between fifteen hundred and two thousand primarily Dagestani Wahhabis, joined by hundreds of Chechen radicals and a smaller number of Arabs, calling themselves the "Islamic International Peace Keeping Brigade" and driving armored personnel carriers and jeeps, crossed into the mountainous Avaristan region of the Russian province of Dagestan. At their head were Basayev, who was styled the "military emir" of the operation, and Khattab, his deputy. Russian television showed images of camouflage-wearing, bearded mujahideen, who were fighting under the black banner of international jihad, not the green wolf flag of Chechnya. Basayev proclaimed, "It is not a Chechen army, but an international corps," while Maskhadov's defense minister said, "We asked Basayev not to attack Dagestan."[43] Tellingly, the name of the military invasion was Operation Ghazi Mogamed (Ghazi Mohammed or Mogamed was a nineteenth-century Dagestani *ghazi*, or holy warrior, who fought to expel the Russian invaders and establish shariah law in the land).[44]

The Wahhabi invaders quickly seized control of twelve villages of Echeda, Gakko, Kedi, Kvanada, Gadiri, and Gigatl in the Tsuamdi district and the villages of Godoberi, Miarso, Shodroda, Ansalta, Rakhata, and Inkhelo in the Botlikhsk district.[45] They also seized two strategic mountain passes from Chechnya into Dagestan and planned to use this captured zone as a bridgehead. From there they planned on taking control of the entire Botlikhsk *rayon* (region) and moving down the Andiskoe Koisu

River into central Dagestan.[46] Basayev solemnly proclaimed the found-
ing of the Islamic Republic of Dagestan and named Sirazhuddin Ram-
azon, a Dagestani Wahhabi, as its prime minister. Basayev then issued
a call for Dagestanis to rise up and overthrow 140 years of occupation
by "Muscovite unbelievers."[47] He also declared war on the "traitorous
Dagestani government and Russian occupation units." Khattab revealed
the invaders' grand ambitions when he proclaimed they were going to
liberate Dagestan and create "an Islamic Caucasian state extending from
the Black Sea to the Caspian Sea."[48]

This represented a real threat to Russia and brought memories of Imam
Shamil's nineteenth-century calls for jihad, which united the Dagestanis
and Chechens in a holy war that shook the empire to its foundation. Moscow's fears were not overblown. As it transpires, Dagestan is three times
the size of Chechnya (roughly the size of Portugal), has two million inhabitants, and contains 70 percent of Russia's coastline on the Caspian Sea;
it provides a vital transit route for pipelines bringing oil from Azerbaijan
to Russia and is home to Russia's only warm-water port, Makhachkala.
The Russians could stand to lose landlocked, tiny Chechnya, but the loss
of strategic Dagestan would be a tremendous blow and might signal a
domino effect as the other small Muslim ethnic republics of the northern
Caucasus were invaded by the anti-Russian Wahhabis. The fall of Dagestan might potentially lead to the formation of an unstable, hostile jihadi
state on Russia's southern border.

As Shamil Basayev's call for a jihad of liberation was televised throughout Dagestan by Movladi Udugov's Kavkaz station, the Russian authorities were slow to react. They seem to have been caught unprepared by
Basayev's audacious invasion.[49]

Then something extraordinary happened: hundreds of armed Dagestani militia volunteers began to gather their weapons and arm themselves
for war. While most of the invading Wahhabis were Dagestani Avars and
Dargins, the armed men came from other Dagestani ethnic groups, which
make up the republic's mosaic of thirty-four ethnic groups. It seemed as
if Moscow's worse nightmare was coming true. Dagestan and Chechnya
were once again united in a holy war to overthrow Russian "infidel" rule.

Only it did not unfold that way. As it happened, the spontaneously
armed Dagestani militias and police were converging on the borders of

the Wahhabi area of Avaristan (it will be recalled that the nineteenth-century Imam Shamil was an ethnic Avar), not to support Basayev and the invading Dagestani-Arab-Chechen force, *but to repel it*. In fact, local militias were established in the surrounding areas to resist the Wahhabi invaders. These volunteers and local police units moved to block strategic mountain passes out of Avaristan down into central Dagestan.

The following is an extraorindary eyewitness account of a local village elder from the Andi tribe, whose people refused to let the Wahhabi invaders through their territory:

They [the Wahhabi invaders] tried to put us under psychological pressure. The [Chechen] soldiers pointed their automatic weapons, machine guns and grenade launchers at us. Shirwani Basayev [Shamil's younger brother], who commanded the soldiers posted in our district, refused to meet with us. Through a transmitter he told us that we had no business being in his headquarters. But if we permitted his squad to go through the Andi village to the pass and bridge near the village of Muni, he would leave us alone.

After a few days I went to meet with the soldiers again. This time I managed to get ahold of Shirwani Basayev. He spoke with me in a conceited manner. He said that they were going to teach us Islam. I answered that we could teach him many things about it. I invited him to visit our village unarmed and see for himself just how highly we honor the Muslim tradition.

Shirwani, however, said that he did not have time for sightseeing trips. He warned me that if we did not let his squad through the Muni Pass, they would walk there over our corpses. I told Basayev that if they killed our men, then our women would tear at their throats as viciously as wildcats.

Basayev wanted to outwit us. So he asked us to let them go through at least to help their dying brothers [Dagestani Wahhabis from Magomedov's divisions] fighting against the Russian army in the villages of Ansalta and Rakhat. I said that the Andis may not permit anyone with bad intentions to set foot on their soil. The soldiers spoke amongst themselves in Chechen. However, I know the language and I understood them, they wanted to kill us. As we were leaving they started shooting at us.[50]

Thus, far from assisting the invaders, the Andis, and many other ethnic groups and even some moderate Avars, joined the local police and MVD units in preventing the invaders from spreading from their occupied areas in the barren mountains of the Botlikhsk region of Avaristan.

The reasons for this were complex. But as Emil Souleimanov distinctly put it, "The [Andi and other moderate Dagestani] villagers considered them [the Avar, Dargin, Chechen, and Arab] occupants and unwelcome religious fanatics."[51] At the time it was reported that "the Andi people are strong adherents of Sufi Islam and detest Wahhabism."[52] Mikhail Roschin has further elaborated on the larger Dagestani rejection of the invaders:

> This [rejection of the invaders] was connected with the fact that traditional [Sufi] folk Islam, which is adhered to by the vast majority of Dagestan's Muslim believers, coexists poorly with radical fundamental Islam . . . Moreover, the majority of the population of Dagestan is extremely hostile and suspicious of anything connected with so-called Wahhabism, that is radical Islam. The local word "Wahhabite" has derogatory and negative connotations. As a result of the events in Botlikhsk when the insurgents were defeated, an unexpected alliance was formed between the Dagestanis and the federalists. Women in Botlikhsk treated Russian soldiers as if they were their own sons.[53]

Robert Bruce Ware and Enver Kishinev, specialists on Dagestan, carried out a poll which found that only 11 percent of Dagestan's multi-ethnic population wanted an Islamic state, while over 63 percent said they wanted socialism.[54] The vast majority of Dagestan's population were religious moderates who feared the disruption of the republic's delicate ethnic balance and the start of both a Bosnian/Lebanese-style ethnic civil war or the introduction of alien Wahhabi Islam. In this respect they mirrored the viewpoint of the majority of their neighbors in Chechnya who had voted for Maskhadov, not the extreme religious candidates Udugov and Yandarbiyev. It should also be mentioned that 80 percent of Dagestan's budget came from Moscow, and its people had not been deported by Stalin, thus most had little historic or economic incentive to break away from the Russian Federation.

Meanwhile, as the local Dagestani police and village volunteers stood up to the Wahhabi invaders and prevented them from moving forward with their plans to come out of the barren mountains, Moscow belatedly reacted to the invasion. First, President Boris Yeltsin fired his prime minister, Sergei Stepashin, who earlier had met with the Wahhabis in the other enclave of the Kadar Zone and effectively allowed them to secede from Dagestan. Fatefully, Yeltsin then promoted a relatively unknown head of the FSB (the new KGB) named Vladimir Putin to be his prime minister. President Yeltsin would state, "Putin was the man of my hopes. He was the man I trusted, to whom I would trust the country."[55]

Prime Minister Putin subsequently flew down to Dagestan and met with Russian military officials and drank a toast on camera to impending victory. By this time the entire North Caucasus Military District had been mobilized, and thousands of Russian Federal troops began to converge on the Botlikhsik district of Avaristan. By August 16 the invaders had been halted and had decided to dig in and stand their occupied ground.

Basayev's men dug trenches into the rocky mountains and prepared to resist the inevitable Russian counterattack. But the fact that the Wahhabi invaders were concentrated in small areas on the side of open mountains gave the Russians a tactical advantage. They began to mercilessly bomb the occupied villages with Sukhoi dive bombers and to strafe them with Hind attack helicopters. Chechnya's moderate foreign minister who had condemned the Wahhabi invasion of Dagestan left the following second-hand account of the brutal Russian bombardment of the fanatical Wahhabi invaders: "As one participant recounted to me you could just hear shouting 'Rejoice! Our brother has become a martyr!' This welcoming attitude towards death is hardly traditional and for many of us it sounded bizarre."[56] It would seem that many of the invaders thus had subscribed to the Arabs' cult of martyrdom, which promises those who die in the name of glorious "holy war" the rewards of paradise.

Regardless of their motivation, Basayev and the invaders were surprised by the lack of popular support across Dagestan. To compound matters, the Russian Federal army then stormed the Wahhabi invaders' positions with ground troops. But these were repulsed by Basayev's men, who had expertly dug defensive trenches. At the time, Russian television featured images from Udugov's Kavkaz network of Wahhabis launching mortars at Russian troops to cries of "Allahu Akbar!" (God is [the] Greatest, an Islamic war cry rarely used by Chechens in the first war) and interviews with Shamil Basayev, who now sported a long Wahhabi-style beard and a cap with the *shahaada* (the first pillar of Islam: "There is no God but Allah") inscribed in Arabic on it. There were also images of women from the Wahhabi villages dressed in long black burqas with even their eyes covered by veils, something that would have been repellant to most Sufi Dagestanis. The Russian news juxtaposed these images of women in alien burqas with images of angry local Dagestani women arming themselves to create "women's battalions" to defeat the invaders, whom they described as "bandits, not Muslims."[57]

As the invasion devolved into a stalemate, the Russians sent in paratroopers, but these were also forced to retreat after coming under determined sniper fire. It was at this time that the Russian Colonel General Viktor Kazanstev, who was in charge of operations, decided to deploy weapons of mass destruction known as FAEs (fuel-air explosives), or vacuum bombs, to dislodge the entrenched Wahhabi invaders. The dropping of these deadly bombs, which even the hardened Chechen fighters and Arab volunteers had not previously encountered, had a devastating effect. One report of their inferno effect on the invaders stated:

> The spectacle is frightening. Even if it is seen a long way off. Over the place where the bomb lands, a huge fireball appears. Although the characteristic and frightening thunder of the explosion is almost inaudible, terror envelops the man. Fear rises within as it were, from the knowledge that a "quiet" fireball inflicts death on every living thing. The weapon is not like napalm. It is possible to hide from napalm, from a vacuum bomb—no. Neither cave, nor strong dug-out, nor hole, nor trench can save a person from it.[58]

These horror weapons seem to have had the desired effect, and the invaders began to withdraw back to Chechnya on August 22 after sustaining significant losses. Basayev then announced that his troops had "redeployed" and would now work toward their objectives in the political arena.

But the Russian military and the Dagestani government were not in a negotiating mood and took advantage of the momentum in the Avaristan-Botlikhsk enclave to turn their attention to the other Wahhabi enclave known as the Kadar Zone. Buoyed by their success in the mountains of

Avaristan, the Russian military then surrounded the Kadar Zone with tanks and mobile artillery and began to bombard it on August 29, 1999.

The Kadar Zone Wahhabis had, however, prepared themselves for combat with the authorities and were armed with infantry weapons and antiaircraft guns. According to one account:

> The fighters' positions took more than a year to prepare with echeloned fire positions protected by reinforced concrete structures and linked together by hidden communication trenches intersecting the terrain, in woods and hollows. Caches of food and weapons were prepared beforehand. "The extremists had turned every house in Karamakhi into an impregnable fortress, and this was especially the case in Chabanmakhi."[59]

As the Russian Federal troops bombed the encircled Kadar Zone with aviation and artillery, the estimated five hundred Wahhabi defenders of the targeted zone put up an "active defense," and then called Chechnya asking for reinforcements on August 31. In Chechnya, the warlords Ruslan "Khamzat" Gelayev and Arbi Barayev responded by sending troops to the border of the Dagestani region where the Kadar Zone was located, the Novolakskoe region.[60] The Russians were alarmed to hear that as many as two thousand fighters had mustered along the border in Chechnya.

By September 2 the Russian attacks had taken their toll on the Wahhabi defenders (an estimated 150 had been killed), and the extremists of the Kadar Zone were sending increasingly desperate calls to the Wahhabis in Chechnya asking for assistance. One pro-Russian militiaman reported: "We considered that in this hell nothing could survive during the bombing."[61] In one instance, an artillery officer spotted some Wahhabi fighters retreating into a house and hit it with a shell, to which he proudly proclaimed, "Now all the Wahhabis have had their beards shaved off."[62] At this time, Emir Khattab's father-in-law, who lived in Karamakhi, was arrested attempting to be smuggled out of the Kadar Zone wrapped in a carpet.[63] The Russians, who were widely supported by surrounding communities who provided them with food and assistance, took great pleasure in targeting Khattab's house with their tanks.

Under the onslaught, surviving radical fighters tried to break out of the Russian encirclement, but were pushed back by Russian *spetsnaz* (special forces). As the besieged Kadari Wahhabis fought back desperately, word came from the border that Shamil Basayev and two thousand fighters had crossed into Dagestan and captured several villages in the heart of the Novolaksoye lowland region on September 5. From there, the invaders intended to move deeper into the populated sections of Dagestan, including the major town of Khasavyurt (whose population of a hundred thousand was one-third Dagestani Chechen), and from there to the capital of Makachkala, which was put on high alert.

The invaders' ultimate aim was to split Dagestan in half and create a corridor to the Caspian Sea, and thus break the Russian blockade around Chechnya. In fact, Basayev's forces pushed to within five kilometers of Khasavyurt, Dagestan's third-largest city, before being repelled by Russian Federal forces in mid-September. This second incursion had been a much greater threat than their previous invasion of the highlands of Avaristan.

But the second invasion from Chechnya, which was launched to distract Russian forces from attacking the Wahhabis in Kadar, Karamakhi, and Chabanmakhi, came too late to save the doomed Kadar Zone. By September 12 the Russians had raised their flag above the ruins of the captured villages and had begun sweeps to arrest Wahhabi fighters.

The Russians followed this up by bombing Khattab and Basayev's bases at Serzhen Yurt and Urus Martan inside Chechnya. Clearly, the new, bellicose Russian prime minister, Vladimir Putin, had come to see the Chechen-Russian peace treaty as irrelevant in light of the Chechnya-based Wahhabi invasions of Dagestan, which cost the Russian side as many as 275 soldiers' lives (with 937 wounded) and had been repulsed only by the mobilization of ten thousand Russian troops.[64]

Putin and most Russians were unmoved by the fact that President Maskhadov, who had been described as "pro-Russian" by Basayev, led a rally of as many as five thousand people against the invasions in Grozny while they were occurring.[65] The Chechen mufti Akhmed Kadyrov also condemned the invasion, but this was not widely reported in Russia. It also meant little to the Russians that Maskhadov officially issued communiques condemning the invasion, which had been carried out largely by exiled Dagestani Wahhabis led by a smaller number of Chechen and Arab extremists who were at war with Chechnya's president too. Few Russians knew or cared about the widespread criticism of Basayev that swept Chechnya after he and his invading force returned home.[66] For many Russians the invasions by a force of Dagestani and Chechen rogue Wahhabis and Arab jihadists had been a "Chechen" invasion of the Russian Federation directed by the Chechen "bandit" government.

But the invasions of Dagestan were not enough to whip up war frenzy among the war-weary Russian population, who were still scarred by the loss of over seventy-five hundred of their soldiers in the unpopular Russian-Chechen War of 1994–1996. It would take more than these minor incursions into a distant Caucasian Muslim republic to awaken a desire for war among the populations of the heartlands of Russia in St. Petersburg, Moscow, and other average Russian cities such as Ryazan and Volgodonsk.

Tragically, such a catalyst for war came as the war in Dagestan was winding down, in the form of a mysterious bombing campaign, subsequently described by Russian authorities as "Russia's 9/11," which took the lives of almost three hundred Russians in towns extending from Dagestan to Moscow itself. History would show that this deadly bombing campaign would provide the new prime minister, Vladimir Putin, with the pretext to launch a full-scale war on Chechnya strongly supported by an increasingly hysterical Russian public.

The Mysterious August to September 1999 Apartment Bombings in Russia

There is no doubt that President Boris Yeltsin had a legitimate *casus belli* (case for war) in defending the Russian citizens of the Federal Republic of Dagestan from the aggression launched by Wahhabi invaders based in the lawless state of Chechnya. Recall if you will that US troops invaded Mexico in 1916 to track down the Mexican bandit Pancho Villa, after his raiding force of five hundred men attacked the New Mexico border town of Columbus (although the Americans did not launch a total war on Mexico). But antiwar sentiment was still not running high in Russia. Few Russian citizens were willing to countenance a full-scale war based on the incursions in the far-off Caucasus. It was not Basayev's easily repulsed invasions that mobilized the Russian public for another round of costly war in Chechnya, but the bombing campaign by unknown culprits that was erroneously blamed on the "Chechen terrorist nation."

The apartment bombing campaign began in the Dagestani garrison town of Buinaksk (Dagestan's second-largest city), which had been filled with Russian troops to fight the nearby Wahhabi invasion. There, on September 4, 1999, a bomb went off next to a five-story apartment building housing Russian troops from the 136th Brigade and their families. Sixty-four people were killed in the explosion (twenty of whom were children), which leveled the building in the evening. Another bomb was found near a second apartment complex and miraculously defused just twelve minutes before it was set to go off.[67]

This bombing took place in the initial days of the suppression of the Kadar Wahhabi Zone, and a Russian minister stated, "The explosion at Buinaksk and the incursion from Chechnya are links in the same chain."[68] The massive bombing was unprecedented in Russia, and nothing like it had occurred during the war of 1994 to 1996.

Worse was yet to come.

The next bombing took place in Moscow itself on the night of September 9 and blew up an apartment building killing another ninety-four people. Investigators at the scene found traces of an explosive known as RX, or hexagon. The bombing was seen as the work of professionals in light of the sheer scale of the explosion and the placement of the bomb, which brought down a nine-story apartment building.

The third bombing took place on September 13, 1999, at 5 AM, when a large bomb exploded in the basement of an apartment building in southern Moscow. Approximately 119 people died and 200 were injured. This was the deadliest blast in the bombing campaign, and it flattened an eight-story building.

The final bombing took place a few days later in the southern city of Volgodonsk, once again around 5 AM, when the building's inhabitants were sleeping. On this occasion the building was seriously damaged, but only seventeen people were killed. In total almost three hundred Russian citizens had been killed by unknown terrorists.

Prime Minister Vladimir Putin did not wait for an investigation and immediately blamed the Chechens. His bold, uncouth threats of retaliation against the Chechens resonated with Russians who were panicked by the mysterious chain of bombings and wanted to blame someone. Putin would rally his grieving people by threatening the Chechens, stating, "If they're in the airport, we'll kill them there. And excuse me, but if we find them in the toilet, we'll exterminate them in their outhouses."[69]

But then something strange occurred in the Russian town of Ryazan that was to forever cast doubt on Putin's sweeping accusations of Chechen involvement. It all began on September 22, when a resident of an apartment building in the city noticed two suspicious men carrying sacks into the basement from a car with fake Ryazan license plates. He then called the police, but by the time they arrived the suspicious men were gone. The policemen then went to the basement and found three 50-kg sacks of white powder there with a detonator and timing device set to go off at 5:30 AM. The white powder was tested by a state-of-the-art explosive detecting device and found to be RX/hexagon. It will be recalled that this was the exact explosive used in all the previous bombings in Russia proper, which also took place at roughly 5 AM.

As the bomb was disconnected from the timer, 30,000 residents of Ryazan were frantically evacuated from the area, and a citywide manhunt was launched to find the culprits. It subsequently was announced on Russian television that the police had thwarted yet another terrorist attack.

But the plot thickened that same evening when an alert telephone employee in Ryazan tapped into a long-distance phone conversation and overheard an out-of-town person suggesting to others on the line that they "split up" and "make their own way." The number was then traced to a local FSB telephone exchange unit. The police raided the venue and arrested three Russian FSB agents who fit the description of those who had earlier deposited the bomb in the basement.

The whole incident was a shock to Russia and was the equivalent of the New York Police Department apprehending FBI agents planting a bomb in Manhattan in the horror-filled days after 9/11. Not surprisingly, the FSB agents were quickly released on orders from above, much to the fury of the local Ryazan police. The FSB then issued a highly implausible statement which claimed that the whole operation had simply been a "training exercise" designed to assess how well the local people and police responded to a possible terror threat. The FSB also claimed the white substance in the hidden bags that was assessed to be RX/hexagon by a $20,000 police detector was in actuality "sugar."[70]

The Ryazan police vehemently denied this claim and stated that their men had earlier tasted the white substance in addition to testing it, and it had not been sugar. The whole episode created a wave of distrust among many Russians. Alexei Kartofelnikov, the alert neighbor who had spotted the bombers and called the police said, "Somebody tried to blow us up. I have no doubt about that. But as for who did it, or why—I don't know what to think. The government started bombing Chechnya the next day. I know Chechens. I served with them in the army. They are good people. How can one suspect them of such a thing?"[71]

Another resident of the building, Ivan Kirilin, similarly stated, "Who should I believe—what the government says or what was in the basement? I don't think the Chechens would blow up a residential house. You have to ask—who is responsible for the war? Who needed the war? The government, of course."[72] Ryazan resident Tatiana Borycheva said, "The authorities are trying hard to hush it up and hide everything. I don't believe the Chechens were behind it. I think it's a big political game. People are fighting for power, and our lives are not worth a kopeck in their game. I think somebody wanted to set up the Chechens to start the war and grab power."[73]

Skepticism of the FSB and government's explanation for the "training exercise" in an unimportant Russian city was not limited to Russia. Headlines in newspapers across the globe reported skepticism. The *Los Angeles Times* headline read "Fears of Bombing Turn to Doubts for Some in Russia," while a headline in Britain's *Independent* read "Did Alexei Stumble across Russian Agents Planting a Bomb to Justify Chechen War?"

To compound matters, a Russian FSB agent named Alexander Litvinenko defected to the UK and claimed that the FSB had been behind the bombing campaign in a book entitled *Blowing Up Russia*. He was subsequently tracked down and killed in London by Russian FSB agents, as was one of the FSB agents involved in the "training exercise." Professor John Dunlop, senior fellow at Stanford University's prestigious Hoover Institution who has written the definitive book on the bombings, boldly stated: "It is my belief that the explosive device placed in the basement in the building in Ryazan did in fact represent a live bomb."[74] David Satter of the *National Review* reported:

To do what they were accused of having done without expert assistance, however, Chechen terrorists would have needed to be able to organize nine explosions (the four that took place and the five that the Russian authorities claimed to have prevented) in widely separated cities in the space of two weeks. They also would have needed the ability to penetrate top-secret Russian-military factories or military units to obtain the hexogen.

Finally, Chechen terrorists would have needed technical virtuosity. In the case of the Moscow apartment buildings, the bombs were placed to destroy the weakest, critical structural elements so each of the buildings would collapse "like a house of cards." Such careful calculations are the mark of skilled specialists, and the only places where such specialists were trained in Russia were the *spetsnaz* forces, military intelligence (GRU), and the FSB.[75]

A commission subsequently was established to investigate the charges, but its chief investigator, Mikhail Trepashkin, was arrested for "revealing state secrets" and sentenced to four years in jail. Two other members of the commission were assassinated. This effectively closed the investigation, and there was no "9/11 Commission"–style inquiry into the worst terrorist attack in Russian history.

What made the whole episode even more mysterious was the fact that the obvious culprit, Russia's most notorious "bandit-terrorist" enemy, the dreaded Shamil Basayev of the 1995 Budyenovsk hospital hostage-seizure fame, adamantly denied any involvement in the bombing campaign. The usually swaggering Basayev mutely stated: "The latest blast in Moscow is not our work, but the work of the Dagestanis. Russia has been openly terrorizing Dagestan, it encircled three villages in the centre of Dagestan, did not allow women and children to leave."[76] Basayev then said, "When we are forced into a corner, we are capable of anything, like Budyonnovsk. But we are not in a corner right now."[77] Basayev even sounded frustrated by the bombings, perhaps sensing that they had hurt his cause, and said, "Part of me wants people to know the truth and why we fight. But people are all confused about terrorists and explosions now."[78]

There is reason to believe Basayev's claim. He had in the past carried out a minor terrorist attack in Moscow to bring attention to himself and his cause. In November of 1995 Basayev ordered that a small radioactive parcel of cesium be buried in Izmailovsky Park in the heart of Moscow. He then gave Russian journalists directions to the spot to prove to the Russians that he was "not bluffing" in his threats to Russia.[79] But on the occasion of the mysterious 1999 apartment bombings in Russia, far from taking credit, Basayev blamed the Dagestanis.

Notably, after the bombings, Basayev's former friend, the moderate foreign minister of Chechnya, Ilyas Akhmadov, asked him off the record if he had ordered the bombings. Akhmadov recorded this extraordinary discussion with Basayev as follows:

> I [Akhmadov speaking] don't claim to know who blew up the buildings, but it wasn't the Chechen government. Moreover, during my last brief encounter with Shamil, shortly before I left Grozny, I asked him directly "I will keep this to myself, but can you tell me who stands behind these explosions?" To which he responded without any hesitation, "Ilyas, I don't know who did it, but I know they are not human."[80]

Dagestani experts Professors Robert Bruce Ware and Enver Kishinev eloquently argued that Basayev was not to blame for the explosions as follows:

> Some observers noted that Chechen leaders such as Shamil Basaev and Salman Raduyev were usually quick to claim responsibility for their exploits. Would Basaev not have taken credit for the apartment blasts if they were his work? Indeed why would any Chechen wish to enrage Russians by attacking civilians in their beds? And why did the explosions stop when Russian troops entered Chechnya? If Chechens were behind the blasts then would the blasts not have continued after war resumed?[81]

By contrast, Emir Khattab, who had a wife and children in the doomed Kadar Zone, seemed to take the blame for the bombing campaign, stating: "The mujahideen of Dagestan are going to carry out reprisals in various places across Russia."[82] He also said, "From now on, we will not only fight against Russian fighter jets and tanks. From now on, they will get our bombs everywhere. Let Russia await our explosions blasting through their cities. I swear we will do it."[83] He then claimed that the war had shifted from Dagestan to "all Russian cities and would be directed against all Russians."[84] Finally, he stated: "When there are a lot of explosions, then they will get scared. We will stop Russia."[85]

The Khattab threats seem plausible in light of the fact that a journalist who earlier visited the Kadar Zone and met with the radicals claimed, "The Wahhabists' trucks go all over Russia. Even one wrong move in Moscow or Makhachkala, they warn, will lead to bombs and bloodshed everywhere." The Dagestani Wahhabis then threatened, "If they [the Russians] start bombing us, we know where our bombs will explode."[86] The fact that the apartment bombing campaign began in nearby Buinaksk, Dagestan, during the attack on these same Wahhabis in the Kadar Zone, lends support to the theory that Dagestani extremists trained by the Arab jihadi Khattab carried out the attacks.

Russian investigators subsequently arrested several Dagestanis and Karachays for the bombings and claimed they worked for Khattab. The Russian investigators claimed that Khattab paid one Achemez Gochiyayev (a Turkic Karachay, i.e., a member of a small ethnic group located to the west of Chechnya, whose people also were deported by Stalin) $500,000 to orchestrate the bombings.

The Russians arrested most of those they claimed were involved in the bombing campaign, and they consisted of two Tatars, five Karachays, a Russian, and eight Dagestanis (mainly Avars).[87] Most were given life sentences for their crimes, but several claimed they were "beaten and threatened by their interrogators before their closed hearing trials."[88] But it must be emphatically stated that *no ethnic Chechens were ever arrested in the investigations or officially accused by investigators of having carried out the 1999 bombings.*[89] Tellingly, the Russians did not even charge Shamil Basayev with a role in the blasts.

But this simple fact did not matter to most Russians, who had become swept up in a level of what has been called "Chechenophobia," which did not exist during the first war, of 1994 to 1996. Russia seemed to have found an easily demonized people to blame for the unsolved bombing campaign, and Putin quickly moved against them. Before the investigation that later led to the arrest of predominantly Avar-Dagestanis and Karachays had even begun, the Russian authorities began mass sweeps of Moscow and other towns to arrest or deport Chechen suspects to

Chechnya. Thousands of Chechens, including women and children, were dragged to police stations and interrogated and arrested. Many were held for months, although they were all ultimately found innocent. Mairbek Vachagayev, the Chechen government's representative in Moscow, stated of the sweep arrests (known as Operation Foreigner): "It was never like this during Russia's war with Chechnya. At that time there was some sort of understanding of our case, and even support for it. Now it's like a mass psychosis."[90] Former Interior Ministry General Aslambek Aslakhanov, a member of the Russian Duma, similarly stated:

> Not even having seen the site of the bombings, the Russian authorities announced that it was done by Chechens and that [the explosive] hexogen was used—about which no one had ever heard anything. I said on the third day afterward in a news conference that I didn't believe Chechens did it. I believe that this is a move directed against Chechens. And that's what actually happened.[91]

Such skeptical voices were, however, drowned out in the wave of anti-Chechen hysteria that swept Russia. The bombings would begin the process of linking the entire Chechen people to terrorism and legitimizing the second, full-scale invasion of Chechnya, under Prime Minister Putin. Thus, either Khattab or the FSB (depending on which version of the bombing guilt one ascribes to—or perhaps *both* as some have argued in a hybrid theory, which suggests that Khattab's Dagestani Wahhabis began the campaign and the FSB capitalized on it and extended it to commence a state of emergency and promote Putin) succeeded in bringing the full wrath of the Russian Federation down on the war-weary Chechen people. Most notably, Emma Gilligan would point out, "The Russian government refused to engage with the complexities of the issue, to recognize Maskhadov's position, to acknowledge that the radicals were not popular among the Chechen population at large."[92]

The Russian government's inability to recognize a friend in President Maskhadov was intentional. History would show that Vladimir Putin, a complete unknown before the 1999 bombings, would exploit the moment to rise to power and win the March 2000 presidential elections based on his tough stance on the "Chechen terror threat." After he declared a popular war on the Chechens to defend Russian citizens from the bombers,

Putin's popularity would skyrocket. Gregory Felfer has reported: "Two things brought about Putin's victory: the bombings and the phrase about wiping out terrorists in the outhouse."[93]

Putin would then take advantage of his newfound popularity to enact emergency laws to dismantle Russia's fragile post-Soviet democracy (which had thrived under Yeltsin) and reconstruct an authoritarian state. Putin's new Russia would be defined by the silencing of the previously free press, mass arrests of dissidents and real or perceived opposition figures and critics, and the overturning of the right of regions to elect their own governors. Former Russian Finance Minister Mikhail Kasyanov would bitterly recount this process of Putin's rebuilding of a police state, saying, "He received carte blanche from the citizens of Russia. They simply closed their eyes and let him do whatever he wanted as long as he saved them from this threat."[94]

The Russians would not, however, be the main ones to suffer under Putin. Tens of thousands of Chechen civilians would die in Putin's subsequent war in Chechnya as a result of the killing of less than three hundred Russians by either the FSB or Khattab's Karachai-Dagestani-Tatar terrorists. The anti-Chechen hysteria would become so extreme that the Russian military would establish "filtration" camps throughout Chechnya where thousands of Chechen were imprisoned, tortured, and in many cases killed, on the mere suspicion that they were terrorists. Several Russian members of the Duma (Parliament) captured the newfound bellicose sentiment of Putin and his people when they called for the use of tactical nuclear weapons to wipe out the Chechens.[95] Others called for the "physical extermination of the whole [Chechen] republic using strategic air strikes, biological weapons, psychotropic gases, napalm."[96]

As the war clouds gathered over the Kremlin and the Russian people bayed for Chechen blood, President Maskhadov tried to reach out to Putin to offer his help in launching a joint campaign against the Wahhabi extremists, who threatened both their people. But Maskhadov's phone calls went unanswered. In a step that captured the cold cynicism of the Putin Kremlin, far from accepting Maskhadov's outstretched hand, the Russians declared the Chechen president a "terrorist," and a warrant was issued for his arrest.[97] In response, Maskhadov said, "I don't want this war. Let it weigh on Russia's conscience."[98] It was clear that Putin would recognize no distinction between the small number of Wahhabi terror-ists led by Khattab on the one hand, and the moderate Chechen majority led by Maskhadov, who wanted peace, on the other hand.

On the very day after the suspicious FSB "sugar" incident in Ryazan, Russian fighter bombers began to indiscriminately bomb and strafe targets across Chechnya. War had once again come to the blood-soaked Caucasus. After three chaotic years that saw the virtual hijacking of the Chechen state by warlords and foreign-funded Wahhabis, the inferno in Chechnya had been reignited.

The Return of the Russians

By what privilege did the Russian government have the
right to kill thousands of [Chechen] civilians for the
sake of an "anti-terrorist operation"?
— Associate Professor Emma Gilligan,
   author of *Terror in Chechnya*[1]

Basayev is a warrior. He is someone who is taking
revenge. He is using the same methods as the enemy,
who uses those methods against the Chechen civilians.
It is an eye for an eye.
— Chechen President Aslan Maskhadov[2]

The Commencement of Russian "Antiterror" Operations in Chechnya

On September 28, 1999, the second war commenced, and transcontinental Russia, a country with eleven time zones and population of 140 million, was at war with tiny Chechnya, with a population of less than a million. The Russian army that was dispatched to Chechnya was a juggernaut of 110,000 troops (80,000 soldiers from the Ministry of Defense and 30,000 from the Ministry of Internal Affairs) and was more than twice the size of the army previously sent to conquer Chechnya in 1994. Putin captured the country's new bellicose spirit and laid out their war aims, stating that their objectives were to "wipe out the Chechen thugs wherever they are, right up to the last shit house."[3] Russia's most popular newspaper actually called for the "physical extermination of the whole [Chechen] republic using strategic air strikes, biological weapons, psychotropic gases, napalm, and everything else available to our once-powerful army."[4]

The war began when a fifty-mile column of Russian troops and armor crossed into northern Chechnya and began to seize control of the easily controlled flatlands located to the north of the Terek River. There they met little opposition from the lowland clans, who had always been more Russified. Simultaneously, a column crossed into Chechnya from Ingushetia to the west. Above them flew squadrons of Mig and Sukhoi fighter bombers that had been systematically bombing villages in the south and the capital of Grozny for several days in advance. Flights of Mil Mi-24 Hind attack helicopters also were given orders to engage in "free hunts" and swarmed the countryside attacking any perceived "bandit-terrorists" from far above.

Hundreds of civilians were killed in the initial missile and aerial bombardments, and they were no less innocent than those Russians killed in the apartment bombings. One US military analyst noted, "There was very little concern for collateral damage [i.e., civilian deaths], despite Russian claims that attacks were more 'precise' than previous battles."[5] As the Russian bombs hit their villages, tens of thousands of panicked refugees fled before the invading Russian behemoth. Ultimately, more than a quarter of a million Chechens, one-third of Chechnya's population, would flee their microrepublic to escape the Russian onslaught.

Russia described this massive invasion as a limited "counterterrorism operation," and for most Russians it was seen as a suitable response to the "Chechen bombing campaign." In other words, it was a justified retaliatory campaign against a nation of "terrorists."

In actuality, the former Russian prime minister later was to announce that the Russian invasion had been in the works for months in advance (i.e., prior to the mysterious Moscow bombings).[6] Sergei Stepashin subsequently would acknowledge: "Regarding Chechnya, I can say the following. The plan for [military] action in this republic has been under development since March [1999]. We planned to move out and reach the Terek [a river in northern Chechnya] by August or September. This would have happened even if there hadn't been explosions in Moscow."[7]

In addition, the Russians had been carrying out large-scale war exercises in all the republics surrounding Chechnya since 1998.[8] The fact that Russia had been planning the invasion all along confirmed the suspicions of Basayev, who had long predicted that the Russians would be back and that peace with them was a sham. The news that Russia had been preparing to invade prior to the Dagestani incursions also undermined President Maskhadov's peace party.

Regardless of when the invasion was planned, it proved to be incredibly favorable to the relatively unknown Prime Minister Putin's approval ratings. John Dunlop has reported that in August of 1999, when he was first chosen by President Yeltsin as prime minister, only 2 percent of Russians saw Putin as viable to be president should Yeltsin retire. Following the mysterious apartment bombings and his tough responsive language, however, Putin's approval rating soared to 21 percent in October; and by the time the invasion was under way in November, a full 45 percent of Russians felt he was suitable to be president.[9] The unsmiling ex-KGB officer Vladimir Putin was seen as the grim defender who would protect Russia from the "Chechen terrorists" who had wreaked so much havoc in the Russian heartlands.

If the Russians were unifying behind Putin and his war, the quarreling Chechen warlords also put aside their differences and, for the first time, rallied to their own beleaguered president. Warlords such as Arbi Barayev, Shamil Basayev, Khattab, Raduyev, and others who had been calling for the overthrow of President Maskhadov just days before, now acknowledged him as their overall leader — although it must be said that their warbands operated semi-independently.

In return, Maskhadov forgave them and assigned several of them to key positions. Basayev and Khattab were given control of the eastern front facing Dagestan. Ruslan "Khamzat" Gelayev was given control of the western front facing Ingushetia. Arbi Barayev and his Wahhabis prepared to defend Urus Martan, while Raduyev swore to fight to the death defending Grozny. Aslanbek Ismailov was put in charge of the defense of Grozny and was joined there by the fighters of Khunkar Pasha Israpilov and Doku Umarov (this latter figure, a Sufi fighter, would later become head of the Chechen resistance and labeled the "Chechen bin Laden" when he created a terror group known as the Caucasian Emirate).

There was, however, no sign of support from the Chechen mufti, Akhmad Kadyrov, and his anti-Wahhabi Sufi supporters, the Yamadayev brothers who controlled the key city of Gudermes. This worried Maskhadov, as the Russian army converged on the capital of Grozny.

By October 15, 1999, the Russians had seized a strategic ridge overlooking Grozny and had begun to systematically bombard the Chechen capital. Andrew Meier, who was in Chechnya at the time, wrote of the Russian bombardment: "The onslaught was designed to lose as few Russian soldiers as possible, while killing as many Chechens, armed or not, as possible."[10]

Hundreds of civilians died as shells rained down on the capital's already shattered neighborhoods. The Russians declared that those who remained in the town would be declared "terrorists and bandits."[11] As there were still as many as fifty thousand civilians trapped in Grozny, the United States and the European Union, however, strongly protested this act of barbarism. Britain's foreign minister "wholeheartedly condemned" the Russian ultimatum to Grozny's citizens and said, "We cannot understand how Russia imagines it can rout out terrorism by attacking a whole population."[12] President Bill Clinton said, "Killing everyone in a city where thousands of helpless civilians were holed up in basements — was totally unacceptable."[13]

Under Western pressure, the Russians belatedly withdrew their blanket threat to the city's trapped civilians. They then opened "humanitarian corridors" to allow civilian "nonterrorists" to evacuate. But word soon spread that the Russians were occasionally bombing and wiping out columns of retreating civilians fleeing through the humanitarian corridors under white flags, and they were arresting all males over the age of ten and transferring them to the dreaded "filtration" camps. Those in convoys that were destroyed were then retroactively labeled "terrorists" or "guerillas."[14] A typical account of Russians attacking fleeing Chechen civilians in these corridors stated:

> Survivor Taisa Aidamirova said the refugees were travelling in a convoy of seven cars and a bus under white flags, when they were stopped at a Russian checkpoint 5 km south of the city. "When the [Russian] troops opened fire, a bullet struck the petrol tank of the bus and it exploded," she told the BBC. "There were bodies everywhere." Most of the victims were women. "We had to leave some of the wounded behind."[15]

After hearing horrific reports like this one in which forty civilians were killed, tens of thousands of Grozny's inhabitants chose to remain in the basements of their homes as the Russians pulverized the city above them, rather than roll the dice by trusting the word of the Russian troops.

For over a month the Russians rained rockets and artillery down on the besieged city as they slowly moved to encircle it in three rings of steel and land mine fields. The UN would call Grozny "the most destroyed city on earth."[16] Shamil Basayev was to later state: "I am confident that the bombardment we were subjected to in Grozny was not witnessed by anyone facing the ordeal of conventional arms during the past century."[17]

In November, American monitors in NORAD (North American Aerospace Defense Command) detected the launch of SS-21 Scarab and Scud B tactical ballistic missiles into downtown Grozny. As these lethal weapons of mass destruction landed in the urban center of Grozny, they wreaked a level of carnage on Chechen civilians that could no longer be kept secret from the outside world. One rare reporter, who succeeded in entering the off-limits Chechen capital in October, reported seeing the mangled bodies of scores of Chechen civilians slain by a Russian missile. These bodies were strewn around the blood-spattered crater of a surface-to-surface missile strike (October 21, 1999), which killed 137 people peacefully shopping in a downtown market.

Although Russian spokesmen proclaimed that their notoriously in-

accurate ballistic missiles were somehow distinguishing between inno-
cent Chechen civilians and fighters, one eyewitness to the marketplace
slaughter recalled, "After the first hit, I saw a man who was sitting in a car.
His head had been blown off, but his hands were still holding the wheel.
Corpses were everywhere in the market. They were lying on the stalls."[18]
After initially denying that they were responsible for the attack, Russia's
generals reluctantly admitted that the slaughter was caused by a Tochka
SS-21 missile carrying an "airburst device" (i.e., cluster bomblets).

As the NORAD observers monitored the events across the globe, they
recorded multiple Russian ballistic missile strikes on Grozny, which were
supplemented by direct tube artillery fire, multiple rocket hailstorms (the
Russian multiple rocket launchers were nicknamed *Grad*, i.e., "hail"),
240-mm mortar rounds, TOS-1 thermobaric warheads, cluster bombs, and
laser-guided iron bombs dropped from Su-24 and Su-25 tactical bombers.

In the process of raining destruction down on Grozny, whole neighborhoods that had barely survived the first Russo-Chechen conflict were
systematically reduced to rubble. As the Russian army attempted to destroy the elusive Chechen fire squads that persisted in firing back on their
positions from the ruins, Grozny came to resemble the futuristic postnu-
clear holocaust setting for a Mad Max movie rather than a European city
about to enter the twenty-first century.

In the meantime, Russia's military planners began to discuss the de-
ployment of chemical and biological weapons to annihilate the elusive
Chechen defenders and meet their strict December deadline. While
many voices in the Russian High Command suggested using biochemi-
cal weapons to flush out the Chechen fighters, this option was vetoed by
Putin, who feared an outraged Western reaction.

But Russia's generals knew that their conventional arsenal held a
variety of terror weapons that were as effective as any unconventional
biological, chemical, or nuclear weapon. Among them was the terror
weapon known in the West as fuel-air explosives, which had already been
deployed to repel Basayev's invaders from the mountains of Dagestan
in August 1999. If the Russians could not expel the tenacious Chechen
defenders of Grozny from the city using traditional means, they would
literally turn the air they breathed into fire.

As they made their debut in Chechnya, Russia's fuel-air explosives (known by the Russians as "vacuum bombs") soon instilled fear in the hearts of even hardened Chechen veterans of the earlier Russian sieges of Grozny. As the name suggests, fuel-air explosives kill by turning the air being breathed by the enemy into an aerosol fuel (the highly toxic ethylene oxide or propylene oxide). This flammable aerosol cloud is subsequently ignited, turning oxygen in the targeted area into a fiery mist that sears the lungs, burns off skin, and incinerates victims over a wider radius than a conventional bomb.

Fuel-air explosives can be delivered by either artillery shell or two component bombs. In the case of third-generation bombs, such as the KAB-500 TV-guided bomb, or the ODS BLU fuel-air cluster bomblet, a weaponized aerosol cloud is exploded over an extensive area by an initial-delivery component. In a matter of microseconds, this fast-spreading cloud then seeps into hardened bunkers, basements, trenches, and cellars. As this deadly mist fills the strike zone, a second component ignites the aerosol cloud, creating a tremendous fireball that engulfs even those hiding in defensive bunkers. The enhanced fireball then courses outward from the epicenter, flattening walls and buildings. The fire waves are then reenforced as further bombs or shells are exploded on the target zone, creating an arcade of explosions.[19]

This lethal fireball is, however, only the first step in the fuel-air process — the subsequent crushing stage of the explosion is just as deadly. As the initial detonation takes place, it creates a tremendous overpressure. Blast waves surge outward, crushing to death those not burnt to death in the primary explosion. One military expert described the effects of this terror weapon on those humans unfortunate enough to be caught in its second wave as follows:

Personnel under the cloud are literally crushed to death. Outside the cloud area, the blast wave travels at some 3,000 meters per second (9,843 feet per second).

As a result, a fuel-air explosive can have the effect of a tactical nuclear weapon without residual radiation. Since a fuel-air mixture flows easily into any cavities, neither natural terrain features nor non-hermetically sealed field fortifications (emplacements, covered slit trenches, bunkers) protect against the effects of fuel-air explosives.[20]

Most frighteningly, the entire blast process also creates a secondary vacuum as the oxygen in the air of the target zone is consumed. Those caught in the resulting vacuum (even victims hiding in bunkers) have the air sucked from their lungs. In most instances, this causes a collapse of the lungs, suffocation, or in the mildest cases (among those farthest from the explosion) inability to breath for several long, and often deadly, seconds.

A CIA study on fuel-air explosives stated: "The effect of an FAE explosion within confined spaces is immense. Those near the ignition point are obliterated. Those at the fringe are likely to suffer many internal, and thus invisible injuries, including burst eardrums and crushed inner ear organs, severe concussions, ruptured lungs and internal organs, and possibly blindness."[21]

As the FAEs were deployed in Grozny in the fall of 1999, the city's hospitals and morgues began to fill with horribly maimed men, women, and children who had had their skin burnt off by these horror weapons, which had not been deployed in the first war. Dr. Khassan Baiev, the village doctor from the hamlet of Alkhan Kala who had previously stated his contempt for Wahhabis, was to record the use of FAEs as follows: "The shock wave from the explosions was so powerful it collapsed buildings and sucked bodies out, smashing them against stationary objects. Colleagues told me how you would find people dead in a cellar with no evident markings on them, though their organs were atomized inside their bodies."[22] One Chechen civilian in the city stated, "I never imagined that war could be worse than what we saw before. But this is not war. It is murder on a state level, it is mass murder."[23]

But even as thousands died around and among them, the small Chechen force of no more than three thousand fighters held firm and repulsed Russian armor and infantry probes into the heart of the city, Minutka Square.[24] Under the skilled direction of the head of military operations in Grozny, Aslambek Ismailov, the highly mobile Chechen fighters dug antitank trenches, constructed interconnected firing positions, planted land mines, placed snipers' nests, dug bunkers, and created passages through the walls of bombed-out apartments to once again turn Grozny into an "urban forest" quagmire for the Russians.

In addition, the Chechens were intimately familiar with the city's sewage system and civil defense tunnel networks, described as this "city-beneath-the-city," and used them to launch ambushes on Russian probes and static positions. Moreover, elusive ten- to twenty-five–man Chechen "hunter-killer" teams fought with dismounted Russian infantry, who were ordered to avoid direct combat with the rebels and call in artillery strikes whenever they encountered Chechens. For their part, the Chechens tried to get into close contact firefights with the Russians in using so-called "flea and dog" tactics (i.e., the flea bites the dog, then escapes).[25]

In these conditions the battles were brutal and, despite the Russians' best efforts, often devolved into close-quarter fighting, with the Russians relying on "*Schmel*" (bumblebee) flamethrowers to root out Chechen "rats." The Russians lost over 530 men by December, a number that far exceeded US losses in the brutal 2004 Battles for Fallujah in Iraq, the heaviest US urban fighting since Vietnam.[26] Russian morale was said to plummet because of the high mortality rate and the fact that Chechens kept reappearing in districts that had already been cleared.[27] Olga Oliker reported that this declining morale was in part because "Overall, artillery proved effective, but it failed to protect Russian ground forces from close combat."[28]

The battle for Grozny clearly demonstrated that the advantages of numbers and advanced military technology were easily mitigated in urban combat by lightly armed guerilla defenders who had a mastery of their home terrain and the willingness to engage in firefights. Despite the Kremlin's best efforts to prevent Russian casualties, by December Russia's young men once again were arriving home in caskets in the hundreds as the Chechens continued to make Moscow pay a steep price in blood for their capital.

In response to Russia's probes into Grozny, the Chechen defenders (many of whom had earlier been trained in Red Army military tactics while serving as conscripts in the Soviet forces) utilized a variety of Russian weapons against their attackers. The Chechens' favored killing tools included the trusty AK-47 and updated 74 (automatic Kalashnikov rifles designed in 1947 and 1974, the sturdy weapon of choice of guerillas throughout the world), the shoulder-fired RPG-7 (Rocket Propelled Grenade, which was used with such deadly effect by the Chechen fighters that it came to be known as the "Chechen atom bomb"), Dragunov sniper rifles fitted with laser scopes, truck-mounted multiple rocket launchers, and remote-controlled antitank land mines.

In his insightful analysis of Chechen battle tactics during the siege of Grozny, Timothy Thomas provides the following description of how the defenders used these and other weapons:

> Privately, one Russian officer told a reporter that "a Chechen company [100 soldiers] can match head for head a Russian brigade [3,000 soldiers]" in Grozny. Reportedly the Chechens were divided into 25-man groups that were subdivided into three smaller groups of eight each that tried to stay close to the Russian force ("hugging" the Russian force as they had during the 1995 battle to minimize the Russian artillery effort) . . .
>
> Snipers also could be found in trenches and under concrete slabs that covered basements. These slabs could be raised with car jacks when Russian forces approached, provide ambush firing positions, and then drop back down. The attacking Russian force struggled to discern what was merely rubble and what was a kill zone . . .
>
> At times, when the fight was dragging on, the Chechen force would move out of the city and attack the Russian force in the rear, especially in cities already taken. This was a daring exploit if one report is accurate— that 50,000 Russian soldiers surrounded the city . . .
>
> Finally, the impressive mobility of the Chechen force included escape routes from firing positions, interconnected firing positions and again the sewer network to move about the city. Russian forces especially feared the nighttime, when the Chechens would move against and reclaim abandoned positions.[29]

Using such asymmetric tactics (including ammonia-based Molotov cocktails—as a counterpoint to horrific fuel-air explosives, handheld grenade launchers—in response to Russia's short-range ballistic missiles, and truck-mounted antiaircraft guns—as a response to the mighty Russian air armada) the Chechen urban guerillas stalled Russia's vaunted effort to crush the "bandit-terrorists" throughout the months of November and December.

The fiercest fighting, however, was between Chechen *boyevik* defenders and a group of pro-Russian Chechens led by a former mayor of

Grozny named Bislan Gantemirov. But the so-called Gantemirovsky were not the only ones to go over to the Russians. In what was seen as perhaps the greatest betrayal in Chechen history, the Sufi mufti of Chechnya, Akhmad Kadyrov, and the Yamadayev brothers, both of whom controlled Chechnya's second-largest city of Gudermes, made an agreement with the Russian invaders on November 11, 1999. They agreed to allow the Russian Federal forces into their city and to work with them.

This move gave the Russians control of the central valley of Chechnya. The mufti then called on Chechens not to resist the Russians. CNN was to report, "Russian officers said some Gudermes residents were cooperating in the occupation of the city because they're tired of the fighting. Russian officials said they are now working to 'clean' the city—searching Gudermes for terrorists."[30]

Gudermes subsequently became the headquarters for the Russian army operations in Chechnya, and the Yamadayev brothers' clan-based militia, now known as Vostok (East), joined the Russians. The five Yamadayev brothers were subsequently given the award "Hero of the Russian Federation," and one of them became a member of the Russian parliament.

For his part, the mufti Akhmad Kadyrov became head of the so-called Russian "puppet" administration in Chechnya and declared the region of Gudermes a "Wahhabi-free territory."[31] Clearly the Yamadayev brothers and Kadyrov had put their fingers to the wind and decided that the Russians would ultimately win the war. They also may have felt that working with the Russians was more favorable than working with the despised Wahhabi warlords, who, if they won, wanted to create a shariah state that was alien to Chechnya's ancient Sufi traditions which they supported.

Thus once again it was the intrusion of the alien strain of fanatical Wahhabi Islam that not only had given Russia a pretext to invade Russia (vis-à-vis the Dagestan invasions of August and September 1999 and the apartment bombings that were pinned on Khattab's radicals), but also had divided and weakened the Chechen resistance.

The loss of Gudermes and the territory surrounding it was a tremendous blow to the *boyeviks* and Maskhadov's government. This loss was compounded by the subsequent fall of the town of Urus Martan. To compound matters, by late November the Russians had fully enveloped

Grozny and had begun to flatten neighborhoods as they moved deeper into the city's center.

But on December 16, 1999, however, the rebels showed they still had some fight in them when the Russians, following the playbook of the first war, sent in a "reconnaissance by fire" armored column to the city center at Minutka Square. This probing column was ambushed by Chechen fighters armed with antitank weapons and annihilated, costing the Russians as many as 350 men. Burning tanks and Russian bodies littered the square in the aftermath of the battle that resembled those of 1994 and 1996.[32]

Two British reporters who witnessed the attack left the following eyewitness account of the Chechen repulse of the Federal forces on December 16, 1999:

> The streets of central Grozny were littered with the corpses of young Russian soldiers early this morning after a column of tanks and armored vehicles suddenly stormed the Chechen capital only to be attacked by entrenched rebel forces wielding rocket-propelled grenades.
>
> Eyewitness reports spoke of at least 100 dead Russian troops at a strategic square south-east of the city centre where a dozen Russian tanks and armored vehicles were said to be ablaze. The battle represented the first major Russian defeat of the current Chechen war and recalled the kind of humiliation suffered by the Russians in the last war for the breakaway territory in 1994–96.
>
> After weeks of aerial bombardment and missile attacks, the ferocity of the Chechen response showed how badly the Russian generals had miscalculated . . . Last night the sky was illuminated by the flash of exploding shells and ordnance. Clouds of black smoke rose from the battlefield.
>
> A journalist for the Reuters news agency on the spot said she saw the bodies of 100 dead Russians in Minutka Square just north of the city centre. A reporter for the Associated Press said that all the Russian vehicles were ablaze, surrounded by dead or wounded soldiers. The Russian armored column was trapped by rebel forces armed with machine guns and shoulder-held anti-tank rockets on the open expanse of the square. A three-hour battle ensued in which the Russians were soundly

beaten for the first time in the current war. It appeared that the Russian troops had been sent to their deaths last night in unfamiliar territory where they were ambushed and trapped on the open expanse of the square by the Chechens who know every inch of their battered city.[33]

This victory was to help consolidate the Chechens' reputation as perhaps the greatest urban guerilla fighters in the world. (After 9/11 this image would come to harm the reputation of Chechens, as many American soldiers mistakenly transplanted the legend of the famed Chechen *boyeviks* of Grozny and claimed that the Chechen highlanders had somehow redeployed their forces across Eurasia to become the ultimate enemy of NATO in the deserts of distant Afghanistan.)

But the Minutka Square ambush was to be the Chechen rebels' final victory as the Russians fell back on the use of artillery and aerial bombardments to flush out Grozny's defenders. By late January 2000, the rebels' southern supply lines had been interdicted by the Russians, and their numbers and morale began to fall. While Basayev wanted to hold out in the city until the symbolic date of February 23, the anniversary of the deportation, other commanders were worried that the entire "army" of now no more than three thousand fighters in Grozny would be trapped and destroyed.

Thus the Chechen "wolves" decided on a desperate breakout plan set for the night of January 30–31.[34] If the small number of rebels escaped, they could live to fight an asymmetric guerilla war from the safety of the southern mountains. If they failed, they would be wiped out by the massive Russian army and the war would be over.

On the designated night, a group of approximately two to three thousand rebels led by the head of the Grozny defense, Aslanbek Ismailov, and Shamil Basayev and the mayor of Grozny Lecha Dudayev (a nephew of the slain president) began to furtively move out of the city following a rail line during a snowstorm. The *boyeviks* sent out an advance party to scout the way toward the nearby village of Alkhan Kala, but it did not return. This was not surprising, since the city was encircled by three rings of tens of thousands of Russian troops armed with everything from artillery to tanks.

Commander Aslanbek Ismailov then made the fateful decision to continue the dangerous night escape in the snow to the southwest regardless. The rebels were attacked briefly while crossing the Sunzha River, but continued to move in a southward direction. Along the way, the group stumbled across an open field that they knew was mined by the Russians (sources have indicated that the Russians had previously dropped small, plastic aerial-delivered land mines known as "butterflies" onto the snow-covered field from helicopters). Someone in the group suggested sending the approximately two hundred Russian prisoners traveling with the group across the minefield to clear it, but this was vetoed by Basayev and the other commanders as being inhumane and against the Geneva Conventions on the handling of prisoners of war.[35]

Instead, Shamil Basayev himself and several other commanders, including Aslanbek Ismailov and several volunteers, decided to lead the group across the minefield in pairs. As Basayev and the other commanders led the way, chaos unfolded as men stepped on the lethal PMF-1 butterfly antipersonnel land mines that were calibrated to blow off a foot or a leg. Chechen reporter Lyoma Turpalove of the *Guardian* reported on the nightmarish scene as the Chechen rebels tried to sneak across the snow-covered minefield close to nearby Russian positions as follows:

> Lyoma Dadayev, a fighter who survived the march, said one commander, Shamil Basayev, turned to his men and said: "Women often tell us, 'You let our sons be killed while you stay alive.' Well, we shall go first."
>
> Khamzat Tisayev, wounded in the foot, said some fighters sacrificed themselves to clear a path, running ahead to deliberately set off mines. "The boys marched on mines and shouted to us: 'Meet you in paradise!'"
>
> After the first mines exploded, Russian artillery shells and rockets screamed into the rebel column, killing scores. The rebels pressed on, leaving their dead and wounded behind, contrary to custom. Some still shudder at the memory. "I was pulling my comrade on a sledge, and then was hit in my leg by a fragment," Mr Dadayev said. "I had to leave him behind, because otherwise I would have died too." Mr Tashayev wrote: "Our wounded comrades pleaded with us not to leave them, but we had to keep going."[36]

Another Chechen fighter claimed, "We had to walk on our dead comrades to avoid stepping on unexploded mines."[37] Dr. Khassan Baiev, the village doctor of the nearby village of Alkhan Kala who was to play such a major role in the event, was to record the tragic incident as follows:

Basayev and his men knew about the mines, but the snow had been disorienting and they lost the trail. The field commanders convened to discuss the best way to continue. Someone suggested sending the Russian prisoners ahead to trigger the mines and forge the path for the others. Lecha Dudayev and several other commanders disagreed. They contended that intentional killing of weaponless Russian soldiers contradicted the spirit of Chechnya's struggle for independence and the Muslim faith. Shamil Basayev agreed, saying that as a senior commander, he should be the one to lead the procession across the minefield.

So they pushed on. To protect the life of their leader, two of his body-guards rushed forward, sacrificing themselves on the mines but opening a safe path. A few yards away, another mine detonated, shattering Basa-yev's right foot and ankle. In the ensuing panic, people started running in different directions, setting of still more mines. Lying in the snow, Basayev called for calm. "Stop running!" he shouted. Volunteers pushed through the snow forging a safe path; many died when they trampled on invisible, live mines.[38]

The main rebel force of two to three thousand made it through the carnage, as the Russians rained artillery and machine gun fire on their retreating column, and escaped to the small town of Alkhan Kala. The retreating rebels, many dressed in white camouflage and carrying scores of wounded comrades, then burst into the sleeping town and asked for assistance. Shocked residents directed them to Dr. Khassan Baiev, who ran a primitive clinic in the basement of his bombed-out apartment. There hundreds of bleeding and horribly mangled rebels gathered out-side of his clinic while the doctor and his overwhelmed staff performed life-saving surgeries, including so many amputations that his hacksaw blade lost its edge.

Dr. Baiev marveled at the courage of the wounded rebels, most of whom were "young boys," who stoically waited for life-saving operations and surgeries.[39] He operated on them with a hacksaw and with no pain-killers or antiseptics.

Dr. Baiev was shocked when the fighters then brought a bearded rebel whose face was covered in soot into his clinic and announced that he was their leader, Shamil Basayev. Basayev, Russia's most-wanted man, was known to Baiev, who ran the only operating clinic in the region and treated both Russian soldiers and Chechens. Dr. Baiev recorded his conversation with the infamous/legendary rebel leader who had a ten-million-dollar bounty on his head as follows:

> "Is that you, Khassan?" he [Basayev] asked as I bent over. The explosion had blinded him. "Don't operate on me first. Deal with the young guys before me."
>
> "You've lost too much blood," I replied. I slipped on the blood pressure cuff: 60 systolic over 40 diastolic, a near-death reading. He had probably lost 50 percent of his blood; another half hour, and he'd be dead. I had to work fast . . . "In pain?" I asked. "You are so quiet."
>
> He shook his head. "I don't want to interfere with your work," he whispered. "I'm going to have to amputate your leg above the ankle," I said.
>
> "Do your work," he said, "but if there are others worse off, take them first."[40]

Basayev survived the amputation of his right foot, but many other commanders who had led the fateful charge through the minefield did not. Among them were Khunkar Pasha Israpilov, who had joined Salman Raduyev in the Dagestan raid in the first war; the mayor of Grozny Lecha Dudayev; and the brilliant commander of Grozny's defenses, Aslanbek Ismailov. In addition, somewhere between 170 and 300 fighters died in the chaos in the minefield.[41]

Salman Raduyev and Khattab, however, remained unscathed, as did President Maskhadov, who had earlier escaped to the mountains. Another three hundred Chechens, including Doku Umarov, who would later take control of the rebellion, were severely wounded in the bloody incident. The losses were unprecedentedly high for a small Chechen "army" of three thousand that could hardly sustain the death and wounding of more than a tenth of its fighting force.

To compound matters, Russian troops chased the fleeing rebels to the village of Alkhan Kala the next morning and prepared to launch a dreaded *zachistka* (cleansing operation). Many immobile, wounded rebels subsequently were captured by the Russians and sent to the dreaded filtration camp of Chernokozovo, where reports of torture were rampant. Most were never heard from again.[42] But most of the retreating Chechen force managed to escape to the southern mountains before the Russians completely encircled the town.

Their escape was seen as a strategic setback by the Russians, who did not initially admit that the main rebel fighting force had broken out of their "ring of steel" in Grozny. In an attempt to downplay reports of the escape, Defense Minister Igor Sergeyev insisted that Russian forces were successfully blocking the rebels from breaking out of Grozny. This source stated, "Nobody will ever allow the rebels to leave the city other than under a white flag and after laying down their weapons."[43] Sergei Yastrzhembsky, the acting Russian president's aide, said of the rebel retreat, "If they left Grozny, we would have informed you by all means."[44]

But the truth was that the main Chechen fighting force of 3,000 fighters had humiliated the Russian army, which was over 110,000 strong, and escaped to fight another day. The Russians were furious and needed someone to lay the blame on. Incredibly, their wrath fell on the simple village doctor of Alkhan Kala, Dr. Khassan Baiev. Russian troops subsequently stormed his makeshift hospital and killed all his civilian patients, including an elderly Russian woman, and booby-trapped their bodies to kill Dr. Baiev should he return. They then put out an arrest warrant for the "bandit doctor."[45]

Ironically, the notorious Chechen Wahhabi warlord Arbi Barayev had previously captured Dr. Baiev and declared, "He deserves to die. He has opened a hospital for Russian soldiers. He is treating our enemies."[46] On that previous occasion, Dr. Baiev's life had been spared after the Chechen warlord's men tortured him for treating wounded Russians. Dr. Baiev would later tell a journalist from the BBC:

One day Chechen fighters and Russian soldiers were brought into my hospital. Of course the situation was very difficult. I always told the fighters: "This place is a peace place. This hospital is open for everybody who needs help, not just for Chechens." Some said, "Why are you treating Russian soldiers? It's the enemy!" I said that for me, it doesn't matter, Chechen or Russian. I take to my operation room first who is seriously wounded. I am a doctor, I took the Hippocratic Oath. That's why I treat everybody.[47]

But now Dr. Baiev was wanted by the Russians, who would certainly either execute him on the spot or, if he was lucky, dispatch him to the dreaded filtration camp at Chernokozovo as a "terrorist," where he would be tortured. He was thus forced to flee Russia and eventually made his way to distant America, where he was given asylum with the support of Physicians for Human Rights, a Boston-based group that honored him for fulfilling his Hippocratic Oath and treating both Russians and Chechens. In America, Dr. Baiev subsequently wrote the most moving and powerful book on the Chechen conflict, *The Oath: A Surgeon under Fire*, which captures all the horrors of the Chechen war from the eyewitness perspective of a civilian doctor.

As for the main force of the retreating Chechen fighters who escaped Grozny and the *zachistka* at Alkhan Kala, they fled southward to the mountains. In an attempt to kill them before they escaped, the Russians indiscriminately carpet bombed the villages in their path, killing 363 civilians. But this failed to wipe out the fast-moving rebels, who by this time had dispersed into the highlands.

Most of the retreating fighters fled up the Vedeno and Argun Gorges into the sheltering mountains, with the Russians in hot pursuit. Among them was Shamil Basayev, whose amputated leg became infected and needed to be further amputated up toward the knee. At the time, Khattab and his media-savvy Arabs took pictures of Basayev riding on horseback through the snow-covered mountain forests and posing with Khattab to show off his bandaged stump. The images, which were posted online at qoqaz.net (the first online global jihad site), and another one released to the press of Basayev holding a hand-carved wooden leg, were meant to show the Russians that the Chechens' most-feared leader was still alive and dedicated to the struggle.

At the time, the pro-Chechen qoqaz.net site posted an interview with Basayev, who appeared to be unbroken by his injuries. Basayev spoke to an Arab interviewer referring to Chechen *boyeviks* as "mujahideen" as follows:

The successful withdrawal from the Capital was a victory for the Mujahideen. We were able to break through three layers of Russian siege lines that were manned by nearly 100,000 enemy soldiers. Breaking through this mass of Russian forces that were backed by large numbers of aircraft, artillery and vehicles is considered a victory, especially since the enemy was given ample time to enforce a complete siege on every part of the city.

Our successful withdrawal is a slap in the face for the Russian Military Command that claimed that it would not allow any of the Mujahideen to exit the city, and that it would kill or capture every single one of the Mujahideen. The Russian Military Command even boasted that a fly could not exit the Capital. How then were we able to break through these lines in large numbers, and to fight a successful rear-guard action that inflicted massive casualties amongst Russians soldiers in the villages south of Grozny? Despite this humiliating defeat, the Russians still claim victory, by Allah, tell me, where was their victory?

The front part of my foot was injured by a "butterfly" mine during our withdrawal from the Capital. This wound was compounded by infection, and the lower part of my foot was amputated. All praise to Allah, I have since recovered. I can fight, but the wound needs time to heal completely. Many brothers fight without one of their legs. My situation is not as difficult as theirs because I have only lost a foot, and not my entire leg. Losing one foot will not hinder my ability to sprint insha-Allah [God willing].

We cleared the withdrawal path several times, but it was re-mined every time it was cleared. What hit us during the withdrawal were not land mines but "butterfly" mines that are deployed by aircraft. These mines do not need to be planted into the ground, and they resemble the colour of the earth.[48]

Seemingly undaunted by his wound, Basayev vowed to continue the fight. But with the exception of Ruslan "Khamzat" Gelayev's fierce defense of the lowland town of Komsomolskoye, which was conquered by the Russians in March 2000 leading to the death of 841 fighters, the Chechen insurgents had abandoned the lowlands to the mighty Russian occupation forces.[49] With the Russian flag raised over the ruins of Grozny and other Chechen towns, the war would devolve into a guerilla campaign designed to make the Russians pay a heavy price for occupying the Chechen homeland.

For their part, the Russians would spread their "counterterrorism" operations throughout Chechnya and arrest tens of thousands of Chechens under the mere suspicion that they were terrorists. Thousands of arrested Chechens were to be tortured or killed in such dreaded "filtration camps" as Chernokozovo. Human rights activists in Russia would harshly accuse their own government of "state-sponsored terrorism" against a people that was increasingly described in broad racist terms as a race of terrorists. Tens of thousands of Chechen civilians also would die in "sadistic" *zachistkas* (cleansing/sweep) operations, indiscriminate bombardments, and night raids known as "disappearances." Chechnya would come to resemble a human rights "black hole" where the indigenous population was terrorized by Russian troops who blamed them for the August-September bombing campaign, which was of course carried out by either Khattab's non-Chechen Wahhabis or the FSB.

For his part, Chechen president Aslan Maskhadov continued to try to reach out to the Russians, even as they put a 300-million-rouble bounty on his head and cynically called for his arrest by Interpol for leading the "terrorist" invasion of Dagestan.[50] Even as the arrest warrant was issued, Maskhadov appealed to the Pope, President Bill Clinton, and US Secretary of State Madeline Albright to mediate.

But while the moderate Chechen president sought peace, he planned war.[51] Maskhadov successfully organized a hit-and-run guerilla rebellion that was to cost the Russians the lives of hundreds of their soldiers. His rebels planted land mines, attacked checkpoints, ambushed columns in the forested mountains, and sniped at patrols in Grozny. They continued to put a lie to the Russian claims that Chechnya had been "pacified."

But it was the always unpredictable Basayev, not Maskhadov, who would ultimately garner headlines across the globe by responding to the Russians' state-sponsored terrorism against his people, which has been described as a racially based "crime against humanity," with his own terror campaign.[52] Basayev's terror operations, which were harshly condemned by Maskhadov, were to gain the Chechens notoriety throughout the world, even as the Russians managed to maintain a comparative news blackout on their own much more systematic, wide-scale terror operations against the Chechen people. A history of the terror campaigns of the Russian government and military and of Basayev's rogue terror wing sheds a fascinating, but tragic light on this dark descent into a shadow war that was to cost tens of thousands of Chechen civilians and hundreds of Russian civilians their lives.

"Welcome to Hell" Russian War Crimes in Chechnya

Russia's state-sponsored terror campaign against the Chechen "terror nation," which it erroneously held responsible for the September apartment bombings (and correctly blamed for defeating the Russians in the first war), began with an indiscriminate barrage of missiles and bombs on Chechnya's hamlets and towns. By October 1999 the number of slain Chechen civilians far surpassed the number of Russians killed in the Khattab/FSB bombing campaign. Just one bombing alone on a civilian-packed market in Grozny by Tochka ballistic missiles alone killed 137 Chechen civilians.[53] An eyewitness to this Russian war crime reported:

> There were lots of people at the market and not only those who were shopping. The Grozny market was also a place where you could meet your friends, exchange the latest bit of news, etc. At 4:30 PM the merchants were getting ready to take down their stands when the bomb was dropped. In the fraction of a second the market became a bloodbath. Pieces of flesh were strewn over the ground; there was screaming, and wounded and dead people everywhere.[54]

Thousands were to die across Chechnya in Russian bombings designed to avenge the death of the approximately three hundred Russians killed in the apartment bombing campaign and terrorize the population into submission. Human Rights Watch estimated that as many as ten thousand Chechen civilians died in the early stages of the Russian bombing campaign alone.[55] At the time viewers of Google Earth who scanned the satellite images of Chechnya on their computers were able to see Grozny and several other Chechen cities to the south of it burning from space.

Having brutally conquered most of Chechnya by February 2000 through an indiscriminate use of force, the massive 110,000-man Russian force then spread throughout the ravaged countryside and towns and began an operation designed to capture or kill all suspected "terrorists" (all Chechen fighters were labeled "terrorists" at this time and the Geneva Conventions were not applied to them).

But how were the Russians to delineate average Chechen men and women from the small number of three thousand fighters/"terrorists"? The Orwellian solution was a countrywide establishment of so-called "filtration camps," where thousands of Chechens were systematically captured and imprisoned under the mere suspicion of being rebels (or more commonly, of having knowledge of or sympathy with them). Most were then tortured and, in hundreds of cases, extrajudicially executed. The lurid reports of the Russian war crimes carried out in these camps put the isolated cases of torture at the Abu Ghraib prison in US-occupied Iraq (which led to the firings and prosecutions of those involved) to shame. Only in the Russian case, no Russian soldiers ever were arrested for their filtration camp war crimes, as in the notorious Abu Ghraib case.

In a nutshell, the Russians set up checkpoints throughout the republic and randomly arrested tens of thousands of Chechens on suspicion that they were terrorists. A report by the Nobel Prize–winning humanitarian group Médecins sans Frontières (Doctors without Borders) described the mass internment of Chechens as follows:

> The war has entered a new phase . . . The Russian forces have transformed Chechnya into a vast ghetto. In this ghetto, terror reigns, every civilian is a suspect, and freedom of movement is denied. Each and every checkpoint is a "Russian roulette" which puts their lives at stake. It is known as *bespredel*, a Russian slang term that means excessive abuse of power, and, in Chechnya especially, "unlimited violence."[56]

This humanitarian group's report described Chechnya as a state-sponsored terror zone characterized by "acts of violence [that] are designed to humiliate civilians: arbitrary executions and mopping-up operations, arrests and disappearances, extortion and racketeering of cadavers." A Chechen woman interviewed for the report stated: "Troops catch everybody, military or not—they just disappear. It's *bespredel* [extreme lawlessness], like the extermination of the nation. If it keeps going on, all the people will either be exterminated, or they will rise up."[57]

Those Chechen men and women who were unfortunate enough to be caught up in the Russian military's sweeps and checkpoints were transferred from their homes and families to filtration camps. Upon arrival they faced a ritual of abuse, where they were forced to run a gauntlet of Russian troops beating them with rifle butts while chanting "Welcome to Hell."[58] Once in the "hell" of a filtration camp, Emma Gilligan writes: "The most common forms of torture practiced included the following: electric shocks to the genitals, toes and fingers with a field telephone; asphyxiation with plastic bags; cutting off ears; filling mouthes with kerosene; setting dogs on the legs of the detained; knife cuts; and carving crosses in the backs of detainees."[59] This source writes "Torture was an official state policy in Chechnya" and was used to create a "broader landscape of fear."[60] Those Chechens who disappeared into the camps faced humiliation, beating, electrocutions, mock executions, imprisonment in holes, and systematic rape of both men and women.[61] Civilians were tortured for evidence on rebel fighters, and many men and women who were raped could not live with the stigma and shame and committed suicide.[62] The sadistic prison guards killed many other prisoners and ran a widely practiced business of selling the bodies of murdered Chechens to their grieving families.[63] Those who were able to ransom the mutilated bodies of their loved ones were the lucky ones. Most grieving families just had to accept that their family member had disappeared and been brutally killed by the Russians, then buried in a hidden mass grave.

Thousands of mutiliated bodies were thrown into mass graves outside of the filtration camps all over Chechnya. According to one account of a typical mass grave:

The grave was astonishing for its location; a heavily guarded area situated just a few hundred yards away from the Russian military headquarters at Khankala, where many had been detained and imprisoned . . . In February 2001, relatives of the detained arrived in Dachnyi to find bodies scattered among deserted summer cottages—in cellars, on verandas, or in the bushes . . . Abdurashid Metaev found his brother Odes and reported "When I found him, he was lying on his stomach, his hands were bound with cord, two of his digits were missing on one of his hands, one of his ears was missing, he had been blindfolded. Odes' ear had been removed when he was alive, because his face was covered in blood."[64]

This Chechnya-wide policy was to go on for years and to see thousands disappear. Of a group of 540 Chechens abducted by the Russians in 2002, only 91 were released, 81 were found murdered, and a stunning 368 were never heard from again.[65] It is not surprising that Chechens considered the disappearance of a loved one in a filtration camp to be a death warrant. Years later, 49 mass graves were found in Chechnya, including one containing 699 bodies.[66]

Considering the scale of the state-sponsored terrorism, it was inevitable, despite the Kremlin's best efforts to enforce a news blackout, that word of what was going on in the filtration camps would leak out. By the summer of 2000, headlines in the West began to describe the horrors being perpetuated in the name of fighting terrorism in Chechnya. Britain's *Guardian* ran a headline that announced: "Tales of torture leak from Russian camps: Escaped Chechen victims tell of rape, beating and humiliation." A *Los Angeles Times* headline would read: "Tales of Horror Emerge from Chechnya Prison: Russia's 'filtration' camp for suspected rebels is a den of torture and humiliation former detainees say." A *Washington Post* headline would state: "Chechens Report Torture in Camps." Britain's *Observer* would have a headline that read: "Cries from Putin's Torture Pit: John Sweeney Reports on the Horror of a Russian Prison Camp in Chechnya." Even the *Moscow Times* would have an article titled, "Inside the Hell of Chernokozovo" (this article was written before Vladimir Putin closed down the free media in Russia and arrested the critics of his policies).

An October 2000 article in the *Observer* reported:

Russian security forces have mounted a series of cover-ups to hide evidence of abuses from the Red Cross and the Council of Europe. In the small Chechen village of Katyr Yurt, a torture victim blinded in one eye spoke of the screams he heard each night while inside Chernokozovo. The screams were so bad local people were forced to move away because they found them unbearable.

"At night," he said, "the things you heard were just terrible. Every night they would take people out of the cells. They screamed. They had their teeth bashed in, their kidneys smashed in. You could hear them being beaten from the cell. So then they would turn the music up loud, so you couldn't hear the screams."[67]

Michael Wines of the *New York Times* would report on the finding of a mass grave in Chechnya: "Local military officials said mines had been placed on many bodies, apparently to kill anyone who sought to retrieve them. Russian reports said three bodies had been identified as those of Chechen residents. Most had been killed by gunfire."[68]

By April 2000, Amnesty International was to condemn the Russians' policies in Chechnya as well and to reveal the location of several secret filtration camps. But the Russian deputy minister of justice steadfastly denounced Amnesty International and claimed there were no filtration camps or torture in the country.[69]

Human rights groups and Western governments also condemned Russia for sweep operations or raids on villages known as *zachistkas* (cleansings). In these surprise operations, Russian troops would suddenly encircle a targeted village or neighborhood and then send in troops to go house to house kicking in doors and arresting "terrorists." These brutal operations all too often ended in massacre and looting. In one typical operation in a Grozny neighborhood, fifty-six civilians were captured and then systematically executed in cold blood by rampaging Russian troops.[70] In a typical *zachistka* carried out in the village of Novye Aldi, "Soldiers were pushing people into their homes, throwing grenades into basements full of civilians, and setting houses alight with people inside."[71] Matthew Evangelista was to report, "In Chechnya, reports of torture, rape, and murder continued to make the 'antiterrorist operation' appear more like an all out war against the civilian population."[72]

By the fall of 2000, the *Los Angeles Times* was to publish an article entitled "War Has No Rules for Russian Forces Fighting in Chechnya," which would include several frank interviews with Russian soldiers who had partaken in *zachistkas* in Chechnya. These interviews reveal gruesome details of the systematic regime of terror in Chechnya that was to cost thousands of Chechen civilians their lives. The *LA Times* article reported:

The summary executions don't just take place against suspected fighters. One 33-year-old army officer recounted how he drowned a family of five—four women and a middle-aged man—in their own well. "You should not believe people who say Chechens are not being exterminated. In this Chechen war, it's done by everyone who can do it," he said. "There are situations when it's not possible. But when an opportunity presents itself, few people miss it.

"I killed a lot. I wouldn't touch women or children, as long as they didn't fire at me. But I would kill all the men I met during mopping-up operations. I didn't feel sorry for them one bit. They deserved it," he says. "I wouldn't even listen to the pleas or see the tears of their women when they asked me to spare their men. I simply took them aside and killed them.

"I remember a Chechen female sniper. She didn't have any chance of making it to the authorities. We just tore her apart with two armored personnel carriers, having tied her ankles with steel cables. There was a lot of blood, but the boys needed it."[73]

By 2003, the Council of Europe had forced Russia to halt *zachistka* sweeps, but hundreds of Chechens continued to be kidnapped and executed in secret night raids that became known as "disappearances." Most "disappearances" essentially were random kidnappings by masked Russian troops, followed by torture and all too frequently, a brutal murder. This was usually followed by demands of payment for the deceased's body.

In a typical case, a young man was taken from his family house in the village of Alkhan Kala by Russians in an armored personnel carrier, and his body was subsequently found floating in a river with his head and leg cut off and covered with stab wounds.[74] Human Rights Watch was to issue a scathing account of this new "subtle" policy designed to replace mass *zachistkas*, which stated:

The "disappearances" of detainees in the custody of Russian federal forces in Chechnya is a major human rights crisis that the Russian government and the international community must address. The discovery of the mutilated corpses of some of the "disappeared" has substantiated fears that they have been tortured and summarily executed. While combat between federal forces and Chechen rebels has for the most part ceased, the "disappearance," torture, and summary execution of detainees continues, marking the transition from a classical internal armed conflict into a classical "dirty war," where human rights violations and not the conquest or defense of territory are the hallmarks . . . The risk of "disappearances" affects everyone in Chechnya. Victims are predominately male and range from fifteen years of age to forty-nine; among them have been dentists, drivers, and auto mechanics.[75]

According to this source, many of the Chechen victims of "disappearances" were found blindfolded with their hands tied behind their back with wire, and with their head scalped, nose cut off, and head, chest, or stomach shot. Women also were executed and mutilated in a similar fashion.

The Chechens' response to these widespread atrocities was not long in coming and would, not surprisingly, come from the rebels' most flamboyant leader, Shamil Basayev. It would take on the form of a terror campaign that would soon bring his followers fame as the most notorious terrorists in Europe.

Retaliation Shamil Basayev's Terror War on Russia

By the spring of 2000, the war had shifted to the highlands as the Russians tried to entrap Chechen fighters operating in the Argun and Vedeno gorges. The Russians already controlled such highland towns as Shatoi and Vedeno, and they were now waging a classic counterinsurgency campaign against the Chechen mountain guerillas. But as the "greening effect" took place in the spring of 2000, the Chechens had the cover of tree foliage to hide themselves from Russian helicopters, and they began to stage ambushes on Russian patrols and convoys. In one ambush, more than eighty Russian troops died, and Moscow continued to lose approximately two hundred soldiers a month.[76]

But it was a smaller ambush by a force of Arabs, Chechens, and Dagestanis from Karamakhi led by Khattab's Arab lieutenant, Abu Quteiba, that was to create headlines and signify a change in tactics among a radical group of the rebels. On March 29, two hundred of Khattab's fighters ambushed a forty-eight man OMON (Special Police) convoy that was on its way to partake in a *zachistka* mop-up near the mountain town of Vedeno. Forty-one Russians were killed in the textbook ambush, nine were captured, and six more were killed in a column sent to relieve them. A Russian soldier in the ambushed convoy who was taking photographs at the time was killed. The rebels then retrieved his camera and kept filming.[77]

While the rebels, especially Basayev, had established a policy of publicly releasing captured conscripts to their mothers during the first war, they were known to be in a less forgiving mood now that it was widely known that the Russians were killing tens of thousands of Chechens in indiscriminate bombardments, *zachistkas*, filtration camps, and "disppearances" throughout the country. Their mood was made even more unforgiving by the widely publicized case of a Russian colonel named Yury Budanov.

Budanov was rather emblematic of the Russian soldiers in Chechnya and was known throughout the Chechen community where his unit was based for sadism. But on the night of March 26, 2000, his all-too-typical actions were to gain the attention of the world. On that night Budanov went on a drinking binge to celebrate his daughter's birthday and the March election of Vladimir Putin as president. During his drinking session, he ordered one of his lieutenants to launch an artillery barrage into the nearby sleeping village to celebrate. It was then that his lieutenant, who seemed to have a conscience, refused. For this Budanov had him beaten and thrown into a pit. This would come back to haunt him, as the lieutenant would later testify against Budanov in the war crime he subsequently committed.[78]

Denied the chance to bombard a village of sleeping "terrorists," Budanov then had his armored personnel carrier driven through the village and randomly stopped at the house of a Chechen family known as the Kungaevs. He and three of his men then broke into the house and kidnapped the family's teenage daughter, Elza Kungaeva. Budanov then took Elza to his tent and tortured, raped, and sodomized her before murdering her. He then ordered his subordinates to throw her mutilated corpse into a nearby forest.

But the crime was reported by his lieutenant, and word was leaked to the press. The Russian authorities were then forced to respond as international outrage grew. Budanov subsequently was arrested for kidnapping and murder, although the rape, torture, and sodomy charges, which were proven in the autopsy, were dropped.

In a sign of the extent of Chechenphobia at the time, Russian society rallied to the accused colonel, and he became a hero and martyr for many. Defense Minister Sergei Ivanov "voiced his support and sympathy" for Budanov and called him a "victim of circumstances."[79] Budanov's commander, Lieutenant General Vladimir Shamanov, lent his support to the accused colonel and described him as "one of my best commanders." He also said, "To [Budanov's] enemies I say: Don't put your paws on the image of a Russian soldier and officer."[80] Forty-two percent of Russians interviewed in a poll said of the rape that Budanov was "justified in doing so and should not be punished."[81]

In his first trial, Budanov was showered with rose petals by cheering Russian supporters and ultimately was found not guilty by reason of insanity. Budanov claimed he believed Elza Kungaeva had been a sniper, and he was merely "interrogating" her following normal procedures when he went insane.[82] To compound matters, the lawyer representing the Kungaev family was shot and killed.

The trial's result caused outrage across the world, but nowhere more so than in the mountains of southern Chechnya, where rape is taboo and conservative Islamic traditions prevail. At the time, Basayev's Arab ally Khattab, who had possession of the nine OMON prisoners captured in an ambush, made a widely publicized offer to release them in exchange for Colonel Budanov. When the Russians refused to do so, an infuriated Khattab had the OMON prisoners executed and posted pictures of their bodies taken with the slain OMON soldier's camera online at qoqaz.net.

This incident, more than anything else, seemed to be the beginning of the descent by the rogue Chechen rebels led by Basayev into terrorism. Thus far, the Chechens were unanimously seen by the West as the clear-cut victims of Russian state-sponsored terrorism. The Chechens' military actions, except for the two raids on Budyenovsk and Pervomasikoe where hostages were taken, were seen as legitimate attacks on armed enemy soldiers invading their homeland. Schaefer was to write in his work, "The Chechens focused exclusively on legitimate military and government targets, and despite Moscow's claim that they were fighting terrorists, at this point the conflict was still a clear guerilla versus government battle that focused on ambushing regular government forces."[83]

But by 2000, a small rogue rebel unit led by Basayev would begin to wage an asymmetric guerilla campaign that would come to have a terror component to it. Ema Gilligan was to write of this transformation by the Chechen fighters to "blood avengers": "The retaliation by Chechen separatists was a cumulative process that grew in response to acts of aggression by the Russian armed forces."[84] John Reuter wrote of this terrorist response to Russian brutality:

> Suicide bombings did not begin until the Second-Russo Chechen war, when Russian forces began systematically targeting Chechen civilians in so-called cleansing operations . . . Ultimately, the Kremlin must come to understand that "counter-terrorism" strategies, which employ abduction, torture, and lawless killing, only serve to radicalize the resistance and humiliate the population, thereby creating a fertile breeding ground for more terrorists.[85]

Similarly, Russian journalist Anna Politkovskaya, who was later murdered for her objective reporting on the war and her exposé of Russian abuses in her book *A Small Corner of Hell: Dispatches from Chechnya*, was to write: "It was the methods that the Feds [i.e., the Russian Federal forces] chose for their antiterrorist operation that compelled them [the Chechens led by Basayev] to take a different road."[86]

The "different road" that Basayev chose to wreak his vengeance on the Russians, after a deadly missile strike in Grozny which killed 223 Chechen civilians, was the autonomous terrorist group composed of no more than a few dozen followers and known as the Riyadus Salihin (Gardens of the Righteous) Reconnaissance and Sabotage Battalion of Chechen Martyrs. This group would begin by carrying out bombing attacks on Russian military targets in Chechnya, then gradually extend its operations to include attacks on civilian targets in Russia proper.

The first guerilla/terrorist attack in this process took place on June 6, 2000, when Khava Barayeva, the female cousin of the notorious Chechen Wahhabi warlord Arbi Barayev, and a female friend drove a truck filled with explosives into a Russian OMON base in the Chechen village of

Alkhan Yurt and killed up to twenty-six soldiers. This was to be the first of the so-called "Chechen Black Widow" suicide bombing attacks.

But it was a rogue attack ordered by Basayev on the Dubrovka theater in the heart of Moscow in October 2002 that was to bring Chechen terrorism to the awareness of most Westerners. John Dunlop has demonstrated that this attack was launched after the Russian government unilaterally cancelled peace talks with the moderate wing of the Chechen resistance led by Maskhadov, which were designed to end the ongoing conflict.[87]

The Dubrovka terrorist incident, which was meant to restart negotiations, began on October 23, 2002, when forty armed Chechen men and women stormed the theater during the performance of a sold-out play known as *Nord Ost*. Chechens firing guns burst onto the stage and told the audience of 850 to 900 people that they were hostages. Among the terrorists were nineteen women dressed in nontraditional black hijabs who had explosives around their waists. They were told to detonate them and blow up the theater should the Russians storm it.

The Chechen terrorists, led by Movsar Barayev, the nephew of the notorious Arabi Barayev, then made their demands to the Kremlin. They called for an end to *zachistkas*, aerial and artillery bombardments, and war in their homeland. They demanded that Putin restart peace negotiations with Maskhadov. In essence, their bold *abrek*-style raid into the very heart of the enemy's territory was a reprisal of Basayev's raid on Budyenovosk in 1995. It was meant to put the Russians in an inescapable position, where they had no choice but to comply with the terrorists' demands. In a goodwill gesture, the terrorists then released 150 people, including women, children, and Muslims, and then began to negotiate the release of foreigners, including one American.

Movsar Barayev's terrorists followed this up by releasing a tape to the media that stated:

> Every nation has the right to their fate. Russia has taken away this right from the Chechens and today we want to reclaim these rights, which Allah has given us, in the same way he has given it to other nations. Allah has given us the right of freedom and the right to choose our destiny. And the Russian occupiers have flooded our land with our children's blood. And we have longed for a just solution. People are unaware of the innocent

who are dying in Chechnya: the sheikhs, the women, the children and the weak ones. And therefore, we have chosen this approach. This approach is for the freedom of the Chechen people and there is no difference in where we die, and therefore we have decided to die here, in Moscow.

As the terrorists stated their demands, their hostages used their cell phones to call loved ones and plead for the Russian authorities to give in to the Chechen hostage takers' demands. Their pleas were then played on local Russian radio stations. One shocked Russian was to ask, "How on earth could it happen that a fully equipped detachment of Chechen rebels entered the heart of Moscow and seized a large building full of people?"[88]

Those hostages inside the theater and their panicked family members feared that the Russian security forces would storm the theater and kill the hostages as they had during Basayev's hostage taking in Budyenovsk and Raduyev's hostage taking in the Dagestani village of Pervomaiskoe. One Russian mother at the scene yelled to a policeman manning barricades around the theater, "What are you doing? My daughter just called me 10 minutes ago, begging you not to attack. Explain what is happening! Is this an attack?"[89] Another family member of a hostage pleaded, "Why don't they just tell the terrorists they are fulfilling their demands. Do this for us. Is it so hard?"[90]

At this time, the hostage takers demanded to meet with General Viktor Kazantsev, head of operations in Chechnya. The Russians promised them he was coming to meet them, but he was not. The elated terrorists told their hostages "Tomorrow at 10 AM Kazantsev will come. Everything will be normal. They have come to an agreement. This suits us. Behave peacefully. We are not beasts. We will not kill you."[91]

But Vladimir Putin was not a man who would give in to the demands of the terrorists when it came to negotiating with Maskhadov to end the war. Instead, Dunlop writes, "In addition to seeking to depict the hostage-taking incident as a second 9/11, a second aim behind the regime's response to the crisis appeared to be to fully discredit Aslan Maskhadov, and thus render the possibility of negotiations with him or other moderate Chechen separatists unthinkable."[92]

The comparison to 9/11 that the Russians made was not, however, apt, as the Al Qaeda nihilists sought to slaughter thousands of innocents on 9/11, not end a bloody war that was taking a massive toll on innocents. Regardless, there would be no peace negotiations. The Russians accused the Chechens of starting to execute the hostages, a charge subsequently refuted by the hostages themselves, and launched an attack on the theater.[93] After an ordeal of three days, Russian Alpha forces pumped an incapacitating "psychochemical" gas known by the nickname of *kolokol* (bell) into the theater and then stormed it. As the gas was pumped in, the terrorists, including sobbing Chechen Black Widows who held the detonators to bombs that were to blow up the theater, realized what was happening. One hostage would subsequently state: "'A panic went up among us and people were screaming, "Gas! Gas!" and, yes, there was shooting,' said theatre director Georgy Vasilyev. 'When the shooting began, they (the rebels) told us to lean forward in the theatre seats and cover our heads behind the seats. But then everyone fell asleep.'"[94]

Remarkably, none of the Chechen men or women chose to set off their bombs strapped to their bellies or placed around the theater and kill everyone, even though they realized they were being gassed and would certainly be executed.

But the danger had not passed, as there still were many armed hostage takers in the side corridors who had not been knocked out by the gas in the theater. The BBC was to report, "It remains unclear why the Chechens did not appear to set off any explosives or fire on their hostages once the assault got under way."[95] The only answer is, as Dunlop states in his definitive account of the event, the terrorists "clearly chose to let the hostages live."[96]

Having knocked most of the people in the theater unconscious, the Russian Alpha forces then stormed the theater and executed the passed-out hostage takers with bullet shots at point-blank range to the head. The remaining terrorists, including Barayev, who were still awake were then killed in several gunfights. It appeared to be a clean victory for the Russians, and hundreds of passed-out hostages were taken to nearby buses to be transported to a hospital.

But then things began to go disastrously wrong. Dozens of hostages began to die from the unknown gas. Doctors frantically tried to revive them and asked the authorities what type of gas had been used in order to find an antidote, but the special forces did not reveal the nature of the gas. Experts believe it was fentanyl, an extremely lethal opioid/chemical gas more toxic than those used in World War I.[97] The *Atlantic Weekly* was to vividly report the horrific aftermath of the gas attack as follows:

> Footage showed how unconscious hostages were clumsily dragged out of the theatre and dumped into buses. The few doctors at the scene, not knowing what type of gas they were dealing with, were unable to save many lives. Countless hostages choked on their own vomit, others swallowed their tongues or suffocated to death in cramped buses.[98]

When it was over, as many as two hundred hostages may have died. Only two or three died at the hands of the terrorists for resisting them, including one suspected FSB agent who entered the theater during the hostage crisis and another Russian woman who sneaked into theater and tried convincing the hostages to rise up.[99] In most accounts of the hostage drama, the Chechens are inaccurately accused of killing the total number of slain hostages, but in actuality it was the Russian security forces who were responsible for the deaths of all but three of the hostages.

After the tragedy, the Russians side tried to implicate President Maskhadov in the notorious terrorist incident (which actually was ordered by Basayev's terrorist wing without consulting with Maskhadov). But during the hostage crisis Maskhadov's government had declared:

> The Chechen leadership headed by President A. Maskhadov decisively condemns all actions against the civilian population. We don't accept the terrorist method for the solution of any kind of problems . . . We call on both sides, both the armed people in the theater and the government of Russia, to find an un-bloody exit from this difficult situation.[100]

In response to the hostage seizure in Moscow, Maskhadov punished Basayev by forcing him to resign from the Chechen military and government. Basayev was once again a rogue warlord on his own.

Meanwhile, the war continued unabated in Chechnya. There Russia suffered one of the greatest losses of the war, and the single greatest loss of life in helicopter aviation history, when a massive Mi-26 Halo cargo helicopter carrying 140 soldiers was shot down by a Chechen guerilla using an *Igla* shoulder-fired antiaircraft missile at Grozny airport. A stunning

127 servicemen were killed in the catastrophe that led to a national day of mourning in Russia. While the Russians initially tried to claim that the helicopter had crashed because of a malfunction, the Chechen rebels gave the media video footage of one of their men shooting it down with the missile and later receiving a pistol from Maskhadov as a reward.

Basayev's guerilla-terrorism campaign also continued in Chechnya on December 27 when two of his Riyadus Salihin suicide bombers rammed a truck carrying a ton of TNT into the headquarters of the pro-Russian Chechen government in Chechnya (which was led by Mufti Akhmad Kadyrov) and destroyed the four-story building, killing 83 in the process. Basayev claimed that he personally triggered the car bomb that also wounded more than 210, including the Russian-appointed deputy prime minister. On May 12, 2003, his suicide bombers, two of them women, also drove a bomb-laden truck into the FSB headquarters in the Chechen town of Znamenskoye and killed 59.

As Basayev gradually morphed from a frontline fighter for his people's freedom into a guerilla terrorist who was willing to send suicide bombers against enemy targets, a Polish journalist published an illuminating interview with him:

> Journalist: Let's talk about your conversion. Five years ago you were famous as a guerilla commander, but back then perhaps no one would have suspected that you would become the leader of a holy war, of a Muslim insurrection in the Caucasus.
>
> Basayev: During the previous war I fought under the banner of "Freedom or Death." Today I fight for the faith as well. I've come to see that the things I believed in were mere fleeting delusions, and that the one eternal value is faith in the Almighty . . . I have matured. Five years ago, when Russia attacked us, the Western world—the sentry of all the holiest values like equality, freedom, justice, fraternity, and civil liberties—turned its back on Chechnya. It betrayed us like a hussy who goes with whomever pays the most. That taught us Chechens a great deal.[101]

Clearly Chechnya's most notorious rebel commander had become disillusioned with the Western democracies, which refused to enact sanctions against Russia for its widespread war crimes in his homeland,

and he had turned to Islam to fortify his sense of mission. This does not, however, mean that he had joined the Arab jihad terrorism movement led by bin Laden known as Al Qaeda, which had declared a holy war on the distant United States and on American influence in Saudi Arabia in 1998. Basayev would always remain grounded in the local Caucasian issues that moved him, namely, the defense of his people and their faith. That, and the historic memory of his people's repression at the hands of the Russians and Soviets, drove him to state: "I need guarantees that tomorrow future Chechen generations won't be deported to Siberia, like they were in 1944."[102] Robert Schaefer would write, "Basayev's true motives were more nationalistic than religious."[103]

Regardless of his localized motives, Basayev held a personal grudge against the "traitor," Chechen mufti Ahkmad Kadyrov, who had been made head of the pro-Russian government in Chechnya. In October 2003, Kadyrov was selected as president of Chechnya by the Russians. While many Americans who discovered Chechens after 9/11 bought into the myth of the Chechen superhuman warriors who fight to the death and never surrender, Kadyrov had been very successful in convincing hundreds of exhausted Chechen fighters to defect from the rebels and join his pro-Russian *Vostok* battalion. Others joined the pro-Russian unit of the Yamadayev brothers or another unit known as *Zapad* (West).

This was seen as a mortal threat to the rebels, and Basayev sent his operatives to kill the pro-Russian "puppet" ruler of Chechnya, who was declared a traitor. Basayev's assassins finally killed President Kadyrov in a bombing on May 9, 2004, carried out on the VIP section of the stands at the Dynamo Stadium in Grozny during a symbolically important Soviet Day parade. The commander of Russia's troops in Chechnya also lost a leg in the explosion. Akhmad Kadyrov's son, Ramazan, who ran his father's increasingly brutal militia, was ultimately chosen by the Russians to be the slain president's successor (he would not become president until 2007) and vowed vengeance on Basayev and the rebels.

Ramazan Kadyrov would bide his time; in the meantime, Basayev continued his guerilla war and led a bold raid beyond the borders of Chechnya into Nazran, the capital of the neighboring republic of Ingushetia (it will be recalled that the Ingush are closely related to the Chechens and also were deported by Stalin in 1944). This raid on fifteen government buildings was far more successful than Basayev's previous raid on Dagestan. During the course of the night attack on June 21, 2004, a group of "at least 100" Chechen and Ingush fighters infiltrated the city of Nazran and killed ninety-eight people.[104] Among them were forty-seven policemen and the acting interior minister. The rebels then escaped with hundreds of firearms they had seized from government arsenals. This signaled the rise of an insurgency in neighboring Ingushetia.

Shamil Basayev also launched a raid on Nalchik, the capital of Kabardino-Balkaria, another small ethnic republic to the west of Chechnya on October 13, 2005. This brazen attack on the local FSB headquarters and other government buildings and the airport led to the death of over 140 people and showed that the Chechen rebels, working in conjunction with sympathizers from neighboring Muslim republics who were chafing under government crackdowns, could strike at Russian targets far beyond the borders of Chechnya.[105] This raid was not, however, a success; and as many as ninety attackers, most of whom were inexperienced locals, were killed by security forces.[106]

In a worrisome development, most of those involved in the raid on Nalchik were actually local Kabardinians and Balkars, who were members of the so-called "Yarmuk Jamaat." This *jamaat*, like the Islamist *jamaats* in Dagestan, increasingly called for a pan-Caucasian jihad against the corrupt, pro-Russian authorities of their republic. It thus appeared as if the original jihad movement founded by exiled Dagestanis, Basayev, Khattab, and Movladi Udugov was metastasizing and spreading across the larger Muslim region of the northern Caucasus, which was plagued by corruption, unemployment, and poverty.

But Basayev was not satisfied with hurting the Russians in the north Caucasus region alone. He began to deploy suicide bombers, many of them Black Widows, into Russia proper to spread the sense of insecurity his people felt to the Russian heartlands. His goal seems to have been to push the Russians into accepting Chechen independence in return for a cessation of the terror attacks. His mantra was "independence for an end to terrorism." Basayev clearly blamed the Russian people for electing Putin as president and strongly supporting the war in his homeland. At one point he stated in an interview with ABC, "Officially, over 40,000 of our children have been killed and tens of thousands mutilated. Is anyone saying anything about that? Responsibility is with the whole Russian nation, which through its silent approval gives a 'yes' [gives its consent]."[107]

Basayev's terror attacks in Russia, which were condemned by Maskhadov, began when two Black Widows set off bombs at a rock concert in Moscow known as *Krylya* (Wings) on June 6, 2003, which killed fourteen people.[108] This was followed by another suicide bombing on a train in the neighboring Russian region to the north of Chechnya known as Stavropol, which killed forty-six people on December 5, 2003. Five days later Basayev dispatched a Black Widow suicide bomber to Red Square in the heart of Moscow, where she killed five people.[109] This attack, which was carried out to commemorate a *zachistka* on a Chechen village, was followed by a suicide bombing at a Moscow metro stop, which killed forty-one on February 6, 2004.

But the Chechen terrorists did not limit themselves to ground targets, and on August 24, 2004, two Black Widows blew up two Tupolev Russian passenger planes, killing forty-three passengers and crewmen on board. It was subsequently reported that both Black Widow bombers had lost brothers to the Russians, one of whom was abducted in a "disappearance."[110]

It would later transpire that many of the Chechen Black Widows had lost their husbands or loved ones to the Russians and had been recruited or brainwashed out of a desire for vengeance. One could say that the Black Widows, also known as *Shahidkas* (female martyrs), who killed as many as two hundred Russian civilians in their remorseless attacks, were as much victims as victimizers; the same could not be said of those who participated in Basayev's next terrorist outrage.

No Chechen terrorist attack received as much notoriety as the 2004 Beslan hostage crisis. This hostage taking began when a group of fifty to seventy predominantly Ingush terrorists with a sprinkling of four or five Chechens stormed into School Number 1 in the town of Beslan in the Christian Caucasian republic of North Ossetia, which was located just to the west of Ingushetia, on September 1, 2004.[111] The terrorists took approximately twelve hundred hostages and herded them into the school's gymnasium. They then set up an elaborate network of explosives around the gym and threatened to blow it up if they were attacked.

The hostage takers were led by an Ingush known as the "Colonel," who gave a message to the Russians from Shamil Basayev that read as follows:

> From Allah's slave Shamil Basayev to President Putin.
>
> Vladimir Putin, it was not you who started this war. But you can finish it if you have enough courage and [the] determination of de Gaulle. We offer you a sensible peace based on mutual benefit by the principle [of] independence in exchange for security. In case of troop withdrawal and acknowledgment of [the] independence of [the] Chechen Republic of Ichkeria, we are obliged not to make any political, military, or economic treaties with anyone against Russia, not to accommodate foreign military bases on our territory even temporarily, not to support and not to finance groups or organizations carrying out a military struggle against RF [Russian Federation], to be present in the united ruble zone, to enter CIS [the Russian-led Commonwealth of Independent States].

The terrorists also would state, "We have only one goal. The Russian army must leave Chechnya."[112] As in the Dubrovka incident, the hostage takers had clear-cut demands, they were not out to senselessly slaughter their victims as in the case of the Al Qaeda mass casualty terror bombings in New York; Washington, DC; Bali; Madrid; Istanbul; Riyadh; Baghdad; and elsewhere or the Taliban slaughter of over 140 students in a school in Pakistan. It was inconceivable to the hostage takers that the Russians would storm a school with over a thousand children held hostage in a gym rigged with explosives. According to Professor John Dunlop, who has written a book on the event, the terrorists seem to have felt that their demands would be met as they were in 1995 at Budyonnovsk and that they could then release most hostages and retreat to nearby Georgia.[113]

But the Russian government pretended that it had not received the terrorists' demands and surrounded the school with tanks, armored personnel carriers, and crack Alpha special forces armed with heavy weapons. As crowds of concerned parents gathered around the scene wailing and praying for their children, many feared that the Russians were more concerned with killing the terrorists than protecting their elementary school-aged children. Considering the history of Russia's previous brutal responses at Budyonnovsk, Pervomaiskoe, and Dubrovka, their fears were not misplaced.

At the time of the three-day siege, Vladimir Putin tried linking the hostage crisis to America's separate war on terrorism against bin Laden's Al Qaeda. He would falsely claim that many of the terrorists were "Arabs and Muslim negroes."[114] *Time* magazine would report "By linking the terrorists to al Qaeda, Putin wants to join George W. Bush's global war on terror."[115] As the Russian government continued to deny that it had received demands from the "Arabs" and claimed that only a few hundred hostages were being held, it became obvious to observers that the Alpha troops were planning a Budyonnovsk-style assault on the booby-trapped gym holding over one thousand children.

John Dunlop was to report that on September 1 at 1 PM, "All hell quite literally broke loose at School No. 1 in Beslan."[116] The Alpha team attack seems to have begun when a Russian sniper killed a terrorist who had his foot on the pedal controlling a bomb. The terrorist fell over dead, and his bomb went off.[117] Then the Russians detonated an explosive in the side of the gym and fired tube-launched "flame thrower" projectiles that were in actuality thermobaric incendiary devices similar to napalm on to the roof of the gym.

The use of this clumsy battlefield weapon known as *Shmel* to attack a school packed with screaming children stunned experts, who couldn't imagine them being used in a close-quarter hostage crisis. One Russian journalist wrote of this horrific weapon that "The intense shock and heat of the resulting blast are devastating even to troops sheltering in entrenchments . . . One can only imagine the effect on a conventional building such as a school."[118] Under the intense heat, the burning roof collapsed onto the children below, and a Russian journalist would report, "The hostages who were present in the gymnasium were literally burned under the collapsed roofing, after which they burned up."[119] One hostage who survived was to report:

> After the first two explosives there was no fire in the hall . . . The glass was knocked out. The walls were damaged. There were many corpses along the walls. But the roof remained intact. The roof began to burn when they [the Russian forces] began to fire at it with some projectiles.[120]

An American journalist who visited the school stated: "Many were struck and killed [when the roof fell], others [were] trapped or buried

THE RETURN OF THE RUSSIANS

alive, burning to death amid the heart wrenching screams of almost a thousand other souls."[121]

The small number of stunned hostage takers who survived this inferno then ran into the cafeteria with the surviving hostages and had these children wave white flags out the windows begging for their lives. But an eyewitness hostage survivor would later state that the Russians fired on the children in the windows with weapons including tanks, "after which there was a mountain of corpses on the window-sill."[122] As many as 110 hostages were mowed down in this indiscriminate Russian fire in the cafeteria, once again proving the maxim that in Russia, hostages have more to fear from the special forces trying to liberate them than their captors.[123]

The Russian storm of the school turned into a massacre that dwarfed the previous special force storms of Budyonnovsk, Pervomaiskoe, and Dubrovka in its unimaginable slaughter of hostages. When the smoldering ruins of the school were later investigated, it turned out that 317 hostages had died in the tragedy, 186 of whom were elementary school-aged children. Most were killed when the burning gym roof fell in on them and incinerated them. Many of the victims were first graders attending their very first day of school. More innocents were to die in this catastrophe than in the mysterious September 1999 apartment bombings, and many observers were outraged when Putin subsequently praised the Russian special forces for their courage.

The Chechen rebels reacted to the massacre with shock and disbelief. Hundreds left the rebel movement after this dark day, no longer believing their cause was just. Shamil Basayev relayed a message describing the event as a "terrible tragedy." He then said of Putin, "The Kremlin vampire destroyed and injured 1,000 children and adults, giving the order to storm the school for the sake of his imperial ambitions and preserving his own throne."[124] Apparently hurt by the fact that the Chechens were blamed for the slaughter, Basayev then boldly proclaimed:

Putin is now trying to blame us for that [the Beslan massacre], accusing us also of international terrorism and appealing to the world for help ... We demand a public investigation into the Beslan events from the United Nations, the European Union and everyone who has one-sidedly condemned our actions. We are prepared to help them in every possible way in the inquiry into the incident and provide them with virtually any kind of information. We insist that the storming was carried out by the Russian special services, which had planned that from the very start . . .

There is all that shouting and outrage. Various words are being said, but there is one magic word which needs to be said to stop all wars and evil on this planet. This word is Justice. We have no choice, they offered war to us, and we will fight till victory despite what they say about us and how they label us. This world will sooner be set on fire than we refuse to fight for our freedom and independence! God is Great![125]

Despite Basayev's efforts to blame the Russians for the massacre, the fact remained that his terrorist force of primarily Ingush had put the hostages in harm's way in a country that was known to indiscriminately attack hostage takers, regardless of the threat to the hostages' lives. Most of the world blamed the Chechens for the massacre, not the attacking Russians, and the number of 317 dead hostages was widely added to the Chechen terrorists' list of victims. A typical unnuanced account of the event that was to come out years later would state:

In 1995, Chechen Islamists attacked a hospital in the southern Russian city of Budyonnovsk and took 2,000 hostages—including women and their newborn infants. (More than 100 hostages died.) A decade later, Chechen and Ingush gunmen attacked a school in the town of Beslan and took over 1,000 hostages—including 777 children. Almost 400 people died. This is terrorism of the most hideous form: Even al-Qaeda does not make a practice of targeting elementary schools and maternity wards.[126]

By this time, Basayev had been declared a terrorist by most Western countries, and his continued impunity had become a bitter pill for Putin and his people to swallow. With a bounty of $10 million on his head, many Russians asked how the one-legged terrorist managed to continue to carry out terror attacks from Moscow to Beslan to tiny Russian-occupied Chechnya. As the pressure on Putin, the army, and the FSB mounted, killing Basayev became a national obsession for Russia.

Wolf Hunt The Killing of the Chechen Leaders

It was only a matter of time before the most prominent Chechen rebels were hunted down and killed by the massive Russian force in Chechnya, which had the insider cooperation of Ramazan Kadyrov and Yamadiyev's pro-Russian Chechen militias. These pro-Russian Chechen militias had begun a policy of kidnapping the families of rebels and torturing them to find their whereabouts.

The first rebel to be killed was the notorious Wahhabi, Arabi Barayev, who was killed by Russian forces in a shoot-out in Alkhan Kala on June 22, 2001. The villagers in his hometown refused to allow the sadistic kidnapper to be buried in their village, and his widow subsequently was killed as one of the Black Widows in the Dubrovka Theater incident.

The next leader to be killed was the "Black Arab" Amir Khattab, who had once seemed immortal (he survived a heavy caliber bullet wound to the stomach, a land mine explosion, and the loss of several fingers on his right hand to a grenade). But the larger-than-life Khattab's time ran out on March 19, 2002, when he opened a poisoned letter from one of his trusted couriers in his mountain hideout. The Russian newspaper *Argumenty i Fakty* (Arguments and Facts) would record the death of this jihadi terrorist as follows:

> Having taken the envelope containing the letter from the courier, Khattab went into his tent. "He came out a half hour later with his face pale, rubbing his face with the stump of his arm, and he then fell into the arms of his bodyguards." Feeling temporarily improved, Khattab gave an order to let Ibragim [the courier], who, along with five others, had been put under arrest, go: "He has to get back to Baku."
>
> An hour later Khattab again felt bad. "He fell into some bushes, and a moment later he was dead. Khattab's people searched for Ibragim in Baku for almost a month. It turned out that [Shamil] Basaev had personally ordered his execution. The bound body of the courier was found in the city outskirts with five bullets in the head."[127]

Photographs of Khattab being buried in an earthen grave were subsequently posted on qoqaz.net, the first online global jihad site, and were cause for mourning among many young Arab men who had idolized him as a holy warrior. The media-savvy Khattab, who was seen as much more of a frontline warrior by Arab online followers than the elderly bin Laden, had become famous through his online biopic "The Life and Times of Khattab," which is still available.

Khattab's role as the head of the decreasing number of foreign fighters in Chechnya, estimated to be no more than fifty, was taken by his *naib amir* (deputy commander) Abu Walid.[128] He was, however, killed on April 16, 2004, when his unit was surrounded by forces from the pro-Russian Yamadayev brothers' militia known as *Vostok*. He was killed in combat and beheaded by his enemies. Abu Walid, a Saudi who previously had fought in Bosnia and had joined Khattab in the Dagestan raid, was then succeeded by a Jordanian named Abu Hafs al Urduni, who was himself killed by Russian forces in a gunfight in Khasavyurt, Dagestan, on November 26, 2006. Urduni's demise, combined with the increasing difficulty of getting into the southern mountains of Russian-controlled Chechnya and the rise of a more accessible jihad closer to home in US-occupied Iraq, led to a gradual disappearance of the Arab Wahhabi fighters in the Chechen conflict.

The next Chechen "wolf" to die was Salman Raduyev, aka "Michael Jackson," the leader of the Pervomaiskoe raid into Dagestan and constant thorn in the side of Aslan Maskhadov. He was arrested by the Russians in 2000 in his hometown of Novogroznensky and sentenced to life in prison for his crimes against Russia. But in December 2002 he died from "internal bleeding" in his prison cell in Siberia. Considering the inhumane treatment of Chechens in Russian prisons, it was assumed by most that he had been beaten to death by his Russian captors.

The next figure to be killed was to be widely mourned in Chechnya (unlike the previous terrorists and jihadis) and was the popularly elected president of Chechnya, Aslan Maskhadov. He had just declared a cease-fire with the Russians and was still hoping to negotiate an end to the Russian quagmire in Chechnya, which had cost the Russians thousands of soldiers' lives in its second round, when he was tracked down. A Russian report stated of his March 8, 2005, death: "Today [we] carried out an operation in the settlement of Tolstoy-Yurt, as a result of which the international jihadist and leader of armed groups Maskhadov was killed, and his closest comrades-in-arms detained."

The Russians' cynical misrepresentation of Maskhadov as an "international jihadist leader" deliberately overlooked the fact that the Chechen president actually had called for the expulsion of Khattab's foreign jihadi fighters from Chechnya and was a moderate secularist, not a jihadist extremist. He apparently was killed by one of his own bodyguards, his nephew, when their house was surrounded by Russian troops and he was wounded by a Russian grenade. Maskhadov's nephew, who was subsequently captured, would state: "My uncle always told me to shoot him if he is wounded and his capture is imminent. He said that if he is taken prisoner, he would be mistreated."[129]

Maskhadov's death symbolized the death of the dreams of the vast majority of his countrymen, who had hoped for a secular, democratic, independent state at peace with Russia. Movladi Udugov's Kavkazcenter .com website would state of his death: "By martyring Maskhadov, the Kremlin killed the last illusion of those Chechens who, despite everything, still believed in a so-called 'international law' and civilized forms of communications with the Moscow thug regime."[130]

While the Russians celebrated the death of President Maskhadov, he was hailed in obituaries in the West as a tragic figure and a moderate who had been caught between the extremists on both sides. Tragically, in death the Russians declared him a "terrorist" and refused to return his body to his grieving widow and family.

Maskhadov would be replaced as president of Chechnya by his vice president, Abdul Halim Sadulayev. Sadulayev was a theologian who had worked to spread Islam in his hometown of Argun and had fought in Argun's militia during the first and second wars. He personally knew the horrors of Russia's *zachistkas*. His wife had been taken by the FSB and executed when his attempts to ransom her failed.[131]

In 2002, Maskhadov selected Sadulayev, who was loyal to Maskhadov in his struggles against the Wahhabis, as his vice president. With the death of President Maskhadov in 2005, President Sadulayev began a policy of creating a Caucasian Front to spread the resistance to Russia to neighboring Muslim republics in the region. This Caucasian Front united jihadi-fighting *jamaats* in the lands of Dagestan, Chechnya, Ingushetia, Kabardino-Balkaria, Karachai-Circassia, Ossetia, and Adyghe. He also ordered the disbanding of Basayev's Riyadus Salihin terror group and put an end to hostage takings and suicide bombings.[132] On June 17, 2006, however, Sadulayev was killed in a firefight with Russians and pro-Russian Kadyrovtsy militamen, but only after he and his bodyguards fought back and killed several Russians.

The killing of Sadulayev, who had brought a halt to Basayev's terror campaign, was, however, to be a strategic mistake for the Russians as he was replaced by Doku Umarov, an Islamist commander who played a key role in both Chechen wars (it will be recalled that he was wounded in the breakout from Grozny). Umarov was to relaunch the terror campaign against Russian civilians with a vengeance (except for a brief hiatus designed to thank Russian protestors for marching against Putin in 2012) and ultimately was to earn the moniker of "Russia's bin Laden." He announced his intentions, stating: "Blood will no longer be limited to our cities and towns. The war is coming to their cities . . . If Russians think the war only happens on television, somewhere far away in the Caucasus where it can't reach them, then God willing, we plan to show them that the war will return to their homes."[133]

Umarov was also to continue the policy of working with the various local Caucasian *jamaats* or larger *vilayets* (administrative regions) to spread jihadi terrorism throughout the north Caucasus. Most important, he was to make the momentous decision to subsume the Chechen struggle for national independence into a wider Caucasian jihad against Russia. He would officially do this on October 31, 2007, when he declared the abolishment of the Chechen Republic of Ichkeria and the creation of the Caucasian Emirate, with himself as emir (military leader).

The creation of a loosely organized, pan-Caucasian Islamic state, or emirate, at the expense of the goal of creating a narrower, secular Chechen republic clashed with the goals of exiled Chechen Foreign Minister Akhmed Zakayev, who was a secularist living in London, and Chechen nationalists (President Dzhokhar Dudayev's widow also called it a betrayal of her slain husband's dream).[134] In essence, it meant that the earlier generation of Chechen nationalists had been replaced by Salafi-Wahhabi Islamists who wanted to establish a pan-Caucasian shariah law state. It also signaled the adoption by Emir Doku Umarov of a more global jihadist rhetoric, even if this was not translated into reality. On one occasion Umarov stated that "all those waging war against Islam and

Muslims are our enemies," a far cry from the Chechens' strict traditional focus on Russia.[135]

But for all of Doku Umarov's boilerplate jihadi rhetoric, which on occasion even mentioned distant Britain, Israel, and the United States, the Caucasian Emirate remained a localized insurgent struggle against Russia, not an Al Qaeda affiliate (as in the case of such bona fide Al Qaeda affiliates as Al Qaeda in the Islamic Maghreb, i.e., North Africa; Al Qaeda in the Arabian Peninsula; Al Qaeda in Iraq; or the Nusra Front in Syria). Tellingly, the Caucasian Emirate commander of Kabardino-Balkaria backpedaled somewhat from Umarov's global jihad rhetoric and declared: "Even if we threaten America and Europe every day, it is clear for anybody who understands politics that we do not have any real clashes of interests (with the West). The people in the White House know very well that we have nothing to do with America at the moment."[136]

In this sense, the Caucasian Emirate umbrella group had many similarities with the East Turkistan Liberation Organization, a regional ethnic-jihad insurgency of Turkic Mongol Uighurs residing in eastern China's Xinjiang Province, who were fighting Beijing for an independent Islamic Uighur state.

Under Umarov, the flames of resistance to Russia were to spread from Chechnya to Dagestan in the east and the other small Muslim ethnic republics to west, especially Ingushetia, even as the war in Chechnya gradually came to an end and was replaced by more targeted Russian raids or a "silent war" on real or suspected rebels' homes. By 2008, Dagestan in particular had become a scene of violence, as Wahhabis from the corrupt, impoverished region carried out scores of bombings and assassinations against local authorities. These terror attacks led to harsh crackdowns and arrests of hundreds of young men suspected of being Islamist insurgents or terrorists. The Dagestani news was full of stories of young Islamists or Wahhabis who "went to the forest" (i.e., joined the *jamaat* rebels of the larger Vilayet of Dagestan) or had their houses besieged and destroyed by Russian security forces.

Tragically, Umarov also restarted the Riyadus Salihin terror war on Russia. The war recommenced with the bombing of a high-speed train known as the Nevsky Express, traveling between Moscow and St. Petersburg on November 27, 2009. The bomb derailed the train and led to the death of twenty-six people. In a sign of the growing importance of non-Chechens in the Caucasian Emirate, the Russian government subsequently charged twelve ethnic Ingush for involvement in the terror attack on the train.[137]

Two Dagestani Black Widows then struck with a suicide bombing during rush hour in Moscow's metro system, killing forty people on March 29, 2010. One of the bombers was a seventeen-year-old widow of a slain Dagestani militant, who posed with him in a picture holding a pistol before their deaths.[138] Doku Umarov claimed that the bombing was in retaliation for the massacre of Chechen and Ingush villagers, who were gathering garlic outside the village of Arshty where they were attacked by Russian special forces. Umarov warned the Russians: "The war will come to your street . . . and you will feel it on your own skins."[139]

The Caucasian Emirate stuck again, this time on January 24, 2011, at Russia's busiest air terminal, Domodedovo International Airport. In this bombing, 35 people were killed and 180 injured by an Ingush suicide bomber. Several of those killed in the attack were foreigners. As with the previous bombings, condolences poured in from across the world along with condemnations of the terrorists. Prime Minister Stephen Harper of Canada, for example, stated: "The use of violence against innocent people must never be tolerated, and we condemn those responsible for this horrible act."

In January 2012, Doku Umarov called for a moratorium on terror attacks, but on July 3, 2013, recommenced his campaign after claiming that the Russians had seen his truce as a sign of weakness. He used the upcoming Winter Olympic Games to be held in nearby Sochi, Russia (scene of the final massacre and retreat of the defeated Circassian highlanders in 1864) as a catalyst for the commencement of his terror campaign. At the time he ordered "all mujahedin fighters in the region and Russia's other subjects not to allow Satanist games to be held on the bones of our ancestors, on the bones of many, many Muslims who died and are buried on our territory along the Black Sea."[140]

On October 21, 2013, a Dagestani Black Widow blew herself up on a bus in the southeastern Russian city of Volgograd, killing seven. This attack was followed by two suicide bombings on December 29 and 30 on a metro station and trolleybus in Volgograd, which killed thirty-four people. In the case of the December 2013 bombings, the two Dagestani male bombers issued a martyrdom videotape of themselves stating that the bombings were a "present" to Putin.

As the February 2014 Winter Olympic games approached, many feared that the Caucasian Emirate would attack this global spectacle, which was Putin's pet project and was designed to show a new face of Russia to the world. But despite fears of Black Widows having infiltrated the games, there were no attacks on the festivities that cost Russia $50 billion to stage and protect. Some have suggested that the Caucasian Emirate's failure to attack this showcase of Putin's power may have been because Umarov was dead.[141] Speculation ended on March 18, 2014, when Movladi Udugov's Kavkazcenter.com website announced the martyrdom of Umarov without providing any explanation of how he died.

His successor was announced in a video as the relatively unknown Ali Abu Muhammad al Dagestani (aka Aliaskhab Kebekov), previously the *qadi* or chief judge of the Caucasian Emirate. He announced that his predecessor Umarov was "with the green birds of paradise" and that the jihad would continue. The appointment of a Dagestani religious scholar was significant, as it indicated that the struggle against Russia, which had begun in the early 1990s under the secular-nationalist Dzhokhar Dudayev in Chechnya, had shifted to Dagestan. The new leader of the Caucasian Emirate proved to be a moderate and called for an end to the suicide bombing campaign and killing of moderate clerics. This may have antagonized some of his more radical followers; in December 2014 six of his commanders turned on him and symbolically swore *bayat* (allegiance) to Abu Bakr al Baghdadi, the head of ISIS (the Islamic State in Iraq and Syria). One of these commanders led an attack on Grozny on December 4, 2014, that involved the capture of the main media center and a school in the usually peaceful capital and killing of 14 policemen before the attackers were killed. On April 19, 2015, however, Kebekov was killed by Russian forces in Dagestan and succeeded by a new emir, Magomed Suleimanov, a Dagestani Avar.

As all these events were taking place, a greater threat to Russia had already been eliminated with the accidental death of Shamil Basayev on July 10, 2006. On this occasion, Basayev was working with a group of fellow rebels/terrorists in Ingushetia to transport land mines and explosives. The Chechens claimed that Basayev, or one of his men, mishandled a land mine and it exploded, blowing up a truck filled with explosives. Thus Basayev ultimately was consumed by the fires of war that he himself had worked so hard to stoke.

The Russian government subsequently would claim that its operatives had somehow booby-trapped the mine to "neutralize" Basayev, but this seems highly improbable. If the Russians had known where Basayev was operating, they would not have risked the chance of possibly not killing him with a mishandled mine; they themselves would have targeted the most-wanted man in Russian directly. Movladi Udugov's Kavkazcenter. com website (which is still up and running in Russian, Turkish, and English) would state that Basayev had become a *shaheed* (martyr) *Inshallah* (God willing) as follows:

> The Chechen commander died as a result of an accidental spontaneous explosion of a truck, loaded with explosives on July 10, 2006, in the region of the village Ekazhevo in Ingushetia. Three other Mujahideen became Shaheeds (insha'Allah) together with him. There was no special operation whatsoever . . . The reason [for the] explosion was a careless use of an explosive.[142]

Russian sources would state that inspectors collected the parts of Basayev's body in a radius of up to a mile and identified it by its head and the prosthetic leg.[143]

Congratulations to Putin for the killing of the notorious Basayev came from throughout the world. President George Bush would state: "If he's in fact the person who ordered the killing of children in Beslan, he deserved it."[144] The BBC would post an obituary that stated: "Basayev's death leaves a gap in Chechnya which no other living rebel figure could fill."[145] The *Economist*'s obituary would state that "no other rebel leader possessed such daring and infamy."[146]

This was certainly true, and the impact of Basayev's death on the rebels was incalculable. Basayev had been a demonic figure to the Russians, but for the several hundred die-hard fighters still holding out in Chechnya and surrounding regions, he was a living symbol of their ability to hurt their Russian adversaries with seeming impunity. But many war-weary Chechens breathed a sigh of relief with his death, and many of his followers subsequently took advantage of amnesties offered by the pro-Russian Ramazan Kadyrov government and came out of the mountains and surrendered (once again disproving the myth that Chechens never surrender). On April 16, 2009, the Russians were confident enough to declare an end to "antiterrorism operations" in Chechnya, and the Second Russo-Chechen War of 1999 to 2009 officially came to a successful conclusion.

Today there are fewer than twenty thousand Russian troops in the relatively subdued Chechen republic, which rarely sees terror attacks or conflicts (there was a rare terror attack in Grozny in December 2014 that killed fourteen policemen just prior to a nationally televised speech by Putin). Chechen government and Russian sources claim that at roughly the time the war ended there were only between 100 and 450 rebels still holding out in the southern mountains.[147] Much of the Russian success has been because of the efforts of the slain Mufti Akhmad Kadyrov's son, Ramazan, who served as Chechen prime minister and later president, in using his large militia to hunt down Chechen rebels.

But this peace has come at a cost. Ramazan Kadyrov, Chechnya's "warlord-in-chief," has been widely accused of human rights abuses, including continuing the policy of "disappearances" of suspected rebels and their families or supporters. He also has hired assassins to kill Chechen opponents and dissidents who have fled abroad. His assasssins have killed so-called "traitors" in venues ranging from Austria to Dubai, where they killed his former pro-Russian ally Sulim Yamadiyev after a falling-out in 2004. In 2006 they most likely killed Russian investigative journalist Anna Politkovskaya in Moscow after she exposed cases of torture and other human rights abuses at the hands of his agents. Russian or Chechen government agents also hunted down and killed the exiled former interim president of Chechnya, the Islamist leader Zelimkhan Yandarbiyev, with a car bomb in Doha, the capital of Qatar.

As of today (summer 2015) a fearful peace is kept by Ramazan Kadyrov's five-thousand-man Kadyrovtsy militia, which is made up of supporters from Gudermes as well as many former rebels who joined his force. This force has been accused of running death squads that have engaged in kidnapping, torture, and murder, in its campaign to hunt down the dwindling number of Chechen rebels. Officially, Chechens voted in large numbers for Kadyrov and Putin in recent elections, but outside observers see election fraud and intimidation. Few Chechens dare speak out against Kadyrov, although one brave Chechen journalist said, "We have to live like this, like it or not. Putin launched his war saying he'd kill us in our outhouses. Tens of thousands of us have been abducted, killed and have disappeared. And now we're forced to say things we don't believe."[148]

Because of his success and his lavish praise of President Putin and Russia (the main street in the newly rebuilt Grozny was named Putin Avenue, and the Russian president's portrait competes with those of Kadyrov on billboards throughout Chechnya), Ramazan Kadyrov has been financially supported by Putin. In return for such as acts as sending up to one thousand pro-Russian Chechens to assist the Russian Federation forces that invaded eastern Ukraine in the summer of 2014, billions of dollars have been pumped into Kadyrov's pet projects, which have included rebuilding the shattered ruins of Grozny, once known as the "Caucasian Hiroshima."[149] Where the rubble of Minutka Square once stood untouched as a memorial to hundreds of Russian soldiers burned to death in their tanks during the previous wars, a gleaming new city has arisen. Now women wearing head scarves (which are mandatory in Chechnya under Kadyrov, who has sought to co-opt some of the Wahhabis' fervor) can eat sushi or pizza at new restaurants in the shadow of Dubai-style skyscrapers that are half empty. New apartment blocks have gone up as well as Europe's largest mosque, the Akhmad Kadyrov mosque, built in the Turkish style. In January 2014 Kadyrov also removed the monument to the deportation of the Chechens, which had been built in Grozny under Dudayev, for fear it would antagonize his Russian masters.

Interestingly, Chechnya also has seen a resurgence of Sufi Islam under Kadyrov, who sees it as an antidote to alien Arab Wahhabism. Sufi shrines have been rebuilt and enlarged, madrassas (theology schools) to teach traditional Sufi Islam have been financed, and *zikirs* (Sufi chanting dances) are promoted, even though the majority of fighters in the Russo-Chechen wars and in Imam Shamil's nineteenth-century war were Sufis. Kadyrov, who is a member of the Qadiriya Sufi brotherhood, has decisively prosecuted his slain father's war against the alien Wahhabis, who infiltrated the republic in the interwar years. Thus the Kadyrov clan has won its war against what it perceived as a greater threat to the Chechens' traditional way of life than the Russians. Sufism once again reigns supreme and unchallenged in Chechnya, despite all the Arab Wahhabi missionaries' efforts to eradicate it and enforce alien Saudi-style Islam.

On some levels, Kadyrov has cunningly constructed a de facto Chechen state run by its own forces and government and under its own terms, even though it is de jure under Russian Federation rule. Chechnya, which is still impoverished, needs Russian support, with over 90 percent of its budget coming from Moscow (most republics receive 30 percent of the budget from the capital).[150] The Russians have thus used the tried-and-true colonial policies of "carrot and stick" and "divide and rule" to gain control of the obstreperous Chechens.

Tragically, this has been accomplished at the cost of roughly seventy-five hundred Russian soldiers' lives in the first war and approximately five thousand during the second war. And the tenuous peace is limited to war-weary Chechnya. The bloodshed in the wider region continues, and in 2013 Russian security forces lost roughly the same number of troops in the northern Caucasus that NATO lost in Afghanistan that year. But it is the Chechens on whose lands the wars were fought who indisputably have suffered the most. As many as sixty-five thousand Chechens may have died in the two wars to keep Chechnya inside of Russia and avenge the deaths of three hundred Russians in the mysterious Moscow apartment bombings.

It remains to be seen how long this new "contract" between this turbulent highlander people and its historic Slavic Christian enemies will survive. One Chechen government official said, "Who knows how long this understanding will last, maybe one or two generations, depending on whether a real threat arises to the personal freedom of Chechens."[151] Fearing the future, a Russian official stated: "My fear is that by giving large quantities of weapons to the former fighters who make up most of Kadyrov's Guard, Russia is creating future problems for itself."[152]

Considering the bad blood between the Chechens and Russians, it is not inconceivable that the pro-Russian Chechen government could collapse like a house of cards should the powerful Kadyrov be assassinated like his father before him. In this case, many of the Kadyrovtsy militiamen/former rebels might once again take the mountains and turn their guns on the Russians who have bought their loyalty . . . at least for the time being.

The Chechen Ghost Army of Afghanistan and Syrian Battalion

Reports of Chechen snipers and bomb-makers appearing in one conflict after another, and of Chechens filling the ranks of armed groups in Iraq, Afghanistan and elsewhere have often proved to be exaggerated.
— C. J. Chivers, *New York Times*[1]

I think it's a kind of misinformation sent to the mass media by Russian secret services to make it seem they are not fighting a small separatist movement, but against the world's radical Islamic community.
— Alexei Malashenko, Russian member of the Carnegie Institute, expressing his skepticism at Moscow's claims that Chechen insurgents are linked to Al Qaeda[2]

Specters The Myth of the Chechen Al Qaeda Army of Afghanistan

As all these events were taking place on the historic fault line between Orthodox Russia and the Dar al-Islam in the northern Caucasus, the distant United States of America found itself confronting the nihilist Arab terrorist group known as Al Qaeda al Sulbah (the Solid Base), which was created to expel the Americans from Saudi Arabia and overthrow the "apostate" Saudi dynasty. Al Qaeda was based in Sudan from 1992 to 1996 and in Taliban-controlled Afghanistan from 1996 until its fiery destruction in November and December 2001, following the 9/11 attacks. Bin Laden's Arab terrorist group made a few pro forma supportive statements about the Chechens' struggle for independence (as it did for other Muslim groups such as the Palestinians, Muslim Kashmiris of India, Uighurs of China's Xinjiang Province, Kosovar Albanians of Serbia, etc.), but it did not have the means or interest in involving itself in any meaningful way in the Chechen struggle for independence that was initially led by secular president Dzhokhar Dudayev.

It will be recalled that Dudayev was previously a Soviet air force general who, like many other Chechen Soviet citizens, fought in the ranks of the Red Army during its war against the mujahideen rebels in Afghanistan in the 1980s. This was at a time when Osama bin Laden was fighting on the other side as an Arab volunteer in the ranks of the Afghan Islamist mujahideen rebels.

After the Soviet war ended in 1989 and Chechnya won its first war with Russia from 1994 to 1996, bin Laden subsequently commenced his jihad on the United States in 1998, from his Afghan base with the local Taliban tribal army/government. The Taliban, it will be recalled, were a group of ethnic Aryan Pashtun fundamentalists, who conquered most of Afghanistan from 1994 to 1999 and turned it into a medieval-style Islamic state. Bin Laden also contributed to his native Pashtun Taliban hosts' war against the anti-Taliban rebels known as the "Northern Alliance," by creating a jihad foreign legion force known as the "055 Brigade." This unit of Arabs, Uighurs, and Uzbekistanis became the cutting edge of the Taliban sword in its battles with the Northern Alliance opposition.

Bin Laden's greatest enemy was not, however, the Northern Alliance, which was led by generals Massoud and Dostum, but the distant United States of America, which he labeled "the Far Enemy." On 9/11, nineteen Arab hijackers attacked the United States and awoke America to the dangers of Al Qaeda and its local tribal allies, the Taliban. This changed America's perception of the world, as the White House suddenly began to view a myriad of complex, preexisting issues through the simplistic black-and-white lenses of the so-called "War on Terror."

Prior to this incident, the Americans had been sympathetic to the Chechens' plight. In 1999, US Republican presidential candidate George W. Bush, for example, categorically condemned Russia's brutal campaign in Chechnya and threatened to cut off IMF and Export-Import Bank loans to Russia as part of a new hard-line policy toward the Kremlin. Of the conflict, candidate Bush said, "They [the Russians] need to resolve the dispute peaceably and not be bombing women and children and causing huge numbers of refugees to flee Chechnya."[3] Right-wing hawks in the United States, such as Senator Jesse Helms, the powerful head of the Senate Foreign Relations Committee, also called for punitive sanctions against Russia, including Moscow's expulsion from the Group of Eight.

In a further move that the Russians saw as provocative, Bush's national security advisor, Condoleeza Rice, tellingly proclaimed that "not every Chechen is a terrorist and the Chechens' legitimate aspirations for a political solution should be pursued by the Russian government."[4] The Americans also gave asylum to the moderate Chechen foreign minister, Ilyas Akhmadov, who moved to New England to represent his people's cause.

In light of the sympathy shown to the Chechens in America, it is not surprising that after 9/11, the Chechen vice premier, Akhmed Zakayev, issued a statement of support for the United States, which read:

I am shocked! I simply cannot believe this! Who lifted his hand in order to commit this crime? Is he a human being? I am simply struck dumb I don't have comments on this. Please notify all that we in Chechnya grieve together with the American people! We share the pain and tragedy with them. I express the feeling of sincere condolence to all relatives of those who have been killed. I want to assure the USA and President G. Bush personally of our condemnation of any act directed against the population, I decisively condemn all terrorist acts, and I consider that [the] countries which connived at the mentioned terrorist acts in the USA must inevitably be punished by the world community.

On behalf of the President and the government of the Chechen Republic of Ichkeria I express deep sympathy and sincere condolences to the entire American people and to the American government. We do not have any doubts that behind the destruction of the Chechen towns and villages, behind the explosions of houses in Moscow, Volgodonsk, and Buynaksk are the same destructive forces. The Chechen government condemns terrorism in any form.[5]

The most resounding Chechen statement condemning Osama bin Laden's terrorist attacks on America, however, came in the form of an official letter from President Maskhadov on September 12, 2001. This letter presciently warned of efforts by the Russians to conflate its historic conflict in Chechnya with the brewing US-led war on Al Qaeda:

Please, accept our sincerest and deepest condolences in connection with the tragic consequences of the most terrible terrorist attack in the history of mankind. We, the Chechens, deeply grieve together with you ... Why do we Chechens so sincerely and deeply grieve together with you, America? Because America is the only country in today's world in which there are traditions to protect oppressed peoples from suppression. You, America, are our only hope for the future, the only hope for peace in our land that is saturated with blood.

We, Chechens, are deeply indignant of the undisguised triumph of Mr. Yasrzhembski [Kremlin spokesman] and of some other public figures in Moscow who are cynically trying to exploit the tragedy in America to justify Russia's own policy of state terror in Chechnya. We are angrily agitated and protest against any kind of deceitful political speculation by any states, first of all by Russia, on the grief of the American people. Mr. Yasrzhembski, in view of, apparently, insufficiency of mind, has tried to draw parallels between the American tragedy and Chechnya.

Naturally, he is doing this to seek justification for Russia's war against the Chechen people who have been branded as terrorists and bandits. If we are to speak about parallels, indeed, there are parallels: the murder of tens of thousands of innocent citizens in the name of Russia's criminal-political intentions, the destruction of thousands of civil objects not only on the territory of Chechnya, but also the blowing up of apartment houses in Moscow, Volgodonsk, Buinaksk in 1999, carried out by terrorists from Moscow with the sole purpose of developing a pretext for the subsequent immoral terrorist war in the Chechen Republic.

We, Chechens, grieve together with you, America. We pray for innocent victims. And we ask God to help you, America, to punish those people and those states that are responsible for this barbarous act.

With deep sorrow, Aslan Maskhadov President of the Chechen Republic of Ichkeria.[6]

But such gestures of support paled in comparison to Russian president Vladimir Putin's offer to allow US military aircraft to be based in his county's backyard in the ex-Soviet Central Asian republics of Uzbekistan and Kyrgyzstan, and for the permission for US aircraft to fly over Russian territory. Putin publicly offered his support for America's war on Afghan-based Al Qaeda and cast it as a part of his own preexisting war on the Chechens, who were similarly described as a race of Islamic nihilist terrorists. In fact, the Russian government began to imply that the Chechens were in actuality Al Qaeda working at the behest of bin Laden.

America lost no time in responding to this quid pro quo agreement and suddenly began to use language that described the Chechens as Al Qaeda–linked terrorists. For example, in June 2002 (months prior to the Dubrovka theater hostage incident and years before the Beslan school tragedy), US Secretary of State Colin Powell would backpedal on Condi Rice's previous pre-9/11 statement that "not all Chechens were terrorists" and state: "Russia is fighting terrorists in Chechnya, there is no question about that, and we understand that."[7]

The *Houston Chronicle* was to point out this cynical about-face by the Americans as follows:

> In its determination to build a broad international coalition to fight terrorism, the White House has adopted a new pragmatism in foreign affairs, sometimes siding with nations it previously cited for abuses. On Wednesday, this approach was evident as the Bush administration tempered its criticism of the harsh way Russia has treated Chechen rebels, and instead blasted the Chechens for harboring terrorists linked with Osama bin Laden . . .

In the past, Bush and his advisers had criticized Putin for the brutal Russian military campaign against the Chechens, saying it amounted to an abuse of human rights. While repeating that Russia should be mindful of such abuses, Bush and his advisers appeared to suddenly change their focus, portraying the Chechens less as victims than as co-conspirators with terrorists. Bush's spokesman Ari Fleischer urged Chechen leaders to "immediately and unconditionally cut all contacts with international terrorist groups, such as Osama bin Laden and the al-Qaida organization."[8]

In light of the total absence of any ties between the embattled Chechen rebel government in the southern mountains of Chechnya and Al Qaeda in Afghanistan, President Maskhadov sarcastically responded that cutting off ties with bin Laden's organization would be "no problem."[9]

It was at this time that Russian and later American media sources began to issue a barrage of vague reports of Chechens "pouring" into distant Afghanistan to form the vanguard of the Taliban army fighting US Central Command/NATO in the Central Asian country of Afghanistan.[10] They also spoke of bin Laden escaping from the massive country of Afghanistan to the Russian-encircled mountains of tiny Chechnya to find sanctuary.[11] It was even reported in one conspiracy-laced book (without a shred of evidence to support the absurd claim) that the Chechens had given Osama bin Laden "suitcase nukes" to be used against the United States of America.[12]

These wild, unverified reports came as a shock to three distinct groups of experts: those studying the Caucasus, Afghanistan, and Al Qaeda. The vague, secondhand accounts of "thousands" of Chechen *boyeviks* in Afghanistan who had somehow broken out of the Russian-dominated mountains and traveled across Eurasia to fight to the death on behalf of the doomed Pashtun fundamentalist Taliban tribesmen made little sense. Neither did the idea of bin Laden escaping the much larger country of Afghanistan and somehow making his way to tiny Chechnya at a time when it was controlled by 110,000 Russian troops who were hunting the remaining rebels.

Such commonsensical issues as the logistical obstacles involved in traveling across Eurasia and the motives that would inspire peoples of vastly different ethnic, religious, linguistic, and political backgrounds to unite forces against the world's lone remaining superpower seem to have been entirely ignored by those sensationalizing the news in America. In the post 9/11 scheme of things in America, any Muslim with a weapon, from Bosnia to Chechnya to Palestine to Kashmir was now "Al Qaeda" or "Taliban."

Among the many dubious accounts of Chechen "Al Qaeda/Taliban" operating in the Afghan theater of conflict was one widely disseminated, secondhand report that claimed, "One source inside Kunduz, Afghanistan told CNN that about sixty Chechens fighting alongside the Taliban drowned themselves in the Amu river rather than give up."[13] Those familiar with the outnumbered Chechens' tenacious defense of Grozny and other dramatic field actions under intense siege conditions found this unsubstantiated, but widely accepted, rumor to be beyond belief. No Chechen bodies were subsequently found in the Amu Darya River, and the Chechen government mocked the idea of such a large number of its troops from the small Chechen "army" committing collective suicide in defense of the Taliban in distant Afghanistan.

As the Western media nonetheless recast such rumors as facts, the Kremlin gleefully provided weekly press conferences supporting unsubstantiated American media claims that Russia's historic Chechen enemies (and not the foreign Arabs, Uzbekistanis, Uighurs, or Pakistanis, who all had a history of involvement in Afghanistan) made up the largest contingent of Al Qaeda's 055 foreign legion. Russian government sources, for example, claimed that "more than three hundred" Chechens had been surrounded in the Taliban's religious headquarters in Kandahar, that "hundreds" of Chechens had been captured by coalition forces, and that "hundreds" of Chechens had arrived in besieged Kunduz to help defend Al Qaeda's 055 Legion.[14]

If one subscribed to the veracity of all of these secondhand reports and applied simple rules of mathematics to them, one would have to accept the bizarre proposition that there were more Chechens reported to be waging war in Afghanistan against Americans and NATO than in their own homeland fighting against the enemy occupying force (recall that the largest Chechen fighting force in the Second Russo-Chechen War that came together to defend its capital of Grozny was made up of only three to four thousand fighters, and that less than a thousand fighters remained active in Chechnya by the time of 2001's Operation Enduring Freedom in Afghanistan).

During our conversations in Boston in 2003, I had the chance to ask the exiled Chechen foreign minister, Ilyas Akhmadov, whether the Chechen Army of Ichkeria had, counterintuitively, given up the battle for its own homeland and deployed hundreds of seemingly unneeded soldiers across Eurasia to the deserts of Afghanistan to defend the Taliban fundamentalists. This uniquely informed Chechen source ridiculed this outlandish notion and told me:

> Chechens are not a people who usually travel the world and we don't know Asia. Most Chechens could not spot Afghanistan on a map had they not fought there in the '80s for the Soviet Union. We have no interest in the Taliban and their extremist regime or its ties to Al Qaeda terrorism, which we condemn. We don't speak Arabic or Pashtun of Al Qaeda and the Taliban. Our enemy is closer to hand, in our own villages and homes. Our enemy is the Russian occupiers who are brutally killing our people, not the USA which we emulate for freeing itself from the British Empire and sharing freedom with the world.
>
> And besides, how would our soldiers escape to Afghanistan through Russian and US controlled airspace even if they had some strange desire to do so? In case you hadn't noticed there is no "Chechen Airlines" flying to Kabul these days from the ruins of Grozny airport. Our remaining fighters are hard pressed in the mountains defending their homes and families from the Russians, not defending the Taliban extremists' homes. This is all Russian disinformation (*dezinformatsiia*) and the Americans are uncritically swallowing it.[15]

Akhmadov was not the only Chechen to ridicule the notion that his people had somehow made a global alliance with Al Qaeda and the Taliban to take on both the Russians *and* the United States and its powerful NATO allies, simultaneously. Even Movladi Udugov, the Islamist who founded the notorious Congress of the Peoples of Chechnya and Dagestan, was to call the rumors that the Chechen rebels were allied to Al Qaeda "nothing but a pack of lies."[16] Udugov's infamous ally, Shamil Basayev, was to frankly (and somewhat belligerently) state: "I have not met Bin Laden. I received no money from him, but I would not have declined the offer."[17] President Maskhadov, no friend of Basayev's, was to state: "Basayev has no links with international terrorism. He has no contacts either with al Qaida or with bin Laden . . . His primary target is the principal structure of the Russian state."[18]

Some have tried to retroactively link Basayev to bin Laden by suggesting that a short training trip that Basayev and a few dozen Chechen fighters took to the Khost region of Afghanistan in 1994 (i.e., on the eve of the first Russian invasion of Chechnya) to learn tactics from Afghan mujahideen means that he was "Al Qaeda." But this is historical revisionism and an anachronism, since the Afghan training camp he visited was run by local Afghan Tajik mujahideen at this time, not Al Qaeda. Al Qaeda was located in the African country of Sudan from 1992 to 1996 (i.e., at the time of Basayev's brief visit).[19] Most important, Basayev's visit to Pakistan and pre-Taliban Afghanistan was a short-lived failure, and he and his small number of men returned home shortly after arriving.[20]

Which brings us to the most obvious person in Chechnya to join Al Qaeda, the Saudi commander, Amir Khattab. Paul Tumelty has written an insightful article for the journal *Terrorism Monitor* on Khattab, who ran his own jihadi unit dedicated to fighting Russians, which states:

> Khattab has often been described as an associate of Osama bin Laden, given that the two Saudis both fought in the anti-Soviet jihad. Yet although they were in Afghanistan at the same time, Khattab was only a 17-year-old mujahid when he arrived in 1987 and he persistently refuted any connection with bin Laden, stating that there is "no relationship because of the long distance and difficult communications." He constantly reiterated this sentiment in interviews, simply referring to bin Laden as a "good Muslim."
>
> There is now evidence, however, that both sides were in contact via representatives during the 1990s and early 2000s. That correspondence amounted to a rigorous debate over strategy, as both men had an entirely different worldview and each attempted to convince the other of the superiority of their respective approaches to jihad. This was also characterized by a personal rivalry between them, particularly as Khattab's stature grew within the Islamist community.

> Although he occasionally highlighted the oppression of Chechnya's
> Muslims, bin Laden was obsessed by the Judeo-Christian alliance [i.e.,
> the United States and Israel] and focused his strategy upon attacking
> the "far enemy" [i.e., the United States]. Khattab on the other hand
> sought to establish an Islamic system in Chechnya and then use it as
> a base from which to forcefully expand into neighboring territories.
> Right up until his death in 2002, Khattab never threatened to attack the
> United States.[21]

It should be clearly stated here that Khattab's separate, Chechnya-based jihadi group never joined bin Laden's "World Islamic Front for Jihad against Jews and Crusaders," which united several militant groups in an umbrella organization controlled by bin Laden in 1998.

Having said that, I have found several examples of individual Arabs and Turks who, having fought jihad in the mountains of Chechnya under Khattab, then left his group and joined Al Qaeda.[22] Several Arabs who joined Al Qaeda, including members of the 9/11 attack team, previously tried to reach the Russian-encircled Chechen mountains to wage jihad with Khattab, and only joined Al Qaeda after they failed to reach Chechnya.[23] In other words, Khattab and bin Laden recruited some militants from the same pool of jihadists.

Most important, before he merged his separate group with Al Qaeda, Egyptian Islamic Jihad leader Ayman al Zawahiri made an exploratory journey to Dagestan in 1997 to see if he could set up a headquarters for his embattled Egyptian terror group there among the like-minded Wahhabis of that region.[24] This mission failed after he was arrested by Russian authorities, and Zawahiri subsequently joined bin Laden in Afghanistan and united his group with Al Qaeda in 1998.[25] Zawahiri then became number two in Al Qaeda.

It should also be stated that several of the Muslim charities (such as Al Haramein, the Islamic Benevolence Foundation, and Al Kifah), which collected *zakat* (tithe) money from Muslim believers to support Khattab's jihadis in Chechnya and other jihad groups across the globe, also donated money to Al Qaeda. Bin Laden also appears to have at one time offered up a small sum of $1,500 per person to assist Arab jihad volunteers who wanted to travel to fight in Chechnya.[26] These are the closest links I have found between the few hundred foreign fighters who fought in Chechnya under Khattab and bin Laden's separate Al Qaeda organization in Sudan and Afghanistan.

As for links between ethnic Chechens and the Taliban/Al Qaeda, they are equally fleeting. The most notable example was when the former interim Chechen president, Zelimkhan Yandarbiyev, made an unofficial funds-collecting trip to Pakistan and Afghanistan in 2000 (this trip was never condoned by the Chechen government). There he met with Taliban officials who symbolically recognized the Chechen government.

A Chechen was also found guilty by a Danish court in 2011 for plotting to bomb a Danish newspaper that had published a controversial cartoon of the Prophet Muhammad in 2005. It also should be noted that in 2012, three Chechens were arrested on suspicion of being involved in a plot to fly remote-control planes into targets in Spain.[27] The failed terror attempts by these four Chechens in Europe appear to have been lone wolf operations, not operations planned by Al Qaeda Central.

There is also the case of approximately 150–200 Chechen fighters who traveled to Syria from 2012 to 2014 to fight against the Shiite regime of President Bashar al Assad alongside the Al Qaeda–linked jihad groups Nusra Front and ISIS (Islamic State in Iraq and Syria), to be discussed.

These tangential examples are as close to a "smoking gun" as we have for direct operational ties between Chechnya and Al Qaeda. Considering that, by contrast, American citizens have actually joined the Taliban (for example, John Walker Lindh, a California convert to Islam who became a Talib fighter before his capture by US troops) and even joined Al Qaeda (for example, Adam Gadhan, an American convert to Islam from Oregon, who became an Al Qaeda spokesman and senior operative), it is remarkable that there has not been any evidence of even a single named Chechen joining the Taliban or Al Qaeda.

In fact, no Chechens were among the over 774 Al Qaeda/Taliban members ultimately detained by Central Command in the US overthrow of the Taliban regime in Afghanistan in the fall of 2001 and sent to the US prison at Guantánamo Bay. The United States and its allies, by contrast, detained twenty-two ethnic Uighurs from Xinjiang, China, seven Uzbekistanis, hundreds of Arabs, nine Brits, and hundreds of Pakistanis, but not one ethnic Chechen was ever apprehended in the 2001 collapse of the Al

Qaeda foreign legion/Taliban army or in the subsequent Afghan War of 2001–2014.[28]

The *Moscow News* was to report on this important development as follows: "The fact that of the 300 people currently kept in Guantánamo only three may possibly be connected to the Chechen conflict—and even these three are not ethnic Chechens [two were ethnic Tatars from the Volga region and one was a Kabardinian]—destroys the myth that linked the conflict in Chechnya to the operation in Afghanistan." This source would also state that "since the war in Afghanistan began, little concrete evidence of an Afghan-Chechen link has surfaced. Journalists who have gone looking for Chechens in Afghan detention centers have so far come up empty-handed."[29]

The *Moscow News*' claim that journalists had traveled to Afghanistan after the successful overthrow of the Taliban in the American/NATO invasion of 2001 in search of the elusive Chechen–Al Qaeda fighters is correct. Among those to visit and interview hundreds of foreign prisoners of war captured by the anti-Taliban Northern Alliance in northern Afghanistan was Robert Young Pelton, a veteran combat reporter for *National Geographic*. Pelton, who had spent time in the trenches with the Chechen separatists during the Russian siege of Grozny (winter 1999), made his way to the deserts of northern Afghanistan in search of Chechen fighters, many of whom he may well have expected to know personally. Although Pelton soon discovered scores of Arabs, Uzbekistanis, Pakistanis, and even uncovered one American among the Al Qaeda 055 Brigade/Taliban prisoners of war, he encountered no Chechens. For his part, John Walker Lindh (aka "the American Taliban" discovered by Pelton), a uniquely qualified source who actually served as a Taliban foot soldier in Kunduz, told Pelton, "Here, in Afghanistan, I haven't seen any Chechens."[30]

Carlotta Gall, another correspondent with firsthand experience in Chechnya, also went to Afghanistan in search of Chechens and came up empty-handed. She had the following to say on the existence of Chechens among the approximately thirty-five hundred Al Qaeda/Taliban prisoners of war held by the Northern Alliance at Sheberghan in Afghanistan:

More than 2,000 of the prisoners are Afghans, of whom only the commanders will probably be of interest to the United States. More than 700 are

Pakistanis, with smaller numbers from other countries of the Islamic world; Saudi Arabia, Kuwait, Yemen, Sudan, Morocco, Iraq, the Muslim republics of Russia, and the countries of Central Asia. Despite assertions by the Afghans that there were many people from Russia's separatist Chechnya region fighting for the Taliban, there is not one Chechen among the prisoners.[31]

As a scholar of Chechnya, Al Qaeda, and Afghanistan, I was so intrigued by the notion of the mysterious Chechen specters of Afghanistan that in the summer of 2003 I myself traveled to the plains of northern Afghanistan and got permission from General Dostum, the Uzbek Northern Alliance warlord who captured the vast majority of the Taliban/Al Qaeda prisoners and still held them, to interview his captives. Against all odds Dostum, a larger-than-life figure who led his horsemen against the Taliban in 2001, agreed to allow me access to the thousands of prisoners he held in a medieval-style fortress prison in his bastion of Sheberghan.[32] There I had the surreal experience of interviewing scores of Taliban prisoners of war from Pakistan and Afghanistan.

Over the course of my interviews with the Taliban prisoners of war, it became obvious that, while they had heard of Uighurs, Uzbekistanis, Arabs, and even John Walker Lindh the American Talib, none had ever heard of, or personally seen, an actual Chechen. This despite the unsubstantiated Russian reports of "hundreds" of Chechens playing a key role in the defense of the north and "hundreds" in the south, reports that were uncritically swallowed by the American media. The same held true for their Northern Alliance captors, who said they had found no Chechens among their foreign prisoners of war.

I felt a little like an eccentric professor in search of the Big Foot–like mythical Chechen Al Qaeda globe-trotting superfighters of Afghanistan until one evening I was having dinner with Dostum's bodyguards in his compound. There I noticed that one of his bodyguards looked distinctly non–Turkic Mongol (Dostum's people, the Uzbeks, are the horse-riding descendants of Genghis Khan's nomadic hordes). When I asked him where he was from in my limited Uzbek, he replied in Russian that he did not speak Uzbek.

Intrigued, I asked him where he was from in Russian, which I speak comfortably. To my shock, he replied that he was from Gudermes and

Urus Martan, Chechnya! I had found an actual Chechen soldier in Afghanistan and was sitting next to him having soup and naan bread. When I excitedly asked him what had taken him from his mountainous homeland to the plains of the pro-American Uzbeks of northern Afghanistan, he told me that he had fought in the First Russian-Chechen War, where he lost a brother. He explained that he was a secularist and no fan of Khattab and his foreign jihadis. During the bleak interwar years, he had departed Chechnya in search of work and had ended up as a paid fighter (*naemnik*, a Russian word also meaning mercenary) in Uzbekistan.

When the United States invaded neighboring Afghanistan after 9/11, the ruler of Uzbekistan, President Islam Karimov, dispatched a group of elite guards to protect General Dostum, a fellow Uzbek. Among them was the Chechen I met, who apologetically refused to give me his name for security reasons.

I then asked him if he had met any Chechen prisoners during his service with Dostum, and he told me that he too had been searching for his countrymen since his insertion in Afghanistan during the route of the Taliban. While he claimed to have discovered jihadis from Uzbekistan among the Taliban prisoners of war (these were sent back to Uzbekistan to face trials), Arabs, and Pakistanis, he had encountered none of his *zemliaki* (countrymen) in his more than a year and half in the employ of Dostum "the Taliban Killer."

When I returned to Boston, I published my findings with the Jamestown Foundation in Washington, DC, and gave a talk on them in London at the International Institute for Strategic Studies, but the vague reports of "fanatical Al Qaeda" Chechen superfighters in Afghanistan continued to emerge in the media. For instance, the Agence France-Presse published a story titled "Americans Hunt for Chechens in Afghanistan," which stated:

> They have been the stuff of nightmares for Russian troops and now U.S. forces face the prospect of trying to combat Chechen fighters in Afghanistan who have thrown their lot in with Osama bin Laden's al Qaeda network. "There are a hell of a lot of them and they sure know how to fight," one senior American officer said after the conclusion of the recent offensive Operation Anaconda against diehard fighters in eastern Paktia province.

Chechen separatists, who have been involved in a fierce war for independence from Russia for the past twenty-nine months, appear to make up the largest contingent of al Qaeda's foreign legion . . .

Following the downfall of his Taliban protectors in Afghanistan, there has been speculation that Osama may now try to seek refuge in Chechnya. "We know the history of the Chechens. They are good fighters and they are very brutal," Hagenbeck said. The general said he has heard of reports out of the Pentagon that a unit of 100–150 Chechens had moved into southern Afghanistan.[33]

The *National Post* similarly reported:

Chechens were among the most bloodthirsty enemies that U.S. special forces and allied troops faced in their campaign to oust the Taliban from power in the months after 9/11 . . . The Afghans who fought alongside the Americans 12 years ago were tough, battle-hardened men inhabiting one of the most violent places on the planet. But they still were absolutely terrified by Chechen jihadis, who were regarded as pitiless and fanatical —even by the standards of Islamist terrorism.[34]

Such accounts became commonplace during the Afghan War of 2001–2014, and a search of "Chechens Afghanistan" on Google led to almost two hundred thousand hits by the fall of 2014. A typical hit was a 2014 ABC News article titled "The Secret Battles of US Forces and Chechen Terrorists," which stated:

For the last 12 years, U.S. Special Operations forces have repeatedly engaged in fierce combat in Afghanistan against ruthless Taliban allies from Chechnya, who have the same pedigree as their terrorist brethren threatening to disrupt the Winter Olympics in Russia, current and former commandos tell ABC News. "I'd say Chechens were a fair percentage of the overall enemy population early in Operation Enduring Freedom," recalled an active-duty senior Special Operations officer, referring to the Pentagon's name for the Afghan war, in which he was among the first ground operatives . . .

Chechens joining the Taliban and al Qaeda–aligned militias stood out for their ferocity and refusal to surrender, operators with considerable experience in eastern Afghanistan revealed in recent interviews.

"Chechens are a different breed," a Special Forces soldier who has fought them told ABC News. "They fight till they die. They have more passion, more discipline and less regard for lives," said the soldier, who did ten tours hunting high-value targets in Afghanistan. "A few of them could have just given up but decided they needed to die."

A U.S. Special Operations officer with nine deployments to Afghanistan compared Chechen jihadists to the Viet Cong guerrillas who fought U.S. Special Forces in the Vietnam War. "What I always appreciated was their lack of tether. They will transplant anywhere. I don't think they ate or were even clear as to why they fight, wherever it is, but they're fighting most of the time. It's just a fire in their bellies. It's what they do," said the veteran Special Forces operator.[35]

For all their appeal to military types, such testosterone-laced, boiler-plate-rhetoric accounts of Chechen "nightmares/fanatics" with "fire in their bellies who never ate and needed to die," of course lack any specific details of the sort US and NATO forces have on other Arab, Uzbekistani, Pakistani or Pashtun Taliban and Al Qaeda fighters, whose names, identities, and characteristics are often known. Tellingly, there have been no US military reports of any Afghan-based Chechen commanders' names or those of any rank-and-file Chechen fighters in the country. (No known Chechen commanders covered in this book ever redeployed or took their troops from the battles in their homeland to distant Afghanistan, so this is perhaps not surprising.)

For all these reasons, it is my firm belief that these vague, ritualized accounts of fierce Chechens in Afghanistan come from US fighting men who began to consider fighting so-called "Chechens" in Afghanistan to be a rite of passage. The lack of any Chechen prisoners at the massive US prisons in Bagram and Kandahar and the Afghan prison Pul-i Charki and complete lack of even a single substantiated Chechen passport or corpse seems to mitigate against the existence of a Chechen fighting presence of any size in Afghanistan. By contrast, we know the actual names of several British, Canadian, and German Muslims who went to Afghanistan to fight jihad against the United States and were killed by US Predator or Reaper drones operating on the Afghanistan-Pakistan frontier.[36]

In the summer of 2009, I myself worked as an intelligence contractor for the US Army's Information Operations team at ISAF HQ (NATO's International Security Assistance Force Headquarters) in Kabul, Afghanistan. There I met US soldiers and heard vague stories of the legendary "Chechen snipers" in the Afghan hills, Chechen Black Widow bombers said to be lurking in Afghanistan's countryside, and die-hard Chechen fanatics who always fought to the death when cornered. "Evidence" of Chechens being in an area of operations usually was provided in the form of secondhand stories of skilled enemy sniping or "radio intercepts." But the commonsensical question is: "How many US troops from places such as Alabama or New Mexico (or more improbably, local Afghan translators from places such as Kandahar who speak Pashtu) are fluent in Nokchi — the complex, ancient, pre-Aryan language of less than a million Chechen highlanders from the distant Caucasus — to corroborate such claims?"

It seems that jargon-filled, pro forma accounts by US troops in the field describing fights against "die-hard Chechen fanatic warriors" have been uncritically accepted as a given fact by the US military establishment in Afghanistan (and Iraq). The US military's fighting men have discovered the legendary, Russian-killing Chechens of the distant Caucasus Mountains in a big way and have transported them in their imaginations to Central Asia to fight US Central Command and NATO in defense of the Taliban and Al Qaeda.

But one US Army major has broken ranks on the myth of the Chechen Army of Afghanistan and has stated that he has seen "zero proof" beyond scattered rumors that there are "any Chechens anywhere in Afghanistan."[37] A platoon commander from the 101st Airborne who fought in Operation Anaconda, where Chechens were rumored to be among the foreign fighters, in 2002 similarly stated: "It was a pervasive rumor at the time. But I never saw a Chechen. In fact, I'm not sure anyone did."[38] A Central Asian expert who was based at Forward Operating Base Salerno in Afghanistan also claimed that "an [Afghan] cultural adviser who grew up in the U.S. told me that many Afghans call fair-skinned foreign fighters 'Chechen' in part because that's what they think the Americans want to hear."[39]

This is not to say definitively that there has not been a single Chechen in Afghanistan. I myself found what seems to be a unique video proof of one Chechen who had joined the Taliban. I found it in a documentary readily available on YouTube titled "Afghanistan: Behind Resistance Lines." On this video, there is a split-second shot of a smiling, non-Pashtun–looking armed fighter with a sleeveless jacket, a Western-style cap, and light skin and a reddish beard. A Taliban fighter points him out and says, "This brother is from Chechnya."[40]

This video would seem to indicate that the Chechen fighter might have been a lone wolf, and it is probable that other Chechens made their way across Eurasia to Afghanistan to fight as individuals or in small groups, along with much larger numbers of Pakistanis, Arabs, North Africans, Uzbekistanis, Uighurs, Canadian Muslims, German Muslims, and British Muslims (who do not appear to have become part of the US military's fighting lore despite the fact that we have specific details on many of them, including some of their names and places of origin).[41] But the unsubstantiated reports of units of up to 150 Chechen fighters attacking US troops and of hundreds of Chechen fighters killing themselves in a frenzy rather than surrendering, however, belong the realm of fantasy.

There is, however, one jihad theater of action closer to the Chechen homeland where there is indisputably a widely verified Chechen fighting presence that contrasts drastically with the total lack of evidence of a Chechen fighting presence of any substantial scale in Afghanistan, and that is Syria. With the commencement of a Sunni rebellion against the Russian-supported Assad Shiite regime in Syria in April 2011, as many as eleven thousand foreign Sunnis have made their way to this country to wage jihad on behalf of the Sunni rebels (including hundreds from Europe and a dozen from the United States). Among them were approximately 150 to 200 Chechens (Chechens are Sunnis), enough to form their own jihadi battalion and make their imprint on this bloody civil war.

The Chechen Jihadi Battalion of Syria

In December 2013 the BBC was to report triumphantly in an online video interview carried out with Chechens, "For the first time evidence has emerged of Chechen fighters away from home. After the attacks of 9/11, many reports alleged Chechens have taken part in jihad battlefields in Afghanistan and Iraq and even training camps in Waziristan. Claims never proven. Today's Syria with its bloody conflict became the first front where

Chechens are taking part in fighting outside of the north Caucasus."[42] The US Army's West Point *Counter Terrorism Sentinel* was to similarly report in March 2014:

> For the first time in the post-9/11 period, there is incontrovertible evidence that Chechens and other Caucasian ethnicities are joining and even heading foreign fighter contingents in a non-contiguous war theater far from their contested homeland. Until recently, Chechen violence was focused almost exclusively on symbols of the Russian state and, to a somewhat lesser extent, Russian civilians.[43]

Among the foreign fighters streaming to Syria were Chechen commanders who have been interviewed or filmed numerous times and who are, in contrast to Afghanistan where we have no names or interviews, well known to the media. The most famous of them is the red-bearded Tarkhan Batirashvili, otherwise known by his *kunya* (nom de guerre) as Abu Omar al Shishani ("al Shishani" translates to "the Chechen" in Arabic). Batirashvili hails from the village of Birkiani in the Pankisi Gorge, located on Georgia's northern border with Chechnya, where there is a community of fifteen thousand Chechens known as the Kists. This area came under the influence of Arab Wahhabis during the early stages of the Second Russo-Chechen War, some with links to Al Qaeda, and also served as a rear-area staging ground and cross-border sanctuary for Chechen insurgents.

Batirashvili appears to have fought alongside Chechens from Chechnya who used his valley as a base during the second war. As a Georgian citizen he also fought as a sergeant in the 2008 Russo-Georgian War and is known to harbor a deep hatred for Russians (who of course support the Shiite Assad regime in Syria in its fight against the Sunni rebels). He was later arrested in 2010 by the Georgian authorities for storing illegal weapons and made a promise that he would wage jihad should he make it out of jail alive.[44]

When he was released sixteen months later in 2012, Batirashvili traveled with his brother to Turkey to fight alongside the Sunni Muslim rebels of neighboring Syria against the Russian-backed Assad regime. The Assad Shiite regime's brutal crackdown on Sunni protestors and the regime's use of death squads known as the Shabiha to kill and terrorize

Sunnis mobilized rebel support from Sunni fighters across the globe on an unprecedented scale. Batirashvili was among them, and he had the added incentive of wanting to fight the Russian-backed Shiite Assad government. It also should be noted that the United States gave nonlethal aid to the Sunni rebels and threatened to bomb the Shiite Assad regime when it used poison gases to kill Sunni civilians in the summer of 2013.

Batirashvili, now known as Omar al Shishani, arrived in Syria in 2012, and his first command was of a unit of foreigners known as the Katibat al Muhajirun (the Brigade of Migrants). This unit, made up of approximately one thousand fighters, fought predominantly in the area of Aleppo in northern Syria.[45] The Chechens seem to have played an important command role in this jihadi foreign legion and several other fighting groups, including the Nusra Front, the Free Syrian Army, and the Islamic State of Iraq and Syria (ISIS), that far outweighs their limited numbers.

A British journalist for the *Guardian* gave an eyewitness account of the Chechen fighters in Syria, which compares drastically with the lack of such detailed specific reporting from Afghanistan:

> Some [foreign fighters], like Abu Omar's Chechens, were allowed to form their own units and simply referred to as the *muhajiroun*, or "immigrants." The Syrians refer to the internationals collectively as the "Turkish brothers." The disparate levels of fighting ability among the men was immediately clear. The Chechens were older, taller, stronger and wore hiking boots and combat trousers. They carried their weapons with confidence and distanced themselves from the rest, moving around in a tight-knit unit-within-a-unit.[46]

The *World Tribune* would similarly report: "The Chechens are regarded as the best of the jihadist fighters and have been used in several campaigns . . . The Chechens were said to be highly disciplined and daring. The sources said at least 17 of them were killed in a battle with the Syrian Army outside Aleppo in February 2013."[47]

The *Long War Journal* reported:

> "Chechen fighters," often described as fighters from the Caucasus and southern Russia, have been spotted on the Syrian battlefield for months. In October, a group of "Chechen emigrants" is known to have

fought, along with an element from the Free Syrian Army unit, under the command of the Al Nusrah Front to take control of a key Syrian air defense and Scud missile base in Aleppo.[48]

There have been numerous detailed news reports and videos of "Chechen emigrants" fighting alongside the Nusra Front (a group that has sworn fealty to Al Qaeda and is among the the largest and most effective groups of Sunni rebels) and alongside Free Syrian Army rebels, who are supported by the United States. For instance, in October 2012 Chechens were reported to have been involved in the successful assault on the 606 Scud Rocket Brigade base.[49] They also fought alongside Nusra Front fighters in the overrunning of the Sheikh Suleiman army base west of Aleppo in December 2012 and in the storming of the Syrian Army's Eightieth Regiment near the airport in Aleppo in February 2013.

In 2013, the *Wall Street Journal* published a fascinating article on Batirashvili, aka Abu Omar al Shishani and his men's role in the conflict with Russia's Syrian ally Assad, which captured some of the impact the legendary Chechen fighters had on the war in Syria:

> For months, Syrian government forces hunkered down at a remote air base north of Aleppo, deftly fending off rebel assaults—until one morning a war machine rumbled out of the countryside, announcing that the Chechens had arrived. The vehicle was notable for its primal scariness: Rebels had welded dozens of oil-drilling pipes to the sides of the armored personnel carrier, and packed it with four tons of high explosives, according to videos released online by the rebels. It was piloted by a suicide driver, who detonated the vehicle at the base, sending a ground-shaking black cloud into the sky in an attack that analysts said finally cleared the way for rebels to storm the airfield.
>
> The final capture of the airport in August [2013] immediately boosted the prestige of its unruly mastermind Tarkhan Batirashvili, according to analysts—an ethnic Chechen whose warring skills, learned in the U.S.-funded Georgian army, are now being put to use by a group deeply at odds with more mainstream Western-backed rebels.
>
> Until recently, Mr. Batirashvili had few outward religious convictions, former colleagues said. But like many Chechens he wanted to fight the Kremlin wherever he had the chance. "He had that kind of hatred for

them," said Malkhaz Topuria, a former commander who has watched his onetime subordinate's stardom grow in videos posted on the Internet. "It was in his genes."[50]

The Chechens in Syria have been most active in posting their stories and photographs on the Internet with such titles as "Caucasian Power in Syria." There is even a webpage devoted to stories of Chechens fighting in Syria, www.chechensinsyria.com, which also has videos of Chechen fighters in the conflict. There are videos on the website designed to galvanize interest in the struggle in Syria, and these seem to be reaching Chechens, Dagestanis, and others in Russia who are interested in fighting jihad against Russia's Shiite allies in the Middle East.

One Chechen fighter in Syria, who allowed himself to be interviewed under the *kunya* of Abu Hamza, gave the following account of his own journey:

"I went there because I saw videos on the Internet of innocent women and children being killed by the regime. I wanted to fight the [Syrian] government and help the opposition; I wanted to kill Bashar," he said.

Wearing a faded Adidas windbreaker over a camouflage T-shirt, Abu Hamza spoke of his two-and-a-half months skirmishing with the Syrian military as if it were a summer-camp adventure at which he had met like-minded men of diverse backgrounds. He declined to tell me the name of his group for fear of compromising his comrades' safety, but he said they included ten other Chechens, several Azeris, Indians, and Arabs, and even one American [a smiling American jihadi named Eric Harroun posted a video of himself riding alongside a red-haired Chechen driver to the site of a Syrian Army helicopter shoot down in Syria], whom he described as a "cool guy" even though the American struggled with languages other than English.[51]

There are other Chechen emirs or commanders who have gained fame in the Syrian civil war as well who usually go by Arabic *kunyas*, including Abu Turabi al Shishani, Abu Jihad al Shishani, Fahd al Qasim, Salahhudin al Shishani, Muslim al Shishani (real name Muslim Margoshvili), Abu-Musa Shishani (the emir of the Ansar al Sham group), and Saifullah al Shishani (Ruslan Machaliashvili). Among the most famous was the last-mentioned Saifullah, whose group broke with Abu Omar al

Shishani's group after Shishani swore an oath of allegiance to the Islamic State in Iraq and Syria (ISIS). But Saifullah was dramatically killed on film by a mortar strike while leading an attack on a Syrian prison near Aleppo. The Nusra Front leader Julani wrote a martyrdom epitaph for him that stated:

> Here the heroic knight has dismounted after a good march of jihad, which began in the Caucasus and ended in the Levant [Syria]. Saifullah was killed while moving with all his might to liberate the Muslim men and women from the prison of the tyrant [Bashar al Assad]. He gave only one condition to me before he extended his hand in pledging allegiance, which was to storm the prison and liberate it, and he did not accept an alternative.[52]

Chechen rank-and-file fighters also have died in the fighting in Syria, and their pictures and jihad obituaries were available online at fisyria .com, a Chechen website dedicated to the jihad in Syria. One of these, titled "Boxing Champion or Mujahid [Holy Warrior]," described the *shaheed* (martyred) Chechen fighter who went by the *kunya* of Abdullah:

> Formerly a famous boxing champion and currently *mujahid shaheed, insha'Allah*—Abdullah from Chechnya. That was his name on the blessed land of *Sham* (Syria). Having left the world behind, all the charm of this perishable world, he left it and made a deal with God. In the last operation at Deir es Zor, our beloved brother Abdullah fell martyred. This was a man who always showed love and hate for the sake of Allah.
>
> I do not remember him avoiding a single fight, even with his wounded leg, he was eager to lead against his enemies, he was cocky. The impression he made was that he was a person that was ready to shoot without stopping. In his last battle, he gave one of the first bursts, but in response to the will of Allah Almighty an [enemy] projectile flew and took his soul.[53]

With all of these eyewitness accounts and dozens of online videos of Chechens being interviewed, asking for donations for their jihadi efforts, bragging of their victories, fighting and dying in Syria (readily available at YouTube or LiveLeak by typing: "Chechens Syria"), the natural question is how many of them are there in this jihadi theater of action?[54] The BBC claims there are two hundred Chechens in Syria (Russian government sources put the number at four hundred Muslims from the former USSR fighting in Syria), although the Chechen website Kavkazcenter.com states that there are only 150 fighters from the entire north Caucasus.[55]

Of these Chechens in Syria, perhaps half come from the Pankisi Gorge in Georgia, with many others coming from the refugee diaspora of as many as 190,000 Chechens found in Europe, and of course some from Chechnya itself. This is a small number considering there are thousands of foreign fighters in Syria, making this the greatest transnational volunteer jihad since the 1980s in Afghanistan. But the skilled Chechen fighters seem to have taken on a leadership and vanguard role in the conflict that far surpasses their meager numbers. Most important, the media-savvy Chechens have lent their prestige as legendary fighters to the jihad and have helped recruit other jihadists via the Internet.

Tragically, the images of bearded Chechen fighters waging war as Allah's foot soldiers in the deserts of Syria that are easily accessed on the Internet (alongside other videos of Chechens and Dagestanis fighting in the forested mountains of the Caucasus) also made their way to the shores of the United States, where there is a small Chechen refugee/immigrant community. There they were viewed in Cambridge, Massachusetts, by one Americanized half-Chechen, half-Dagestani named Tamerlan Tsarnaev. These images glorifying jihad for the sake of Allah and sermons by an Al Qaeda recruiter may have helped to radicalize this Boston Chechen-Dagestani and drive him to wage a lone wolf terror jihad in the name of his faith. The story of how Tamerlan Tsarnaev and his younger brother, Dzhokhar, came from the war-torn Caucasus to Boston and turned on the very society that gave them sanctuary is one of the most unexpected and bizarre spin-offs of the preceding story of warfare and bloodshed in Chechnya.

The Strange Saga of the Boston Marathon Bombers

These guys look like home-grown terrorists
to me—not Chechens on a mission.
— Charles King, professor at Georgetown University's
  Foreign Service School[1]

There is any number of paths towards violence, and
this seems to have been their own. Two young people
dreaming dreams of glory, with
a sense of moral outrage, looking for identity, and
extremely difficult to detect.
— Dr. Marc Sageman, author of *Understanding
  Terrorist Networks* and *Leaderless Jihad*[2]

The Elusive Chechen Connection
to the Boston Marathon Bombing

Perhaps the most unexpected story to come out of the previous account of tsarist conquest, Sovietization, genocide, warfare, and terrorism in the Caucasus is the story of the Boston Marathon bombers, Dzhokhar and Tamerlan Tsarnaev. In light of the previous history, there seems to be no rationale for explaining the April 15, 2013, Boston Marathon bombing in the context of Chechen/north Caucasian insurgencies aimed at the Russian Federation. The complete lack of any Chechen threats against the US mainland or previous attacks by Chechens on American targets makes the bombing inexplicable to those studying warfare and terrorism in the Caucasus region. Simply put, there was no rational reason for the flames of hatred that had been stoked in the Caucasus since the tsarist times to spread to the shores of America.

But for all of its incongruence with the previous history, the Tsarnaevs' story starts out being rather typical of Chechens who have been scattered across the globe by ethnic cleansing, state-sponsored terrorism, and warfare. For starters, the Tsarnaev brothers' father, Anzor, came from a family of Chechens that was deported to the Central Asian republic of Kyrgyzstan during Stalin's genocidal assault on his people. Anzor Tsarnaev grew up in the Kyrgyz town of Tokmok, not in Chechnya. This town of fifty thousand, which lies near the border of neighboring Kazakhstan, was flooded with Chechen exiles in February and March of 1944. As many as eighty-five thousand Chechens were forcefully settled in the region by Soviet dictator Josef Stalin as "special settlers." Today there is still a remnant of approximately twenty-five hundred Chechens in this town.[3]

While most Chechens returned to Chechnya when Nikita Khrushchev came to power and released them from their exile camps in the mid-1950s, the Tsarnaev family stayed among the Turko-Mongol-Muslim Kyrgyz. A fellow Chechen who had lived next door said of the Tsarnaevs, "This was a very good family. They all strove to get a higher education, to somehow set themselves up in life."[4] They were not a particularly religious family, and a neighbor said she did not recall seeing them ever go to the mosque.[5] This was typical of the time because of the antireligious policies of the Soviets, which led to the secularization of millions of Muslims in the USSR.

The Tsarnaevs raised cattle and sheep in Kyrgyzstan, and one of their family members later said, "We were pretty much farmers in an urban area."[6] Like most Chechens in exile, the Tsarnaevs got by on little, but ultimately managed to rebuild their lives after the brutal disruption of the deportation. Tragically, however, Anzor Tsarnaev's father, Zaindy—who was deported to Kyrgyzstan when he was only eleven—was killed in 1988, when a shell exploded as he was scavenging in a trash heap for metal that could be sold as scrap.[7]

For his part, Anzor Tsarnaev ended up meeting his wife, Zubeidat, while serving in the Soviet army in the Siberian town of Novosibirsk.[8] They later got married in Elista, the capital of the Kalmyk ASSR, a Mongol Buddhist republic lying just to the north of Dagestan, whose inhabitants also were deported by Stalin during the war. Zubeidat was an ethnic Avar from Dagestan's largest ethnic group, who grew up in a village named Chokh. She fled an arranged marriage to marry Anzor, who was a talented boxer.

After having a son named Tamerlan in 1986, the Tsarnaevs then moved back to Kyrgyzstan to raise him in this mountainous Central Asian Soviet Socialist Republic. When the Soviet Union collapsed, the family moved back to Anzor's ancestral village of Chiri Yurt, Chechnya, for a short period in 1992 to be with his family and *teyip* (clan). They then briefly moved back to Kyrgyzstan in 1993 to have a second baby, named Dzhokhar, probably evoking the name of the famous secular Chechen president, Dzhokhar Dudayev, who was in power at the time.[9] After giving birth to Dzhokhar, the family returned to Chechnya, but not for long. As war clouds loomed on the eve of the First Russian-Chechen War of 1994–96, they were forced to flee back to Kyrgyzstan. A neighbor in Kyrgyzstan recalled how "they were in clothes they would wear only around the house and fled the bombing, managing only to grab their documents and a few things."[10]

In 1999 the family again moved back to what was by then a de facto independent Chechen Republic of Ichkeria to be with Anzor's family. But the timing of their move was unpropitious, as the republic had descended into chaos as radical warlords such as Salman Raduyev, Arbi Barayev, and Shamil Basayev clashed with President Aslan Maskhadov's moderate secular government. As the Russians once again invaded Chechnya following Shamil Basayev's rogue invasions of Dagestan in August and September 1999, the family fled to neighboring Dagestan.[11]

This brief six-month period in Chechnya would be the young Dzhokhar and Tamerlan's only real memory of time spent living in the homeland of their grandparents on their father's side (recall that their father grew up in Kyrgyzstan, and even their grandfather was deported from Chechnya when he was only eleven). The brothers would, however, have been much more familiar with Dagestan, where they lived and attended school in the seaside capital of Makhachkala from 1999 until 2002.

The Tsarnaev brothers' father, Anzor, was more profoundly affected, however, by the conflict in Chechnya and Dagestan than they were. He later claimed he had been detained by Russian troops and tortured.[12] This all-too-common experience for Chechen men, many of whom suffer from PTSD, led him to see a psychiatrist for help in succeeding years.

In 2002 the Tsarnaevs made the fateful decision to emigrate to the United States, claiming asylum on the basis of anti-Chechen discrimination in Kyrgyzstan. I did not see any overt anti-Chechen discrimination in the region against them in my own time spent in Kazakhstan and Kyrgyzstan and suspect that their asylum request was based more on the allure of living in America. As it transpires, Anzor's brothers, Ruslan and Alvi Tsarni, had earlier moved to Montgomery Village, Maryland, and had fulfilled the American dream by becoming extremely successful. Ruslan, a corporate lawyer who came to love America, spoke in glowing terms of his new homeland, and Anzor dreamed of moving his family there for the opportunities and safety it offered. One of Anzor's relatives was to say as much when he explained Anzor's motives for moving to the United States: "He wanted a better life for the children. That's why he went to the United States."[13] Anzor also seems to have had a run-in with the Russian mafia, who beat him so badly that he ended up in the hospital and also beheaded his German Shepherd.[14] There may have thus been both a "push" and a "pull" to the Tsarnaevs' decision to emigrate.

It is extremely rare that Chechens make it to the United States. America did give asylum to the moderate Chechen foreign minister Ilyas Akhmadov (who was, however, denied a green card because of Russian pressure and claims that he was a "terrorist envoy" and "similar to Bin Laden"). But Akhmadov's asylum came only after lobbying from prominent Americans, including Secretary of State Madeline Albright and Senator John McCain. The *Washington Post* was to write in this case:

> Mr. Akhmadov is well known for denouncing terrorism, for opposing the use of suicide bombs and for working, as he puts it, for a "negotiated peace" in his country. To turn him over to the Russian government for arrest, interrogation and possible execution would have meant accepting the Russian definition of all independent Chechen leaders as terrorists, a definition that simply doesn't hold up to the facts.[15]

There was also the case of the famous Chechen surgeon Khassan Baiev, who was given asylum with the backing of the Boston-based Physicians for Humanity, after being honored for treating both sides in the Russian-Chechen conflict and subsequently being labeled a "terrorist" by the Russians as a result.

But these are the rare exceptions. In fact, only about two hundred Chechens live in America, with the largest concentration (about thirty to forty) being in the Boston area.[16] This contrasts drastically to Austria, where there are thirty thousand Chechen refugees.[17] There are also thousands of Chechen refugees in other countries in Europe that are closer to Russia. Of those Chechens who have settled in America, approximately 70 percent are women. Most of them came to America from 2000 to 2002, as their homeland was devastated by Russian *zachistkas*, bombings, and "disappearances" at the hands of brutal Russian troops in the Second Russo-Chechen War.

The Tsarnaev brothers, however, avoided all the conflict in their grandfather's homeland and arrived in New Jersey. They were later given hospitality and a temporary place to live for a month in the Boston area by the famous Dr. Khassan Baiev.[18] Ultimately they settled in Cambridge, Massachusetts, a welcoming, multiethnic town across the Charles River from downtown Boston that is home to both MIT and Harvard. Anzor's brother Ruslan claimed, "When he came here, Anzor loved it. He appreciated the opportunity very, very much. He never complained."[19] Anzor and his family later became lawful permanent residents (LPRs) of the United States (green card holders), and on September 11, 2012, Dzhokhar became a naturalized American citizen in a ceremony in Boston's TD Garden sports arena.

By all accounts, Tamerlan and Dzhokhar initially adapted well in their new American home. Tamerlan, or "Tam" or "Timmy" as he was known to his friends, excelled at boxing, a sport that is often practiced by Chechen men, and took to smoking pot and drinking in nightclubs with his American friends. One of Tamerlan's friends said of the cocky immigrant from Russia, "He used to be more dressed like a pimp, kind of Eurotrash."[20] Tamerlan won Golden Glove boxing competitions in New England and dreamed of joining the US Olympic team. A coach at the Harvard Boxing Club claimed he was "one of the top amateur boxers in the U.S."[21]

His younger brother Dzhokhar was known as a relaxed "pothead," "normal American kid," and a "sweetheart," who was well liked in his high school at Cambridge Rindge and Latin School and later at the University of Massachusetts–Dartmouth.[22] One of his classmates described Dzhokhar, or "Jahar" or "Jizz" as he was known, as "a very goofy kid, a gentle-giant sort of person. He liked to talk, always had his arm around your shoulders." Importantly, his friend said, "He didn't impose any religious things on you, never talked about it."[23]

For his part, the father, Anzor, worked as a freelance auto mechanic fixing cars on the street for ten dollars an hour. Janet Reitman has written of him in her groundbreaking essay on Dzhokhar published in *Rolling Stone*, "Though Islam is the dominant religion of the North Caucasus, religion played virtually no role in the life of Anzor Tsarnaev, a tough, wiry man who'd grown up during Soviet times."[24] The mother, Zubeidat, went to cosmetology school and began providing facials at a local salon to supplement their income. She was described by a fellow Chechen in Boston as a "very open, modern lady."[25]

The two sons initially seemed to epitomize the successful melting-pot influence of America in general, and the multiethnic area of the town of Cambridge in particular. This was facilitated by the fact that their Sovietized secular parents did not impart strict Islamic traditions on them to create barriers to assimilation in mainstream American society, as some devout Muslim emigrants to the United States do. And the Tsarnaev brothers, for all their moves across the former Soviet Union, did not actually experience the horror of the wars that had devastated their grandfather's homeland of Chechnya. They did not bring the baggage of psychological wounds with them or intense identification with a struggle in the former homeland as many war refugees do. During an interview with the *New York Times*, for example, Anzor and Zubeidat Tsarnaev were asked whether the conflicts in Chechnya might have shaped their sons' identities and answered in the negative as follows:

> Question: Did your kids suffer from the war?
> Answer: No, my children did not see the war. They grew up in Kyrgyzstan.
> Question: They never saw the war?
> Answer: Yes, we left, ran away from the war. We did not need it, you see?[26]

On another occasion, a journalist asked Anzor Tsarnaev whether his sons were interested in Chechnya, and he replied in the negative as follows:

> Question: Was he [Tamerlan] interested in the history of the Chechen wars?
> Mr. Tsarnaev: He was not interested. There is a different life in the States.
> Ms. Tsarnaeva: He was absolutely young. He left when he was a small boy.
> Question: Maybe an ethnic or historical interest?
> Mr. Tsarnaev: But we were not interested in it as well.[27]

A Chechen friend of the Tsarnaevs in Cambridge said of the family, "They weren't Chechen" — they had not come from Chechnya, as she and others had — "and I don't think the other families accepted them as Chechens."[28]

In addition, while Dzhokhar was in high school in Cambridge, his English teacher, Steve Matteo, gave his class an assignment to write a paper on any topic that interested them. Dzhokhar initially chose to write the paper on Chechnya. Matteo, who is a friend of mine, then advised Dzhokhar to contact me to learn more about Chechnya since I taught a rare class on this specific topic at the University of Massachusetts–Dartmouth. But Matteo later told me (after the bombing) that Dzhokhar ultimately wrote a paper on another topic instead, and while Dzhokhar was a student at my university (the University of Massachusetts–Dartmouth), he never came to see me to discuss my popular course on warfare and terrorism in Chechnya. This is all the more intriguing when one considers that his family friend Dr. Khassan Baiev was a guest speaker in the class and Baiev's book *The Oath* was required reading. This was a potential opportunity for deradicalization that was missed since the class offered a stark, cautionary tale on the evils of Arab-inspired jihadi radicalism/ Wahhabism and terrorism.

Most interestingly, while the Tsarnaev parents visited relatives in Dagestan regularly during their ten years spent in the United States, they did not bring their children with them on their trips back to their homeland. In other words, the brothers did not maintain a strong diasporic-familial link to their mother's former homeland in Dagestan, much less to their grandfather's childhood home of Chechnya. And even the older brother, Tamerlan, who would have had more exposure to the Chechen language before he arrived in the American melting pot, admitted that he could "hardly speak Chechen."[29]

For all these reasons, friends, family, and neighbors were therefore stunned by the news on April 19, 2013, that the two seemingly Americanized "Chechen" brothers had carried out such a barbaric terror attack on the very community that had embraced them and offered them a welcome home for over a decade. Not surprisingly, in light of the Chechens' notoriety following the Beslan school massacre, many Americans honed in on the brothers' Chechen ancestry on their father's side in an attempt to explain the Boston Marathon bombings, which killed three and injured or maimed over 250 (there was initially little interest, however, in their Dagestani or Kyrgyzstani origins, which were actually far more significant in terms of their own life experience).

Former US ambassador to the United Nations under President George W. Bush, John Bolton, captured the distrust of many when he said of the Chechens, "These people are killers." After warning that more attacks would come to other cities, he also stated: "Chechnya maintains a deep terror network, and the two Boston bombing suspects were likely taking direction from overseas."[30] Bolton was not the only one to suspect that there was someone else, presumably Chechen terrorists in Russia, behind the Marathon bombing plot. Representative Michael McCaul, a Texas Republican and chairman of the House Homeland Security Committee, told Fox News that "the level of sophistication" of the homemade pressure-cooker bombs used at the marathon "leads me to believe that there was a trainer."[31]

As suspicion of Chechens spread through such headlines as "Boston

Attacks Turn Spotlight on Troubled Region of Chechnya" or "Bombings' Chechen Connections," America's small emigrant community worried that the Chechenphobia that had swept Russia following the mysterious 1999 Moscow apartment bombings (that were erroneously blamed on Chechens) had followed them to their new homeland. An alarmist USA Today article fulfilled their worst fears, stating:

> Are the Chechens trying to bring their cause to the international stage? Or are they just Muslim recruits in the global jihad against the western Satan? Probably the latter . . . No matter what, it wouldn't be surprising if some Chechens joined an al-Qaeda-style jihad. Oppressed, war-ravaged nations are the breeding ground for great warriors as well as evil terrorists, from Afghanistan to Palestine.[32]

An article in the *National Post* similarly stated: "This week's killing of three Marathon-watchers in Boston, including an eight-year-old boy, was seen in the West as an epic act of savagery. But by the standards of Chechen terrorists, it was standard fare."[33]

When the FBI later descended on Chechens in the Boston area to question them on their ties to the bombers, their worst fears seemed to be coming true. After a Chechen friend of Tamerlan's named Ibrahim Todashev was killed by FBI agents in Orlando during an interview about Tamerlan's possible involvement in a previous murder in the nearby town of Waltham, a chill descended on Boston's Chechen community. The famous Chechen doctor Khassan Baiev was so worried about the FBI's scrutiny that he decided to stay in Chechnya, where he had returned to open a clinic to treat children with war wounds. (His family, however, remained in the Boston suburb of Needham, where they were very well assimilated.)

Boston's small community of Chechens had been interviewed by the FBI prior to this at the urging of the Russian government, and they had been quite cooperative. (Baiev always gave the FBI agents a copy of his powerful autobiography, *The Oath: A Surgeon Under Fire*, to explain his personal journey from his home village of Alkhan Kala to Boston.) Khassan Baiev was nonetheless moved to say, "I can barely find words to express my sorrow over this event, which has left us mortally ashamed."[34] Baiev would go even further in a subsequent letter to the *New York Times*, which stated:

As a Chechen surgeon who was granted American citizenship in 2012, I want to condemn in the strongest terms the terrorist act at the Boston Marathon. The actions of Dzhokhar and Tamerlan Tsarnaev, suspects in the bombing, were truly despicable. We who live in America want our children, educated in the United States, to be a credit to American society. This ghastly catastrophe has cast a terrible shadow over all the Chechen people and Chechnya. I can barely find words to express my sorrow and shame over this event. We who have deep ties to our original homeland, Chechnya, and our adopted country, the United States, want everyone to know that our hearts go out to all the victims of this tragedy.

On behalf of myself, my family and many Chechens, I am sure, I thank the United States for granting us political asylum and assistance when we fled the horrific conflicts in the Caucasus region of Russia. The United States government and the American people we have come to know have welcomed us with open, friendly arms. We will always be grateful for your generosity.[35]

Baiev's friend, the former Chechen foreign minister Ilyas Akhmadov, who also had a deep appreciation for America, was equally horrified by the attack, which he called "hideous savagery," and stated of the bombers: "They were notional Chechens. They never lived in Chechnya."[36]

The most widely televised American-Chechen response to the bombings, however, came from the bombers' uncle, Ruslan Tsarni of Maryland. On the morning the bombers were identified as his nephews (April 18, 2013)—thus leading to an unprecedented citywide lockdown and massive manhunt for Dzhokhar in Boston—Tsarni urged his nephew, "If you're alive, turn yourself in and ask for forgiveness from the victims. You put a shame on our entire family—the Tsarnaev family—and you put a shame on the entire Chechen ethnicity."[37]

Tsarni then told reporters he taught his own children to love America because it gives everyone the chance to be "treated as a human being." He also said, "I respect this country, I love this country" and offered his condolences to the bombing victims, stating: "We share with them their grief. I'm ready just to meet with them. I'm ready just to bend in front of them, to kneel in front of them seeking their forgiveness."[38] When asked by journalists what provoked the bombings, Tsarni stated: "Being losers, hatred to those who were able to settle themselves — these are the only reasons I can imagine . . . Somebody radicalized them, but it's not my brother who just moved back to Russia, who spent his life bringing bread to their table, fixing cars. He didn't have time or chance or anything, options. He's been working."[39]

In addition, many average Chechens living in America who had no ties to the bombers also came out strongly against the terrorists, who were widely reported in the media to be Chechen. The *New York Times* published a remarkable interview with one of these average Chechens which provided considerable insight into this small community's views on the terror attack that killed and maimed so many people in their new homeland. This article included an interview with Ali Tepsurkaev of Cape Cod, Massachusetts:

> For Mr. Tepsurkaev, 33, who fled the wars in Chechnya more than a decade ago, immediate disbelief turned quickly to fear and despair. The violence that had once consumed his homeland had found him again, this time shattering the quiet refuge he had found here in New England. "I was so upset, I couldn't work," said Mr Tepsurkaev, who soon left his Nantucket home to be with his extended family here in Needham, a Boston suburb. "I left my guys. I couldn't finish. It felt so horrible." "Most of us would be dead right now if it wasn't for the United States giving us a home and saving us from all the violence," he said. "It feels embarrassing for us. After all this hospitality we're getting from Americans, to hear that some Chechen . . ." he said, breaking off. "It's hard. It's difficult to explain . . ."
>
> "I remember them in the dungeon just hiding from the bombs," Mr. Tepsurkaev said of his cousins. "They've seen the screaming, they've seen the blood, but as you see they're getting educated here, trying to get into college and living their lives. No hate, no violence. They've seen it, that's why they appreciate it even more." "But these guys who haven't seen anything," he said about the bombing suspects, "I have no idea what kind of crazy ideas they have going on in their head."[40]

It was not just America's small diaspora of Chechen refugees who wondered what was going on in the bombers' heads and how they came to hate their adopted homeland so much that they were willing to kill and maim civilians in their hometown. As a veritable media frenzy occurred in the aftermath of the bombing, it was soon discovered that there was a Russian link to one of the brothers that might explain his radicalization. Media sources quickly uncovered the fact that twenty-six-year-old Tamerlan, who was clearly dominant and led his malleable nineteen-year-old brother Dzhokhar, had been interrogated by the FBI at the behest of the Russian FSB intelligence services in March 2011.

As it transpires, the FSB had secretly recorded a phone call from Tamerlan to his mother, who was in Dagestan. In the phone call, Tamerlan reportedly talked vaguely about jihad with his mother, Zubeidat. The FSB also recorded Tamerlan's mother talking to someone in the Caucasus, who was under FBI investigation in an unrelated case.

Based on this information, in March 2011 the FSB contacted the FBI "legat" (legal attaché) in Moscow and in September contacted the CIA and provided them with a most unusual Russian language memorandum.[41] The memorandum claimed that Tamerlan "was a follower of radical Islam and a strong believer, and that he had changed drastically since 2010 as he prepared to leave the United States for travel to the country's [Russia's] region to join unspecified underground groups."[42] The FSB did not, however, tell the FBI that the information had come from intercepted phone calls, and when the FBI asked for further information, none was forthcoming. This lapse in communication was to be significant. Had the FBI had more detailed information on the source and nature of the Russians' warning, they might have subjected Tamerlan to greater scrutiny.

Regardless, the FBI investigated Tamerlan and checked "U.S. government databases and other information to look for such things as derogatory telephone communications, possible use of online sites associated with the promotion of radical activity, associations with other persons of interest, travel history and plans and education history."[43] They also scrutinized his Internet activity as part of what is known as an "assessment," the least invasive of three types of investigations. According to a newly declassified report from the CIA, Department of Justice, and Department of Homeland Security, "The CT [Counter Terrorism] Agent also conducted database searches, reviewed references to Tsarnaev and his family in closed FBI counterterrorism cases, performed 'drive-bys' of Tsarnaev's residence, made an on-site visit to his former college [Bunker Hill Community College], and interviewed Tsarnaev and his parents."[44]

As this report clearly states, the FBI interviewed Tamerlan, who had become a born-again Muslim by this time, in his third-floor apartment in Cambridge. His father would later recall his son saying, "They told me they were watching everything—what we look at on the computers, what we talked about on the phone. I said that's fine. That's what they should be doing."[45]

Tamerlan's mother recalled that he was defiant in his meetings with FBI investigators and told them, "I am in a country that gives me the right to read whatever I want and watch whatever I want." She also recalled her son saying, "He was even trying to get the FBI [agent] to convert to Islam."[46] Zubeidat further claimed that the FBI regularly visited them and recalled, "They were telling me that Tamerlan was really an extremist leader and that they were afraid of him. They told me whatever information he is getting, he gets from these extremist [web]sites. They were [watching] his every step."[47] Anzor Tsarnaev recalls the FBI stating that the questioning was "prophylactic, so that no one sets off bombs on the streets of Boston."[48]

But the FBI/Boston Joint Terrorism Task Force (JTTF) did not find any information to indicate that Tamerlan was a terrorist threat to the United States during the three-month investigation. The FBI concluded that its review of the available evidence at the time "did not find any terrorism activity, domestic or foreign, and those results were provided to the foreign government in the summer of 2011."[49]

Having found "no link or nexus to terrorism," the case file was then closed. The FBI nonetheless added Tamerlan and his mother to the Terrorist Identities Datamart Environment (TIDE) database as a precaution on October 19, 2011. Being one of over five hundred thousand people on this list, Tamerlan, however, was not subjected to any further scrutiny after spring 2011. But an electronic alert was set up to notify the JTTF in the event that Tamerlan tried to leave the country.

Nine months later Tamerlan purchased a ticket to travel to Russia. The purchase of the ticket set off the alert for the FBI special agent tasked with his case, but she never requested that Tamerlan be questioned or inspected. On the evening of January 21, 2012, Tamerlan Tsarnaev boarded a plane in New York and flew from there to Moscow to renew his Russian passport (he was born in Kalmykia, a province of Russia). Once in Russia, he disappeared off the American radar since the United States cannot track its citizens' movements in foreign countries once they leave American soil. But unbeknownst to the Americans, Tamerlan's seemingly innocuous journey took on a potentially more sinister aspect after he then made his way down to the Caucasus region of Dagestan, the heart of the Caucasian Emirate's jihad insurgency against Russia.

It was this mysterious journey that was to lead many people to believe that Tamerlan might have been radicalized and trained to carry out the Boston Marathon bombing while in this war-torn Caucasian land. For example, Texas Republican representative Michael McCaul said, "What I'm very concerned about is that when he went over there, he very well may have been radicalized and trained by these Chechen rebels, who are the fiercest jihad warriors."[50] House Intelligence Committee chair Mike Rogers, a Republican from Michigan, similarly said of Tamerlan Tsarnaev's trip to Dagestan, "It would lead one to believe that's probably where he got that final radicalization to push him to commit acts of violence and where he may have received training on what we ultimately saw last Monday."[51] An exploration of this murky journey to Dagestan sheds crucial light on Tamerlan Tsarnaev's Islamist activities in this low-level insurgency zone and goes a long way toward answering the question of whether or not he was radicalized and trained by "the fiercest jihad warriors."

Tamerlan in Dagestan

At first glance Dagestan seems like the perfect setting for a young Americanized Russian citizen who was rediscovering his faith to fall in with militants, become radicalized, and train to carry out a terror attack on the United States of America. By the time Tamerlan Tsarnaev arrived in Dagestan in March of 2012, which was two months after arriving in Russia according to his aunt, this Russian republic had become the epicenter of the Caucasian Emirate's low-level insurgency.[52] Bombings like the one in Boston, only on a larger scale, were not unusual in this blood-soaked region that was ground zero for Emir Doku Umarov's struggle to create a pan-Caucasian imamate. One bombing alone, the March 9, 2002 bombing at a Victory Day parade in the town of Kaspisk, killed 43 and wounded or maimed more than 150.[53]

In 2012, the year Tamerlan visited Dagestan, at least 700 people were killed in the region and over 500 wounded, according to one study.[54] Dagestan, a republic that has roughly the same population as the Boston metropolitan area (three million), was also the scene of a shocking 262 terrorist attacks in the year Tamerlan visited it.[55] Approximately 217 armed militants also were killed in the region in 2012.[56]

By the time Tamerlan arrived in Dagestan, the Russian authorities had commenced a large-scale crackdown designed to eradicate Wahhabi-Salafite militants in preparation for the upcoming 2013 Winter Olympics in nearby Sochi. Just prior to Tamerlan's arrival, in February 2012, the Russian authorities carried out a four-day operation to wipe out local militant bands that left seventeen police and twenty militants dead.[57] In May, while Tamerlan was in the Dagestani capital, Makhachkala, Russia's most dangerous city, two car bombs exploded killing 13 people and wounding 130 more.[58] Smaller bombings and drive-by shootings would have been an almost daily occurrence during Tamerlan's visit to this bastion of Wahhabi-Salafite jihad in Russia.

The *Washington Post* was to capture the tension in the city of Makhachkala between the Wahhabi-Salafite extremists and secular authorities as follows:

> The city Tamerlan came to in search of his roots is beset by intrigue and contradiction. Makhachkala is Muslim but known for its cognac. Weekly shootouts produce a heavy murder toll. Many Dagestanis are turning toward Salafism, a strict fundamentalist sect. Police gun down fundamentalists they say have turned militant. Police are methodically blown up with makeshift bombs. Habib Magomedov, a member of the Dagestan government's anti-terrorism committee, said Tamerlan did not come to official attention during his stay. "Maybe he is unusual in America," he said, "but there are many such young people in Dagestan. Here he would be a lot like many others."[59]

One Dagestani interviewed after the Marathon bombings summed up the chaotic nature of Makhachkala when he said, "No one is talking about the Boston bombing because such things happen every day here."[60]

When Tamerlan arrived in Makhachkala in March 2012, he could not have failed to sense the simmering tension in the city between the growing number of radical Wahhabi-Salafites and the Sovietized Sufi secular majority that had long dominated this port city. He would have seen women enveloped in dark *hijabs* sharing the streets with women in short skirts, restaurants selling sushi near radical mosques, and young men with Wahhabi beards, who feared being arrested by camouflaged heavily armed soldiers manning ubiquitous checkpoints. He also would have seen wireless cafes juxtaposed against Islamist graffiti with such stark messages as "Fear Allah, cover yourselves!" "Allah sees all!" "Know, you dogs, there will be jihad before judgment day!"[61]

Most important, Tamerlan certainly would have heard of young Wahhabis who "went to the forest" (i.e., joined the local Vilayat of Dagestan branch of the Caucasian Emirate) and became jihadi guerillas in the struggle against the "infidel" Dagestani authorities. All too often the lives of these young militants ended tragically when they were tracked down by Federal troops or police and killed in their homes in deadly shootouts. As a policy, the police destroyed the houses of militants, leaving their grieving families homeless, thus perpetuating the cycle of repression and violence. One observer noted of the Russian government's crackdown, "We are seeing in Dagestan the explosion of homes of relatives of militants, enforced disappearances and torture."[62]

The Makhachkala of 2012 had become a much more violent place since Tamerlan last saw it as a child in 2002. But Tamerlan, who by now spoke American-accented Russian and dressed in the flamboyant "Eurotrash" style that was alien to Makhachkala, was welcomed to this city by his father, Anzor, who had moved there in 2011 following his divorce with Zubeidat and a health scare. Ironically, Anzor, an ardent secularist, had divorced Zubeidat in part because of her increasing religiosity, which affected her eldest son.

Tamerlan and his father lived in Anzor's modest apartment in a typical neighborhood in Makhachkala while Tamerlan awaited the issuing of his new Russian passport. But not all of those who welcomed Tamerlan in Dagestan that spring were so innocent. He was also welcomed by his third cousin on his mother's side, Magomed Kartashov. Kartashov was the leader of a Salafite group known as the "Union of the Just" that called for the overthrow of secular governments and the establishment of a worldwide, shariah-based caliphate. This group was essentially the

245

local face of the Hizb ut-Tahrir, a global fundamentalist movement that is banned in Russia.[63] The Union of the Just subscribed to a global Islamist ideology, which is opposed to American intervention in Iraq and Afghanistan. The group led the largest protests against the United States following the release of the incendiary anti-Islamic movie made in California, "Innocence of the Muslims," which led to riots in places ranging from Benghazi, Libya, to Cairo, Egypt. One Union of the Just member proudly proclaimed after the protest that "we burned an American flag that day."[64]

Recalling Tamerlan's relationship with his cousin Kartashov, the head of the Union of the Just, his mother, Zubeidat, would state that "the two became very close" during Tamerlan's spring/summer 2012 visit.[65] Kartashov was ultimately arrested in 2013 for flying black Islamic flags (which were banned in Russia) in his movement's headquarters in Kizlyar, north of Makhachkala where Tamerlan visited him.

But perhaps the most interesting Islamist Tamerlan is reported to have met with during his stay in Dagestan was a shadowy militant named Mahmud Mansur Nidal. Nidal was part Kumyk (one of Dagestan's ethnic groups) and part Palestinian. On April 27, 2013, Russia's *Novaya Gazeta* newspaper reported that Tamerlan met multiple times with Nidal, who was said to be a recruiter for the Vilayat of Dagestan underground. Local authorities reported they were seen together "more than once."[66] Their meetings led to Tamerlan being put under surveillance by the local Anti-Extremism Unit, and he would later report to his mother that on at least one occasion he was stopped on the street by the local police and questioned.[67] An FSB source would subsequently report, "We pay special attention to foreign or ethnic Russian converts. They are extremely ideological and psychologically vulnerable; they're more easily persuaded to do anything, even suicide bombing."[68] But remarkably, in light of the fact that the Russian FSB warned the CIA and FBI about Tamerlan's radicalization in 2011, Tamerlan was never arrested or interrogated by the FSB. This may be because in Tamerlan's case, a Russian security source said Russia's secret police were tracking Tamerlan's movements, but did not consider him "a high risk, just a point of interest."[69]

We will never know definitively whether or not Tamerlan was trying to join the insurgency via this contact, however, because the nineteen-year-old Nidal went underground after being suspected of being involved in a bombing that killed thirteen people in May 2012.[70] Then, on May 18, 2012, the police got a tip that Nidal was visiting his house. They quickly surrounded it and demanded that he surrender. As many Caucasian highlanders had done in the past, however, Nidal chose to go down fighting and threw a grenade at the police. He subsequently died in a fusillade of police bullets as his house burned down around him. His death must have affected Tamerlan, who similarly made a last stand throwing IEDs at the Boston-Waltham police and died in a hail of bullets.[71]

The Russians reported that Tamerlan was seen meeting with Nidal at a Salafist mosque in Makhachkala that they had under surveillance. The mosque on Kotrova Street where they met was known as the al-Nadiria mosque and was named in honor of the man who built it, Nadirshah Khachilaev. Khachilaev, it will be recalled, was an Islamist radical who was involved in the defense of the Kadar Zone secessionist Islamic "republic" in southern Dagestan in 1999. It was this Russian-besieged Wahhabi zone that Khattab and Basayev sought to assist with their second invasion of Dagestan in September of 1999. Khachilaev was subsequently shot down by unknown assailants outside of his home in 2003. His large concrete home was then turned into a mosque and became a "meeting place for Salafists."[72]

But there was more. It seems likely that Tamerlan, who had undergone a transformation from being a marijuana-smoking brash boxer to a devout Muslim by 2011, may have tried to link up with the Dagestani insurgents even before he got to Makhachkala. Russian officials accused him of being in communication via the Internet with one Russian-born Muslim convert from Canada named William Plotnikov. In 2011 Plotnikov, who was also a boxer, traveled to Dagestan from Canada to join the insurgency. Plotnikov's story has many parallels with Tamerlan's, only he succeeded in joining the insurgency, whereas Tamerlan ultimately failed.

At the age of fifteen, William Plotnikov moved with his parents from Siberia to Toronto, Canada, to build a new life and escape local thugs. In Canada he seemed to integrate well and won local youth boxing championships. His coach subsequently would state that he had the potential to "be a good Olympian."[73] The parents were granted Canadian citizenship in 2008, so he could have fought for the Canadian team.

But in 2009 Plotnikov's search for his religious identity took him to a Toronto mosque. His father would subsequently report, "He just got caught up with a mullah who had very radical views."[74] By September 2010 Plotnikov, who had grown a Muslim-style beard and was praying five times a day, had left his Christian family and traveled to Moscow. His father would report, "William started expressing his radical views, that basically from here he was already a ready-to-go, prepped fighter. He only was looking for a chance to get inside, into mujahed [jihadist] forces."[75]

Plotnikov found his jihad sixteen hundred miles south of Moscow in the mountains of Dagestan. He moved to an ethnic Kumyk village of three thousand south of Makhachkala called Utamysh. There he stood out and ultimately was apprehended by the authorities, who acquired access to his list of Internet contacts from Europe and the United States. Among those he contacted on an Internet social site known as the World Assembly of Muslim Youth was one Tamerlan Tsarnaev.[76]

Although Plotnikov was expelled from Dagestan by the Russian authorities, he later returned and joined a group of local insurgents outside of Utamysh. He was given the *kunya* of "the Canadian" and posted online photos of himself and fellow rebels in the forests of Dagestan armed with assault rifles. At one time he wrote online, "I ask Allah that the next season he'll give us the opportunity to kill as many *kafirs* [nonbelievers] as we can, just to shred them to pieces. Allah is almighty."[77]

But the authorities caught wind of the movement of Plotnikov's unit first and ambushed it in the forests outside of Utamysh on July 13, 2012. During the ensuing firefight, Plotnikov and six other insurgents, including two wanted terrorist leaders, were killed and one security officer was slain. The death of Plotnikov seems to have spooked his Internet contact Tamerlan, who abruptly departed from Dagestan just two days later without waiting for his new Russian passport. An FSB source would later state:

> It seems that Tamerlan Tsarnaev came to Dagestan with the aim of joining the insurgents. It didn't work out. First you need to contact an intermediary, then there is a period of "quarantine" before they take someone. The insurgents check him out over several months. After Nidal and Plotnikov were destroyed and he lost his contacts, Tsarnaev got frightened and fled.[78]

Thus it seems that Tamerlan did not come into direct physical contact with any Dagestani insurgents, much less receive training from them to make the Boston Marathon bomb as the previously quoted US congressmen suggested. In fact, much of his actions in Dagestan seem less threatening than they might appear at first blush. According to most sources, Tamerlan actually was something between a distrusted outsider and an aspirational or "wannabe" jihadi during his stay in Dagestan. Habib Magomedov, a member of Dagestan's antiterrorism commission, stated: "My presumed theory is that he evidently came here, he was looking for contacts, but he did not find serious contacts, and if he did, they didn't trust him."[79] A Russian security source similarly stated, "At the moment, we have no credible information about the Tsarnaev brothers' involvement with the Caucasus Emirate movement."[80] The head of Dagestan's Security Council, Magomed Baachilov, also said there was "no evidence Tamerlan associated with Caucasian Emirate militants."[81] A spokesman for the Dagestani Security Council said, "If this young man had indeed been mixed up in something, and if his activities undermined the country's security, he would not have left the country."[82] The FBI carried out its own investigation in Dagestan after the Marathon bombing, and one senior official summed up its findings as follows: "At this point it looks like they [the Tsarnaev brothers] were homegrown violent extremists. We certainly aren't in a position to rule anything out, but at this point we haven't found anything substantive that ties them to a terrorist group."[83]

Support for this theory of a lack of Caucasian Emirate connections to Tamerlan and the Boston Marathon bombing plot also came from a most unexpected source, the local branch of this terrorist organization, the Vilayat of Dagestan. This terrorist group, which typically claimed its terrorist attacks, adamantly denied any link to the Boston Marathon bombing, stating:

After the events in Boston, the US, information has been distributed in the press saying that one of the Tsarnaev brothers spent 6 months in Dagestan in 2012. On this basis, there are speculative assumptions that he may have been associated with the Mujahideen of the Caucasus Emirate, in particular with the Mujahideen of Dagestan. The Command of the Province of Dagestan indicates in this regard that the Caucasian

Mujahideen are not fighting against the United States of America. We are
at war with Russia, which is not only responsible for the occupation of the
Caucasus, but also for heinous crimes against Muslims. Also, remember
that even in respect to the enemy state of Russia, which is fighting the
Caucasus Emirate, there is an order by the Emir Dokku Umarov, which
prohibits strikes on civilian targets. In this regard, the Command of the
Mujahideen of the Province of Dagestan urges the media, primarily the
American, to halt speculations and promotion of Russian propaganda.[84]

As this statement indicates, the Caucasian Emirate had in fact issued
a moratorium on terror strikes against civilians in January of 2012. Its last
major terrorist strike had been the Domodedovo International Airport
attack of January 2011. At the time of the April 15, 2013, Boston Marathon
bombing, this order banning attacks on civilians was still in effect (it was
not lifted again until the summer of 2013 on the eve of the Sochi Olympics). To compound matters, the Caucasian Emirate had never before
carried out attacks on Western targets. While the Caucasian Emirate occasionally issued boilerplate diatribes against the US occupation of Iraq
and Afghanistan, these were never translated to terror attacks on the distant United States of America. There was no precedent for the Caucasian
Emirate to the attack the distant United States, especially at a time when
it had declared a moratorium on terror attacks on civilians.

Scholars of the Caucasus tend to agree with the Emirate's statements.
Professor Jean-Francois Ratelle at George Washington University, who
has spent time in Dagestan, stated that while the Caucasian Emirate sees
America as an enemy of Islam in the generic sense (because of its occupation of Muslim Iraq and Afghanistan), "They wouldn't be likely to
provide training for an attack on the U.S."[85]

We can thus rule out the idea that Tamerlan was actively recruited and
trained to attack the United States by the Dagestani branch of the Caucasian Emirate. But was Tamerlan radicalized by other extremists while he
was in Dagestan? Was he somehow inspired to carry out this act of senseless terrorism in Boston by someone else in this notorious epicenter of
jihadi radicalism in the Russian Federation?

The seemingly unanimous opinion of Dagestanis who met Tamerlan
was that he already had become an ardent convert to the idea of wag-

ing holy war *prior* to his arrival in their land. One of the members of the Islamist group the "Union of the Just," with whom Tamerlan associated while in Dagestan, for example, stated: "He already had jihad views when he came."[86] Another friend of Tamerlan said, "He was not radicalized here; there was no big change in his mentality. He left here the same as he came."[87] In addition, the imam (chief priest) at the al-Nadiria Salafite mosque on Kotrova Street that Tamerlan attended was adamant that his mosque "had nothing to do with Tsarnaev's turn to radicalism or with the Boston bombings."[88]

The conventional wisdom in Dagestan and Chechnya among neighbors of Tamerlan and Anzor and friends whom Tamerlan met during his stay in Dagestan in the spring and summer of 2012 is that he brought his beliefs on jihad with him when he arrived. Both Chechens and Dagestanis reject the implication that Tamerlan became radicalized during his brief stay in Dagestan and during several brief visits to family in neighboring Chechnya. Ramazan Kadyrov, the president of Chechnya, captured this prevailing viewpoint and distanced the Chechens from the Boston Marathon attack when he said, "Any attempt to make a link between Chechnya and the Tsarnaevs, if they are guilty, is in vain. They grew up in the United States, their views and beliefs were formed there. The roots of evil must be searched for in America."[89] A Dagestani minister similarly stated, "The desire to present the situation in a way that shows Tsarnaev took up radical Islam in the Caucasus is an attempt to cast blame on others."[90]

As previously noted, the very Islamist group that Tamerlan associated with during his stay in Dagestan agrees with these assessments. Far from radicalizing Tamerlan, the members of the Union of the Just claim that he tried converting them to a more radical path. As it transpires, the Union of the Just is not a militant jihadist group. According to a *Time* magazine account of the Union of the Just, which was founded by Tamerlan's cousin Magomed Kartashov, "Kartashov's group has never been linked to any acts of terrorism. It is seen in the region as a civil-society organization, which argues that nonviolent resistance is more effective than militancy in spreading the principles of Shari'a."[91] According to Kartashov's lawyer, Tamerlan tried to "pull him to extremism," and Kartashov "tried to talk [Tsarnaev] out of his interest in extremism."[92] The *New York Times* similarly reported that Tamerlan "was apparently interested in radicalism well before he came to Russia, and that they [the five members of the Union of the Just] tried to dissuade him from supporting local militant groups."[93] The Union of the Just's founder, Kartashov, is reported to have spent hours trying to convince Tamerlan not to "go to the forest" (i.e., join the militants).[94] Kartashov and his followers considered the jihadists' insurgency to be "banditry" and a civil war that only resulted in Muslims killing each other. He urged Tamerlan to "embrace nonviolence and forget about Dagestan's troubles."[95]

Thus the members of the Union of the Just did not radicalize Tamerlan or inspire him to become a terrorist since they themselves did not support violent jihad. But they may have impacted him in another sense. While the Union of the Just did not support the insurgency in Dagestan or Tamerlan's efforts to join it, it will be recalled that its members proudly burned American flags in protest against the production of the American-made, anti-Islamic movie *The Innocence of the Muslims*. They were also known for their globalist rhetoric attacking the United States for its occupation of the Muslim lands of Iraq and Afghanistan. Several sources have reported that as Tamerlan heeded Kartashov's advice to "forget about Dagestan's troubles," he began to adopt a more globalist view on jihad. *Time* magazine, for example, reports: "The members of Kartashov's circle say they tried to disabuse Tsarnaev of his sympathies for local militants. By the end of his time in Dagestan, Tsarnaev's interests seem to have shifted from the local insurgency to a more global notion of Islamic struggle — closer to the one espoused by Kartashov's organization."[96]

In her important article on the younger brother, Dzhokhar Tsarnaev (who of course never travelled to Dagestan to be radicalized), Janet Reitman of *Rolling Stone* similarly writes, "By early summer [2012], Tamerlan was talking about holy war 'in a global context.'"[97] She then writes, "Dissuaded from his quest to wage jihad in Dagestan, he apparently turned his gaze upon America, the country that, in his estimation, had caused so much suffering, most of all his own."[98] As Tamerlan began to subscribe to the globalist Islamic ideology of the Union of the Just, instead of the localized jihad against the pro-Russian secular authorities, he appears to have focused his attention on the "Great Satan," America.

Outward signs of Tamerlan's transformation from what has been described as a "dandy" by neighbors in Makhachkala into a global-style

Islamist came in his appearance. When he arrived in Dagestan, Tamerlan stood out wearing his "Eurotrash" flashy clothing. One neighbor said, "He dressed in a very refined way. His boots were the same color as his clothes. They were summer boots, light, with little holes punched in the leather."[99] Another neighbor stated, "It was 40°C (104° Fahrenheit) and he was wearing these American boots. He was stylish, kind, good-looking."[100] On one occasion he almost got into fight in a mosque because of his garish Euro clothing.[101]

But then Tamerlan suddenly changed his look and began to dress like a global jihadist. A friend of his from the Kortova Street al-Nadiria mosque claimed that Tamerlan began to grease his hair with olive oil and wear dark kohl underliner makeup in an effort to "affect contemporary jihadist fashion."[102] He also grew a Wahhabi-Salafist–style beard as he underwent his transformation and began to don a *shalwar kameez* (a baggy shirt and pants worn by Pakistanis and Afghans that was adopted by Arab jihadists who fought in these countries).[103] His newfound jihadist look did not, however, win him over to the local Salafite Dagestanis who, while wearing long beards, tend to wear tracksuits and T-shirts.[104] His fellow congregants at the al-Nadiria mosque found his affectation to be brash and feared it would bring them to the attention of the authorities. One of them would later state of Tamerlan, "There are some people who take things too far. Everyone is being watched."[105]

With the deaths of Plotnikov and Nidal severing his limited ties to local jihadist insurgents, Tamerlan the wannabe jihadist with a newfound sense of global (as opposed to Dagestani) vision and mission returned to Cambridge in July 2012. Donning his new Wahhabi-style beard, he also brought with him knowledge of how jihadists in Dagestan waged war against *kafir* (infidel) societies like the one waiting for him back in America. They did so with bombs like the ones that killed 13 people and wounded more than 130 while he was in Dagestan.

The next step was to learn how to create a bomb like the ones that the Dagestani jihadists regularly set off in Makhachkala to shred the sense of security of the *kafir* secular-Sufi society around them. This was easier to do than one might imagine because of the efforts of a fellow American-turned-Al Qaeda-recruiter named Anwar al-Awlaki. Awlaki was a Yemeni American born in Las Cruces, New Mexico, who traveled to his ancestral homeland, joined Al Qaeda in the Arabian Peninsula, and became known as the "bin Laden of the Internet." In addition to fiery, hate-filled sermons posted on the Internet in English that were said to inspire such terrorists as Nidal Hassan (an American Arab who killed thirteen people in 2009 at an army base in Texas), he and his coauthor Samir Khan (a Pakistani American who claimed he was "proud to be a traitor to America") also created an online magazine titled *Inspire*.

Inspire, which came online in the fall of 2010, claimed to promote "open source jihad" and served as a virtual training camp for English-speaking would-be jihadists across the globe. In its pages, Muslim extremists could read such inspirational articles as "The Ultimate Mowing Machine," which taught its readers how to mow down infidels in crowded places by driving a car into them. Other articles were on how to blow up buildings. But perhaps the most dangerous article was one in the summer 2010 issue titled, "How to Build a Bomb in the Kitchen of Your Mom." This article provided instructions on how to use a pressure cooker, fireworks, and shrapnel made from nails and steel pellets to create a deadly IED-style bomb. Ominously, the article then advised, "The ideal location [for a bombing] is a place where there are a maximum number of pedestrians and the least number of vehicles. In fact if you can get through to 'pedestrian only' locations that exist in some downtown areas, that would be fabulous."[106]

Fortunately, Awlaki and his coauthor Samir Khan were killed by a CIA drone strike in Yemen in 2011, but their poisonous message lived on via the Internet for homegrown, self-radicalized terrorists known as "lone wolves" to learn from.[107]

Meanwhile, back in Cambridge, Tamerlan's mother would subsequently report that her son "was reading, always in front of the computer — he was taking classes on the Koran," and his ex-girlfriend would later testify to his "growing interest in videos about Islam."[108] But his Internet search history reveals that he was listening to more than just sermons denouncing such evils as Harry Potter or promoting the myth that America carried out the 9/11 attacks as an excuse to conquer Iraq and seize its oil.[109] Among the Internet sites he visited was a website featuring a Dagestani jihadist named Abu Dujana and his gun-toting comrades, who called on young men to embrace jihad. Dujana boldly stated in his online message: "If you think Islam can be spread without spilling a single drop of blood, you're wrong" and "only cowards and hypocrites seek excuses not to join the jihad."[110] A YouTube account by Tamerlan in August 2012, a month after he returned from Dagestan, also included in one playlist a video dedicated to the prophecy of the Black Banners of Khorasan.[111] This prophecy, which predicts that the "soldiers of Allah" will march from Khorasan (modern-day Afghanistan vicinity) and liberate Jerusalem at the end of time, has been a central message embraced by Al Qaeda members and other jihadists.[112]

It was perhaps only a matter of time before Tamerlan, or "Timmy," whose American friends said had gone from "hanging out and partying all the time" to someone described as "anti-fun," discovered Awlaki's online instructions on how to make a crude bomb during his Internet searches on jihad.[113] These instructions would enable the wannabe jihadi who had spent the summer in Dagestan to act out his dream of becoming a holy warrior against the *kafir* society that he blamed for invading Iraq and Afghanistan.

The Inspectors General of the Intelligence Community (i.e., the FBI, CIA, NSA, Homeland Security, DIA, etc.) would later report that Tamerlan had seven copies of "How to Make a Pressure Cooker in the Kitchen of Your Mom" on his computer.[114] The House Homeland Security Committee would report that Tamerlan followed the step-by-step instructions in this online manual to construct a replica of the bomb described by Awlaki.[115]

As horrible as it was, the death toll of three from the Boston Marathon bombs set off on April 15, 2013, paled in comparison to those that regularly devastated Dagestan (largely because there were so many paramedic first responders at the bombing site and some of the best hospitals in the world within a few miles). The Boston attack nonetheless was to be the largest terror bombing on US soil since 9/11. Many Americans discovered Chechens for the first time in this context and were at a loss to explain why this people would want to attack their country after the Tsarnaevs had received sanctuary from the wars devastating their homeland. As a delighted Al Qaeda published an issue of *Inspire* dedicated to Tamerlan, his younger brother Dzhokhar, who was wounded in the shoot-out and hiding from the police in nearby Waltham, scribbled out a manifesto that

explained his motives. It stated: "The US government is killing our innocent civilians. I can't stand to see such evil go unpunished . . . we Muslims
are one body, you hurt one you hurt us all. Now I don't like killing innocent people it is forbidden in Islam but stop killing our innocent people
and we will stop."

He then summed up his feelings toward his adopted homeland, writing "Fuck America."[116]

Conclusion

Thus a three-dimensional picture finally emerges of an actual Chechen–
Al Qaeda nexus that finally led to a bona fide attack on the United States.
Only the reality is that the human link between these two vastly different
groups, Tamerlan Tsarnaev, had spent the formative years of sixteen to
twenty-six in the United States, did not really speak Chechen, and had
lived in Chechnya for only six months as a child. He was hardly an in-
strument that represented the will of the Chechen people or the goals of
the Chechen rebels' largely defeated terror wing. Tamerlan was far more
American than Chechen and was inspired not by any Chechen strategic
objectives, but by globalist anti-American Islamist ideology. He essentially succumbed to the allure of terroristic jihad in its most nihilistic
form and acted out his own personal mission.

To compound matters, Tamerlan's only real connection with Al Qaeda
seems to have been vicarious, that is, it was via the Internet (and via a
fellow radicalized American named Anwar al-Awlaki). For all the base-
less hype on Chechens as anti-American henchmen doing the bidding
for Al Qaeda, the prosaic reality that emerges is that the extremely weak
case of Tamerlan Tsarnaev is as close as one gets to an example of an
actual Al Qaeda–Chechen collaboration in an attack on the United States
of America.

But the fact that the Tsarnaev brothers' attack in Boston, Massachusetts, had absolutely nothing to do with the aspirations of the war-weary
Chechens will have little impact on most casual observers, who are likely
to define it as yet another example of this "terror race's" fanaticism. Thus
the Chechens, who have indisputably been the primary victims of the
bloody wars with Russia that have been outlined in this history, will con-

tinue to be demonized in the common imagination. Only now they will be defined not just as a barbaric race of highland raiders, hostage takers, suicide bombers, or killers of schoolchildren, but as anti-American terrorists.

This would be a sad fate for a proud people who suffered from brutal colonial subjugation and the loss of their ancient freedom to imperial Russia, a genocidal assault during the Soviet period, and two bloody wars on their small homeland against a much larger enemy that systematically engaged in state-sponsored terrorism and war crimes against them. To help prevent this misperception from taking root, perhaps it is time for the Russian Federation and the West to stop portraying the Chechens as "walking symbols of violent conflict" defined by a "culture of terror" and come to see them for who they are: human beings.[117]

Notes

EPIGRAPH

Wojciech Jagielski, *Towers of Stone: The Battle of Wills in Chechnya* (New York: Seven Stories Press, 2004), 209.

CHAPTER 1. FIRST BLOOD

1 Abdurahman Avtorkhanov, "The Chechens and Ingush during the Soviet Period and Its Antecedents," In *The North Caucasus Barrier*, ed. Marie Bennigsen Broxup (New York: St. Martin's Press. 1992), 153.

2 Robert Schaefer, *From Ghazavat to Jihad: The Insurgency in Chechnya and the North Caucasus* (Santa Barbara, CA: Praeger, 2011), 57.

3 Vladimir Bobrovnikov, *Musulman Severnogo Kavkaza* (Muslims of the Northern Caucasus) (Moscow: Ran, 2002), 19.

4 For more on the Pashtuns, see Brian Glyn Williams. *Afghanistan Declassified: A Guide to America's Longest War* (Pittsburgh: University of Pennsylvania Press. 2011).

5 The feared Crimean Tatar riders known as *akincis* (those who flow over the enemies' lands) had kept the Russians off the southern steppes for hundreds of years. With the fall of this Muslim Tatar khanate, Europe's last descendants of Genghis Khan began to migrate to the lands of their overlords, the Ottoman sultans, and this cleared the way for the Russians to move into the Caucasus. For a history of the Crimean Tatars and their extraordinary experiences under the Ottoman sultans, Russian tsars, and Soviet commissars, and in their post-Soviet struggle to overcome the effects of ethnic cleansing during the Soviet period, see Brian Glyn Williams, *The Crimean Tatars: From Soviet Genocide to Putin's Conquest* (London: Hurst, 2015).

6 The feared Crimean Tatar riders known as *akincis* (those who flow over the enemies' lands) had kept the Russians off the southern steppes for hundreds of years. With the fall of this Muslim Tatar khanate, Europe's last descendants of Genghis Khan began to migrate to the lands of their overlords, the Ottoman sultans, and this cleared the way for the Russians to move into the Caucasus. For a history of the Crimean Tatars and their extraordinary experiences under the Ottoman sultans, Russian tsars, and Soviet commissars, and in their post-Soviet struggle to overcome the effects of ethnic cleansing during the Soviet period, see Brian Glyn Williams. *The Crimean Tatars: From Soviet Genocide to Putin's Conquest* (London: Hurst, 2015).

7 See Brian Glyn Williams, *The Crimean Tatars: The Diaspora Experience and the Forging of a Nation* (Leiden/Boston: Brill, 2001), 159–60, for eyewitness accounts of this migration of the last of the great Islamic nomadic tribes descended from the Huns and Mongols.

8 John Baddeley, *The Russian Conquest of the Caucasus* (London: Curzon, 1992), 487–88.

9 Valery Tishkov, *Chechnya: Life in a War-Torn Society* (Berkeley: University of California Press, 2004), 18–19.

10 V. I. Desiaterik, *Kavkaz v Serdtse Rossi* (The Caucasus in Russia) (Moscow: Pashkov Dom, 2000).

11 Schaefer, *From Ghazavat to Jihad*, 59.

12 Moshe Gammer, "Russian Strategies in the Conquest of Chechnia and Daghestan, 1825-1859," in *The North Caucasus Barrier*, ed. Marie Bennigsen Broxup (New York: St. Martin's Press, 1992), 47.

13 Ibid.

14 Schaefer, *From Ghazavat to Jihad*, 61.

15 For an account of modern Europe's first genocide, see the excellent work by Walter Richmond Commins, *The Circassian Genocide* (New Brunswick, NJ: Rutgers University Press, 2013).

16 Barsabi Baytugan, "The North Caucasus," *Studies on the Soviet Union* 11, no. 1 (1971): 10.

17 Commins, *Circassian Genocide*, 2.

18 "Islamist Rebels Vows Maximum Force to Stop Sochi Olympics," Reuters, July 3, 2013.

19 Baddeley, *Russian Conquest of the Caucasus*, 112.

CHAPTER 2. RESISTANCE

1 Robert Seeley, Russo-Chechen Conflict, 1800–2000: *A Deadly Embrace* (London: Frank Cass, 2001), 13.

2 Baddeley, *Russian Conquest of the Caucasus*, 266.

3 The Russians were, however, strongly shaped by the experience of 240 years of rule by the Mongol Tatars, who dominated their lands from 1238 to 1480.

4 Shamil, however, underestimated the Russians' tremendous capacity to sustain losses and keep fighting.

5 Baddeley, *Russian Conquest of the Caucasus*, 364 n. 27.

6 Moshe Gammer, *Muslim Resistance to the Tsar: Shamil and the Russian Conquest of Chechnia and Dagestan* (London: Cass, 1994), 118–19.

7 Ibid.

8 Moshe Gammer, "Vorontsov's 1845 Expedition against Shamil: A British Report," *Central Asian Survey* 4, no. 4 (1985): 13-33.

9 Anna Zelkina, *In Quest for God and Freedom: Sufi Responses to the Russian Advance in the North Caucasus* (London: Hurst, 2000), 120.

10 Captain Spencer, *Turkey, Russia and the Caucasus* (London: George Routledge, 1854), 362, 365.

11 Seeley, *Russo-Chechen Conflict*, 62 n. 26.

12 Lesley Blanch, *The Sabres of Paradise* (New York: Carroll and Graf, 1960), 267.

13 Leo Tolstoy, *Hadji Murat: A Tale of the Caucasus* (New York: McGraw-Hill, 1965), 132.

14 Ibid., 288–89.

15 Baytugan, "The North Caucasus," 11 n. 23.

16 Richard Pierce, *Russian Central Asia, 1867–1917: A Study in Colonial Rule* (Berkeley: University of California Press, 1960), 1.

CHAPTER 3. GENOCIDE

1 Yo'av Karny, "Chechen Nightmare, Russian Amnesia: Memories of a Day No One Should Forget," *Washington Post*, February 20, 2000.

2 Fred Weir, "Chechenya's Warrior Tradition," *Christian Science Monitor*, March 26, 2002, http://www.csmonitor.com/2002/0326/p06s01-woeu.html.

3 The short-lived Mountain Republic included all the nationalities of the northern Caucasus, including the animist-Christian Ossetians.

4 While many of the Communists in the region were outsiders, there were many Chechen progressives and intellectuals from the lowlands who joined the Communist Party out of a genuine desire to overcome the stifling influence of their traditional leaders and bring the benefits of modernity to their backward people.

5 The "right" of the fifteen Soviet Socialist Republics (SSRs) to secede from the USSR was of course purely theoretical and limited to the Soviet constitution.

6 "A Report by the Commissioner of the People's Commissariat of Finance Who Visited Daghestan in April 23," in *Chechnya: The White Book*, ed. M. Margolev (Moscow, 2000), accessed February 2002, http://www.amina.com/article/whitebook.html.

7 Abdurahman Avtorkhanov, "The Chechens and Ingush during the Soviet Period and Its Antecedents," in *The North Caucasus Barrier*, ed. Marie Bennigsen (New York: St. Martin's Press, 1992), 157–59.

8 "Report on an Operation 1925," in *Chechnya: The White Book*, ed. M. Margolev (Moscow, 2000), accessed Feburary 2002, http://www.amina.com/article/whitebook.html.

9 Anatol Lieven, *Chechnya: Tombstone of Russian Power* (New Haven, CT: Yale University Press, 1998), 318.

10 Avtorkhanov, "The Chechens and Ingush during the Soviet Period and Its Antecedents," 182.

11 J. Otto Pohl, *The Stalinist Penal System: A Statistical History of Soviet Repression and Terror, 1930–1953* (London: Macfarland, 1997), 100.

12 Mark Elliot, "Soviet Military Collaborators during World War II," *Ukraine during World War II: History and Its Aftermath* (Edmonton: Canadian Institute of Ukrainian Studies, 1986), 92.

13 Avtorkhanov, "The Chechens and Ingush during the Soviet Period and Its Antecedents," 183.

14 The Crimean Tatars are not purely Mongols, but are actually part Turkic and descended from the pre-Mongol, Turkic tribes who have roamed the plains of Eurasia since the time of Attila the Hun and his Turkic warriors.

15 Avtorkhanov, *Karta*, 12.

16 It must also be mentioned that hundreds of thousands of Slavic Russians, Ukrainians, and Belorussians collaborated with the Germans during the Second World War and formed whole armies within the Wehrmacht, but the Slavic nations never were punished for their betrayal.

17 Pohl, *Stalinist Penal System*, 100–101 n. 58.

18 Alexander Nekrich, *The Punished Peoples* (New York: W. W. Norton, 1978), 73.

19 Carlotta Gall and Thomas de Waal, *Chechnya: Calamity in the Caucasus* (New York: New York University Press, 1998), 240.

20 "Attn: Comrade Stalin, February 22, 1944," in *Chechnya: The White Book*, ed. M. Margolev (Moscow, 2000), accessed February 2003, www.amina.com/article /whitebook.html.

21 Gall and de Waal, *Chechnya*, 253.

22 Iu. A. Aidev, ed., *Chechentsy: Istoriia i Sovremennost'* (The Chechens: History and Modern Times) (Moscow, 1996), 262.

23 D. Khodzhaev, "Genotsid" (Genocide), in *Tak eto Bylo: Natsional'nye Repressi v SSSR 1919–1952* (Thus It Was: National Repression in the USSR) (Moscow, 1993), 169.

24 Avtorkhanov, *Karta*, 166 n. 54.

25 Ibid., 169.

26 Iu. Manzur, *Chechnia. Tak eto Bylo* (Chechnya: Thus It Was), vol. 2 (Odessa, RU: 1996), 11.

27 Lieven, *Chechnya*, 321 n. 4.

28 D. Khodzhaev, "Genotsid," 178–79.

29 Carlotta Gall and Thomas de Waal, *A Small Victorious War* (Basingstoke, UK: Pan Books, 1997), 66–67.

30 Yo'av Karny, *Highlanders: A Journey to the Caucasus in Quest of Memory* (New York: Farrar, Straus and Giroux, 2000), 227.

31 Sebastian Smith, *Allah's Mountains: The Battle for Chechnya* (London: IB Tauris Publishers, 2001), 61.

32 Avtorkhanov, "The Chechens and Ingush during the Soviet Period and Its Antecedents," 185.

33 Vladimir Bobrovnikov, "Abreki i Gosudarstvo: Kultura Nasiliia na Kavkaze"(Bandits and the State: The Culture of Violence in the Caucasus), *Vestnik Evrazii* 8, no. 1 (2000): 37.

34 Deportees explained to me that all Soviet citizens were identified on the fifth line of their internal passport by their nationality.

35 Yo'av Karny, "Chechen Nightmare, Russian Amnesia: Memories of a Day No One Should Forget," *Washington Post*, February 20, 2000.

36 Mark Taplin, *Open Lands: Travels Through Russia's Once Forbidden Places* (South Royalton, VT: Steerforth Press, 1997), 175.

37 Gall and de Waal, *Chechnya: Calamity in the Caucasus*, 253.

38 Manzur, *Chechnia*, 222 n. 72.

39 Khodzhaev, "Genotsid," 195 n. 75.

40 Smith, *Allah's Mountains*, 61.

41 Karny, "Chechen Nightmare, Russian Amnesia," 244 n. 77.

42 Khodzhaev, "Genotsid," 170 n. 75.

43 Tishkov, *Chechnya*, 28.

44 Brian Glyn Williams, *The Crimean Tatars: The Diaspora Experience and the Forging of a Nation* (Leiden, NL: Brill, 2001), 386–99.

45 J. Otto Pohl, *Ethnic Cleansing in the Soviet Union, 1937–1949* (Westport, CT: Greenwood Press, 1999), 96.

46 Vanora Bennett, *Crying Wolf: The Return of War to Chechnya* (Basingstoke, UK: Picador, 1998), 182.

47 Ironically, many Chechens came to see Kazakhstan as a second home after finally being accepted by the local Kazakhs, who are known for their hospitality. While living in Kazakhstan in 1996, I encountered Chechens on several occasions and found that they had warm feelings toward the local population.

48 Alexander Solzhenitsyn, *The Gulag Archipelago*, vol. 3 (Boulder, CO: Westview Press, 1998), 402.

49 Vitaly Naumkin, *State, Religion and Society in Central Asia: A Post-Soviet Critique* (Reading, NY: Ithaca Press, 1993), 147.

50 For an analysis of the Crimean Tatar deportation and struggle for repatriation based on fieldwork among survivors of this peoples' exile in Uzbekistan and the Tatars' squatter camps in the post-Soviet Crimea, see Williams, *The Crimean Tatars*, chap. 11.

CHAPTER 4. THE FIRST RUSSIAN-CHECHEN WAR

1 Emma Gilligan, *Terror in Chechnya* (Princeton, NJ: Princeton University Press, 2010), 71.

2 Smith, *Allah's Mountains*, 161–62.

3 Gall and de Waal, *Chechnya: A Small Victorious War*, 67.

4 Lieven, *Chechnya: Tombstone of Russian Power*, 322.

5 Gall and de Waal, *Chechnya*, 79.

6 James Hughes, *Chechnya: From Nationalism to Jihad* (Philadelphia: University of Pennsylvania Press, 2007), 12.

7 Ibid.

8 Tishkov, *Chechnya*, 45.

9 Ibid., 25.

10 Brian Glyn Williams, "Commemorating the Deportation in Post-Soviet Chechnya: The Role of Memorialization and Collective Memory in the 1994–96 and

1999–2000 Russo-Chechen Wars," *History and Memory* 12, no. 1 (spring/summer 2000).

11 Ibid.

12 Tony Barber, "Dzokhar Dudayev," *Independent,* April 25, 1996.

13 Tishkov, *Chechnya,* 166.

14 Ibid., 53.

15 Djohkar Dudayev, *Ternisty Put'k Svobode* (The Thorny Road to Freedom) (Vilnius, RU: 1993), 197.

16 Ibid., 63.

17 Ibid., 64.

18 Tishkov, *Chechnya,* 169.

19 Ibid.

20 Smith, *Allah's Mountains,* 125.

21 Alexei Malashenko, "Does Islamic Extremism Exist in Russia?" *Muslim Eurasia: Conflicting Legacies,* ed. Yaacov Roi (London: Frank Cass, 1995), 46.

22 Lieven, *Chechnya,* 357.

23 "Fighting for Chechnya: Is Islam a Factor?" *Wide Angle,* PBS Video, 2001.

24 Lorenzo Vidino, "The Arab Fighters and the Sacralization of the Chechen Conflict," *Al Naklah* (spring 2006).

25 Hughes, *Chechnya,* 65. Gilligan, *Terror in Chechnya,* 25.

26 Svante Cornell, "The Afghanization of the North Caucasus: Causes and Implications of a Changing Conflict," in *Russia's Home Grown Insurgency: Jihad in the North Caucasus,* ed. Stephen Blank (Carlisle Barracks, PA: US Army War College, 2012), 129. Hughes, *Chechnya,* 24.

27 Tishkov, *Chechnya,* 70.

28 Ibid., 73.

29 Gall and de Waal, *Chechnya,* 193.

30 Smith, *Allah's Mountains,* 149.

31 Emil Payin and Arkady Popov, "Chechnya" (Washington, DC: RAND Corp., 1999).

32 Robert Seely, *Russo-Chechen Conflict 1800–2000: A Deadly Embrace* (London: Frank Cass, 2001), 230.

33 Anna Politkovskaya, *A Dirty War* (London: Havrill Press, 2001), 166.

34 Smith, *Allah's Mountains,* 149.

35 "Russia-Chechnya-Massacre," Associated Press, December 18, 1994.

36 Lieven, *Chechnya,* 43.

37 Ibid.

38 Seely, *Russo-Chechen Conflict,* 250.

39 Ibid.

40 "The Siege of Grozny," BBC, December 15, 2010, http://www.bbc.co.uk/programmes/poocc3zn.

41 Politkovskaya, *A Dirty War,* 157.

42 "The First Bloody Battle," *BBC*, March 16, 2000, http://www.bbc.co.uk/programmes/.

43 Ibid.

44 Ibid.

45 Seely, *Russo-Chechen Conflict*, 231.

46 Smith, *Allah's Mountains*, 152–53.

47 Gall and de Waal, *Chechnya*, 167.

48 Smith, *Allah's Mountains*, 152.

49 Lester Grau and Timothy Thomas, "Russian Lessons Learned from the Battle of Grozny," *Marine Corps Gazette*, April 2000.

50 Seely, *Russo-Chechen Conflict*, 230.

51 Lieven, *Chechnya*, 44.

52 Gall and de Waal, *Chechnya*, 9.

53 Ibid., 154.

54 Ibid.

55 Ibid.

56 Ibid.

57 Gall and de Waal, *Chechnya*, 201.

58 Lieven, *Chechnya*, 109.

59 Seely, *Russo-Chechen Conflict*, 243–44.

60 Ibid., 245.

61 "Soldiers on the Front Line and Military Men in Mozdok," *Izvestiia*, January 11, 1995.

62 Ibid., 110.

63 Timothy Thomas, "The Battle of Grozny: Deadly Classroom for Urban Combat," *Parameters* (summer 1999).

64 Gall and de Waal, *Chechnya*, 5.

65 Ibid., 18.

66 Ibid.

67 Ibid., 216.

68 Seely, *Russo-Chechen Conflict*, 255.

69 Ibid., 158.

70 Ibid., 164.

71 Lieven, *Chechnya*, 118.

72 Gall and de Waal, *Chechnya*, 206.

73 Nicholas Clayton, "Portrait of a Chechen Jihadist," *Foreign Policy*, April 19, 2013, http://www.foreignpolicy.com.

74 Thomas, "The Battle of Grozny."

75 Lieven, *Chechnya*, 122.

76 Smith, *Allah's Mountains*, 165.

77 "The Battle(s) of Grozny," *Baltic Defense Review*, no. 2 (1999): 81.

78 Smith, *Allah's Mountains*, 174.

79 Lieven, *Chechnya*, 122.

80 Ibid.

81 Gall and de Waal, *Chechnya*, 242.

82 "The Situation of Human Rights in the Republic of Chechnya in the Russian Federation: Report of the Secretary General," United Nations Commission on Human Rights, Geneva, March 26, 1996, http://www1.umn.edu.

83 Smith, *Allah's Mountains*, 197.

84 Paul Murphy, *The Wolves of Islam* (Washington, DC: Brasseys, 2007), 20.

85 Lieven, *Chechnya*, 33.

86 David Zucchino, "Chechen Commando Chief Recounts Budyonnovsk Raid, Events That Proceeded It," *Baltimore Sun*, July 16, 1995.

87 Richard Beeston, "The Day I Met the Terrorist Mastermind," *Times* (UK), September 4, 2004.

88 Miriam Lanskoy and Ilyas Akhmadov, *The Chechen Struggle: Independence Won and Lost* (New York: Palgrave Macmillan, 2010), 49.

89 Gall and de Waal, *Chechnya*, 265.

90 Smith, *Allah's Mountains*, 203.

91 Kristin M. Bakke, "Copying and Learning from Outsiders?" in *Transnational Dynamics of Civil War*, ed. Jeffrey T. Checkel (Cambridge: Cambridge University Press, 2013), 54.

92 Michael Specter, "Chechen Rebels Said to Kill Hostages at Russian Hospital," *New York Times*, June 16, 1995.

93 Lanskoy and Akhmadov, *The Chechen Struggle*, 53.

94 Lyudmila Leontyeva, "Budyonnovsk: Striking at Rears," *Moscow News*, June 23–29, 1995, 1–2.

95 Ibid.

96 Gall and de Waal, *Chechnya*, 266.

97 Smith, *Allah's Mountains*, 203.

98 "Yelstin Draws Bitter Wrath of Chechens," *New York Times*, April 22, 1996.

99 Smith, *Allah's Mountains*, 204.

100 Steven Erlanger, "Russia Allows Rebels to Leave with Hostages," *New York Times*, June 20, 1995.

101 Gall and de Waal, *Chechnya*, 273.

102 Erlanger, "Russia Allows Rebels to Leave with Hostages."

103 Schaefer, *From Ghazavat to Jihad*, 135.

104 Zucchino, "Chechen Commando Chief Recounts Budyonnovsk Raid."

105 Gall and de Waal, *Chechnya*, 285.

106 Michael Specter, "10 Days That Shook Russia: Siege in the Caucasus," *New York Times*, January 22, 1966.

107 Ibid.

108 Ibid. Gall and de Waal, *Chechnya*, 294.

109 Specter, "10 Days That Shook Russia."

110 Ibid.

111 Seely, *Russo-Chechen Conflict*, 283.

112 Gall and de Waal, *Chechnya*, 303.

113 Paul Tumelty, "The Rise and Fall of the Foreign Fighters in Chechnya," *Terrorism Monitor* 4, no. 2 (January 26, 2002).

114 Fawaz Gerges, *The Far Enemy: Why Jihad Went Global* (Cambridge: Cambridge University Press, 2006), 58.

115 Brian Glyn Williams, "Allah's Footsoldiers: An Assessment of Foreign Fighters and Al Qaida in the Chechen Insurgency," in *Ethno-Nationalism, Islam and the State in the Caucasus: Post-Soviet Disorder*, ed. Moshe Gammer (London: Routledge, 2007).

116 Thomas de Waal, "Greetings from Grozny," PBS.org.

117 Lieven, *Chechnya*, 141.

118 Gall and de Waal, *Chechnya*, 334.

119 Ibid.

120 "Obituary: Dzhokhar Dudayev," *Independent*, April 25, 1996.

121 Tishkov, *Chechnya*, xvi.

122 Brian Glyn Williams, "The Russo Chechen War: A Threat to Stability in the Middle East and Eurasia?" *Middle East Policy* 8, no. 1 (March 2001).

CHAPTER 5. CHAOSISTAN

1 "The 1997 Presidential and Parliamentary Elections in Chechnya," *Prague Watchdog*, January 27, 2007, http://www.watchdog.cz.

2 Emil Souleimanov, "Chechnya, Wahhabism and the Invasion of Dagestan," *MERIA* 9, no. 4 (December 2005).

3 Dmitri Trenin and Alexei Malashenko, *Russia's Restless Frontier: The Chechen Factor in Post-Soviet Russia* (Washington, DC: Carnegie Endowment for International Peace, 2004), 30.

4 "Obituary: Aslan Maskhadov," BBC News, March 8, 2005, http://news.bbc.co.uk.

5 Trenin and Malashenko, *Russia's Restless Frontier*, 30.

6 Ibid., 31.

7 Oleg Lukin, "The 1997 Presidential and Parliamentary Elections in Chechnya," *Prague Watchdog*, January 27, 2007, http://www.watchdog.cz.

8 Akhmadov and Lanskoy, *The Chechen Struggle*, 76.

9 Ibid., 82.

10 Emil Souleimanov, "Chechnya, Wahhabism and the Invasion of Dagestan," *Middle East Review of International Affairs* 9, no. 4 (December 2005): 11.

11 Akhmadov and Lanskoy, *The Chechen Struggle*, 90.

12 Olga Oliker, *Russia's Chechen Wars 1994–2000: Lessons from Urban Combat* (Santa Monica, CA: RAND, 2001), 40, http://www.rand.org.

13 Souleimanov, "Chechnya, Wahhabism and the Invasion of Dagestan," 9.

14 Matthew Evangelista, *The Chechen Wars; Will Russia Go the Way of the Soviet Union?* (Washington, DC: Brookings Institution Press, 2002), 73.

15 Robert Bruce Ware and Enver Kisriev, *Dagestan: Russian Hegemony and Islamic Resistance in the North Caucasus* (London: M. E. Sharpe, 2010), 106.

16 Wojciech Jagielski, *Towers of Stone: The Battle of Wills in Chechnya* (New York: Seven Stories Press, 2004), 63.

17 For an account of the role of foreign fighters in the conflict, see Brian Glyn Williams, "Allah's Foot Soldiers: An Assessment of the Role of Foreign Fighters and Al Qaida in the Chechen Insurgency," in Ethno-Nationalism, Islam and the State in the Caucasus: Post-Soviet Disorder, ed. Moshe Gammer (London: Routledge, 2007).

18 Dimitri Nikolaev, "Terroristy Zdhut Signala," *Nezavisimaia Gazeta* 137, no. 29 (July 1999): 1.

19 Lorenzo Vidino, "The Arab Fighters and the Sacralization of the Chechen Conflict," *Al Naklah* (spring 2006).

20 Sanobar Shermatova, "Tak Nazyvaemye Vakhkhabity" (The So Called Wahhabis), in *Chechnia i Rossiia: Obshchestva i Gosudarstva* (Chechnya and Russia: Societies and States), vol. 3, ed. Dimitri Furman (Moscow: Mysl', 1999), 408–10.

21 John B. Dunlop, *The Moscow Bombings of September 1999* (Stuttgart, DE: Ibidem, 2012), 71.

22 Robert Bruce Ware and Enver Kisriev, *Dagestan: Russian Hegemony and Islamic Resistance in the North Caucasus* (London: M. E. Sharpe, 2010).

23 Khassan Baiev, *The Oath: A Surgeon under Fire* (New York: Walker, 2003), 212–13.

24 Akhmadov and Lanskoy, *The Chechen Struggle*, 16–118.

25 Julie Wilhelmsen, "When Separatists Become Islamists: The Case for Chechnya," Norwegian Defense Research Establishment, Kjeller, Norway, 2004, 30–31.

26 Murphy, *The Wolves of Islam*, 42.

27 Ibid., 62.

28 Emil Souleimanov, "Chechnya, Wahhabism and the Invasion of Dagestan," *Middle East Review of International Affairs* 9, no. 4 (December 2005): 56, http://www.gloria-center.org.

29 Murphy, *The Wolves of Islam*, 41.

30 Ibid., 42.

31 Ibid.

32 Ibid. Akhmadov and Lanskoy, *The Chechen Struggle*, 134.

33 Ibid., 43.

34 Akhmadov and Lanskoy, *The Chechen Struggle*, 138.

35 Ibid., 143.

36 Schaefer, *From Ghazavat to Jihad*, 165.

37 Trenin and Malashenko, *Russia's Restless Frontier*, 33.

38 Murphy, *The Wolves of Islam*, 97.

39 *Gazeta Wybrozca*, June 17, 1999, 3.

40 Ibid., 92.

41 Evangelista, *The Chechen Wars*, 79.

42 Akhmadov and Lanskoy, *The Chechen Struggle*, 152.

43 Murphy, *The Wolves of Islam*, 98–99.

44 Akhmadov and Lanskoy, *The Chechen Struggle*, 153.

45 "Russian Army Operations during the Second Military Campaign in Chechnya," *Moscow Defense Brief*, March 2002, http://mdb.cast.ru.

46 Mikhail Roschin, "Dagestan and the War Next Door," *Perspective* 11, no. 1 (September–October 2000), http://www.bu.edu.

47 Brian Glyn Williams, "The Russo-Chechen War: A Threat to Security in Eurasia?" *Middle East Policy* 3, no. 1 (March 2001), http://www.brianglynwilliams.com.

48 Emil Souleimanov, "Chechnya, Wahhabism and the Invasion of Dagestan," *Middle East Review of International Affairs* 9, no. 4 (December 2005), http://www.gloria-center.org.

49 It has been suggested that the Russians may have allowed Basayev into Dagestan to provide a pretext for invading Chechnya.

50 Ibid.

51 Ibid.

52 Ibid.

53 Mikhail Roschin, "Religious War in Dagestan," Keston News Service, September 15, 1999, http://www.keston.org.uk.

54 Robert Bruce Ware, "A Multitude of Evils: Mythology and Political Failure in Chechnya," in *Chechnya from Past to Future*, ed. Richard Sakwa (London: Anthem Press, 2004), 84.

55 Dunlop, *The Moscow Bombings of September 1999*, 74.

56 Akhmadov and Lanskoy, *The Chechen Struggle*, 154.

57 "The Begin [*sic*] of Second Chechen Conflict 1999 — Russia," Liveleak, http://www.liveleak.com.

58 Charles W. Blandy, "Dagestan the Storm Part I: The 'Invasion' of Dagestan," Conflict Studies Centre, Royal Military Academy Sandhurst, Sandhurst, Berkshire, UK, http://www.network54.com/Forum.

59 Charles Blandy, "Dagestan the Storm Part 2: The Federal Assault on the Kadar Complex," Conflict Studies Centre, Royal Military Academy Sandhurst, Sandhurst, Berkshire, UK, http://www.da.mod.uk/colleges/arag/document-listings/caucasus/P32/view.

60 Ibid.

61 Ibid.

62 Ibid.

63 Ibid.

64 "Russian Army Operations during the Second Military Campaign in Chechnya," *Moscow Defense Brief*, March 2002, http://mdb.cast.ru/mdb/3-2002/ac/raowdsmcc. Marcel de Haas, *Russian Security and Air Power: 1992–2002* (London: Routledge, 2004), 150.

65 Akhmadov and Lanskoy, *The Chechen Struggle*, 156.

66 Baiev, *The Oath*, 246.

67 Dunlop, *The Moscow Bombings of September 1999*, 217.

68 "Russia Hit by New Islamic Offensive," BBC News, September 5, 1999, http://news.bbc.co.uk.

69 Gregory Felfer, "Ten Years on Troubling Questions Linger over Russia's Apartment Bombings," Radio Free Europe/Radio Liberty, September 9, 2009, http://www.rferl.org.

70 Gregrory Felfer, "Three Years Later Russia Apartment Bombings Remain Unsolved," Radio Free Europe/Radio Liberty, September 6, 2002.

71 Maura Reynolds, "Fear of Bombing Turns to Doubt for Some in Russia," *Los Angeles Times*, January 15, 2000, http://articles.latimes.com.

72 Ibid.

73 Ibid.

74 Dunlop, *The Moscow Bombings of September 1999*, 79.

75 David Satter, "The Shadow of Ryazan: Is the Putin Government Legitimate?" *National Review*, April 30, 2002, http://old.nationalreview.com.

76 Tom de Waal, "Russia's Bombs: Who Is to Blame?" BBC News, September 30, 1999, http://news.bbc.co.uk.

77 Carlotta Gall, "Rebel Leader, Denying Terror, Fights to Free Chechnya," *New York Times*, October 16, 1999, http://www.nytimes.com.

78 Ibid.

79 Michael Specter, "Chechen Insurgents Take Their Struggle to Moscow Park," *New York Times*, November 24, 1995.

80 Akhmadov and Lanskoy, *The Chechen Struggle*, 162.

81 Robert Bruce Ware and Enver Kisriev, *Dagestan: Russian Hegemony and Islamic Resistance in the North Caucasus* (London: M. E. Sharpe, 2010), 125.

82 Edward Walker, "Ethnic War, Holy War, War o War," University of California, Berkeley, February 1, 2006.

83 Reuven Paz, "Al Khattab: From Afghanistan to Dagestan," International Policy Institute for Counter Terrorism, September 20, 1999, http://web.archive.org/web/20001217021000/ and http://www.ict.org.il.

84 Murphy, *The Wolves of Islam*, 105.

85 Will Englund, "Wave of Apartment Bombings in Russia Appears Unstoppable," *Baltimore Sun*, September 17, 1999.

86 Peter Reddaway and Dmitri Glinski, *The Tragedy of Russia's Reforms: Market Bolshevism against Democracy* (Washington, DC: United States Institute of Peace, 2001), 615–16.

87 "Na Svobode Ostalsia tol'ko odin vzryvnik," *Kommersant*, October 12, 2002, http://kommersant.ru/doc/355437.

88 Nabi Abullaev, "Buinaksk Apartment Bombers Convicted," *Moscow Times*, no. 2164 (March 20, 2001),| http://www.themoscowtimes.com. Seidula Abdulaev,

"Buinaksk Bombers Jailed," Institute for War and Peace Reporting, March 23, 2001, http://iwpr.net.

89 Gilligan, *Terror in Chechnya*, 31. de Haas, *Russian Security and Air Power*, 159.

90 "Chechens Rounded up in Moscow," *Guardian*, September 17, 1999, http://www.theguardian.com.

91 Gregory Felfer, "Ten Years on Troubling Questions Linger over Russia's Apartment Bombings," Radio Free Europe/Radio Liberty, September 9, 2009, http://www.rferl.org.

92 Gilligan, *Terror in Chechnya*, 32.

93 Felfer, "Ten Years on Troubling Questions Linger over Russia's Apartment Bombings."

94 Simon Shuster, "How the War on Terrorism Did Russia a Favor," *Time*, September 19, 2011, http://content.time.com.

95 Dunlop, *The Moscow Bombings of September 1999*, 81.

96 Andrei Piontikowsky, "Russia Goes Nuclear over Chechnya," *Jamestown Foundation Prism*, no. 17 (September 1999): 3.

97 David Hoffman, "Miscalculations Paved Path to Chechen War," *Washington Post*, March 20, 2000.

98 Jagielski, *Towers of Stone*, 99.

CHAPTER 6. THE RETURN OF THE RUSSIANS

1 Gilligan, Terror in Chechnya, 46.

2 Hughes, *Chechnya*, 158.

3 John Coffey, "Putin's Statecraft," *American Diplomacy* (January 2012). "Putin's Language Is Becoming the Talk of the Vulgar," *Telegraph* (UK), November 8, 2003.

4 Andrei Piontikowsky, "Russia Goes Nuclear over Chechnya," *Jamestown Foundation Prism*, no. 17 (September 1999): 3.

5 Timothy L. Thomas, "Grozny 2000: Urban Combat Lessons Learned," *Military Review* (July–August 2000).

6 Dunlop, *The Moscow Bombings of September 1999*, 62.

7 Schaefer, *From Ghazavat to Jihad*, 179.

8 Oliker, *Russia's Chechen Wars 1994–2000*, 37.

9 Dunlop, *The Moscow Bombings of September 1999*, 81.

10 Andrew Meier, *Black Earth: A Journey through Russia after the Fall* (New York: W. W. Norton, 2003), 96.

11 Michael Gordon, "Russians Issue an Ultimatum to Rebel City," *New York Times*, December 7, 1999, http://www.nytimes.com.

12 "UK Condemns Chechnya Ultimatum," BBC News, December 7, 1999, http://news.bbc.co.uk/2/hi/uk_news/politics/554075.stm.

13 Evangelista, *The Chechen Wars*, 148.

14 Ibid., 159.

15 "Russians Fired on Refugees," BBC News, December 4, 1999, http://news.bbc.co
.uk/2/hi/europe/549893.stm.

16 Schaefer, *From Ghazavat to Jihad*, 189.

17 "Interview with Field Commander Shamil Basayev," *Cecna.webpartk*, February
20, 2000, http://cecna.webpark.cz/chechenwar_fil/html/basayev2.html (origi-
nally posted on the Chechen website qoqaz.net).

18 Amnesty International, "Russian Federation: Chechnya: For the Motherland—
Reported Grave Breaches of International Humanitarian Law," December 1999,
p. 5, www.amnesty.org.

19 For a demonstration of an FAE explosion, see US Naval Air Warfare Center
Weapons Division, China Lake, California, http://www.nawcwpns.navy.mil
/clmf/faeseq.html.

20 Lester Grau and Timothy Smith, "Crushing Victory: Fuel-Air Explosives and
Grozny 2000," *Marine Corps Gazette*, August 2000.

21 "Backgrounder on Fuel Air Explosives (Vacuum Bombs)," *Human Rights Watch*,
February 1, 2000.

22 Baiev, *The Oath*, 260.

23 Meier, *Black Earth*, 97.

24 Oliker, *Russia's Chechen Wars 1994–2000*, 40.

25 Ibid., 67.

26 "Russian Tanks Pounding Grozny from 3 Directions," *New York Times*, December 18, 1999.

27 Oliker, *Russia's Chechen Wars 1994–2000*, 50.

28 Ibid., 58.

29 Timothy L. Thomas, "Grozny 2000: Urban Combat Lessons Learned," *Military
Review* (July–August 2000).

30 "Russia Seizes Chechnya's Second-Largest City," CNN, November 12, 1999,
http://edition.cnn.com.

31 John Hughes, "The Peace Process in Chechnya," in *Chechnya: From the Past to
the Future*, ed. Richard Sakwa (London: Anthem Press, 2005), 284.

32 "Russians Ambushed in Grozny," BBC News, December 16, 1999, http://news
.bbc.co.uk/2/hi/europe/566842.stm.

33 Ian Traynor and Amelia Gentleman, "Russians in Grozny Bloodbath," *Guardian*,
US edition, December 15, 1999, http://www.theguardian.com.

34 While other sources put the breakout on the night of January 31/February 1, I
have gone with the dates used by Chechen sources, including Ilyas Akhmadov
and Khassan Baiev, not by Western media sources.

35 Lanskoy and Akhmadov, *The Chechen Struggle*, 176.

36 Lyoma Turpalov, "Carnage on the Road Out of Grozny," *Guardian*, US edition,
February 4, 2000, http://www.theguardian.com.

37 Schaefer, *From Ghazavat to Jihad*, 191.

38 Baiev, *The Oath*, 294.

39 Ibid., 294.

40 Ibid.

41 Ibid. Lanskoy and Akhmadov, *The Chechen Struggle*, 176.

42 Ibid.

43 "Chechen Rebels Break Out of Grozny," *Moscow Times*, February 1, 2000, http://www.themoscowtimes.com.

44 "Chechen Fighters 'Abandon Grozny,'" BBC News, February 1, 2000, http://news.bbc.co.uk/2/hi/europe/626959.stm.

45 Baiev, *The Oath*, 306–309.

46 Ibid., 280.

47 Steve Rosenberg, "Operating on the Enemy in the Two Chechen Wars," BBC News, October 7, 2012, http://www.bbc.co.uk/news/magazine-19811823.

48 "Interview with Field Commander Shamil Basayev," *Cecna.webpartk*, February 20, 2000, http://cecna.webpark.cz/chechenwar_fil/html/basayev2.html (first posted on the Chechen website qoqaz.net).

49 Schaefer, *From Ghazavat to Jihad*, 193.

50 "The Case of Maskhodova and Others *vs.* Russia," European Court of Human Rights, Strasbourg, France, June 6, 2013, http://hudoc.echr.coe.int/.

51 "Maskhadov Calls for Halt to Military Operations in Chechnya," *Interfax*, December 15, 1999.

52 Gilligan, *Terror in Chechnya*, 48.

53 Ibid., 35.

54 Paul Murphy, *Allah's Angels: Chechen Women in War* (Annapolis, MD: Naval Institute Press, 2010), 36.

55 Gilligan, *Terror in Chechnya*, 45.

56 Scott Peterson, "Heavy Civilian Toll in Chechnya's 'Unlimited Violence,'" *Christian Science Monitor*, December 11, 2000, http://www.csmonitor.com/2000/1211/p7s1.html.

57 Ibid.

58 Gilligan, *Terror in Chechnya*, 3.

59 Ibid., 63.

60 Ibid., 70.

61 Ibid.

62 Ibid., 69.

63 Ibid., 74.

64 Ibid., 91.

65 Ibid., 80.

66 Ibid., 92.

67 "Cries from Putin's Torture Pit: John Sweeney Reports on the Horror of a Russian Prison Camp in Chechnya," *Observer*, October 14, 2000.

68 Michael Wines, "Russia to Investigate a Mass Grave in Chechnya," *New York Times*, February 26, 2001.

69 Amnesty International, "Chechnya: Crime and Punishment," April 5, 2000, http://www.amnesty.org.uk.

70 Gilligan, *Terror in Chechnya*, 58.

71 Ibid.

72 Evangelista, *The Chechen Wars*, 193.

73 Maura Reynolds, "War Has No Rules for Fighting Forces in Chechnya," *Los Angeles Times*, September 17, 2000.

74 Gilligan, *Terror in Chechnya*, 79.

75 "The 'Dirty War' in Chechnya: Forced Disappearances, Torture and Summary Executions," *Human Rights Watch* 13, no. 1 (March 2001), http://www.hrw.org.

76 Schaefer, *From Ghazavat to Jihad*, 193.

77 "All Captured on Camera: The Last Shots of the Perm Omon," *St. Petersburg Times*, May 14, 2002.

78 Evangelista, *The Chechen Wars*, 152.

79 Ibid.

80 "Military Super Hawk Speaks Out on Chechnya," *Chechnya Weekly*, November 20, 2000, http://archive.is/dFPfJ#selection-1141.401–1141.562.

81 Ibid.

82 Budanov was later sentenced to eight years in jail, but was released early for good behavior.

83 Schaefer, *From Ghazavat to Jihad*, 193

84 Gilligan, *Terror in Chechnya*, 125.

85 John Reuter, "Chechnya's Suicide Bombers: Desperate, Devout, or Deceived?" American Committee for Peace in Chechnya, August 23, 2004, accessed December 4, 2014, http://www.radicalparty.org.

86 Anna Politkovskaya, *A Small Corner of Hell: Dispatches from Chechnya* (Chicago: University of Chicago Press, 2002), 181.

87 John Dunlop, *The 2002 Dubrovka and 2004 Beslan Hostage Crises* (Stuttgart, DE: Ibidem, 2006), 109.

88 Fred Weir, "Hostage Crisis Refuels Chechnya Debate," *Christian Science Monitor*, October 25, 2002.

89 Sabrina Tavernise, "Cellphones Let Families Hear Ordeal of Captives," *New York Times*, October 25, 2002.

90 Ibid.

91 Dunlop, *The 2002 Dubrovka and 2004 Beslan Hostage Crises*, 141.

92 Ibid., 136.

93 Ibid., 144.

94 "How Special Forces Ended Seige," BBC News, October 29, 2002, http://news.bbc.co.uk.

95 Ibid.

96 Ibid.

97 Susan Glasser, "Russia Confirms Suspicions about Gas Used in Raid," *Washington Post*, October 31, 2002.

98 Claire Bigg, "The Dubrovka Theater Seige in Moscow, a Decade Later," *Atlantic Monthly*, October 23, 2012, http://www.theatlantic.com.

99 Ibid., 146.

100 Dunlop, *The 2002 Dubrovka and 2004 Beslan Hostage Crises*, 137.

101 Jagielski, *Towers of Stone*, 206.

102 Kristin M. Bakke, "Copying and Learning from Outsiders?" in *Transnational Dynamics of Civil War*, ed. Jeffrey T. Checkel (Cambridge: Cambridge University Press, 2009), 50.

103 Schaefer, *From Ghazavat to Jihad*, 168.

104 "Dozens Killed in Raid by Chechen Rebels on Ingushetia," *Guardian*, June 22, 2004.

105 "Napeadenie na Nalchik" (Attack on Nalchik), Agentura.ru, http://www.agentura.ru.

106 "Nalchik Raid Leaves Painful Legacy," Radio Free Europe/Radio Liberty, March 13, 2014, http://www.rferl.org.

107 "Chechen Guerilla Leader Calls Russians Terrorists," ABC News, July 25, 2009, http://abcnews.go.com/Nightline/International.

108 "Two Moscow Concert Bombers Kill 14," CNN.com, July 6, 2003, http://edition.cnn.com.

109 Steven Lee Myers, "Suicide Bomber Kills 5 in Moscow Near Red Square," *New York Times*, December 10, 2003.

110 "Russian Plane Crash Caused by Explosives," NBCNews.com, August 30, 2004, http://www.nbcnews.com.

111 Dunlop, *The 2002 Dubrovka and 2004 Beslan Hostage Crises*, 43.

112 Ibid., 52.

113 Ibid., 78. But it must be stated that this group of predominantly Ingush terrorists were no angels, and during the course of the three-day siege, they executed twenty of their hostages (adult males, not children).

114 Ibid., 64.

115 "The Whole World Is Crying," *Time*, September 20, 2004.

116 Ibid., 82.

117 Ibid., 83, 87.

118 *Chechnya Weekly*, October 11, 2004.

119 Ibid., 92.

120 Ibid., 88.

121 John Giduck, *Terror at Beslan* (Toronto: Archangel Group, 2005), 148.

122 Ibid., 95, 96.

123 David Satter, "The Truth about Beslan: What Putin's Government Is Covering Up," *Weekly Standard*, November 13, 2006, http://www.weeklystandard.com.

124 "Chechen Claims Beslan Attack," CNN.com, September 17, 2004, http://edition
.cnn.com.

125 "Excerpt: Basayev Claims Beslan," BBC News, September 17, 2004, http://news
.bbc.co.uk.

126 Jonathan Kay, "How Did Chechya's Culture of Terror Come to Boston?" *National Post*, April 19, 2013.

127 "Who Ordered Khattab's Death?" *North Caucasus Analyst*, May 29, 2002, http://
www.webcitation.org.

128 Paul Tumelty, "The Rise and Fall of the Foreign Fighters in Chechnya," *Terrorism Monitor* 4, no. 2 (January 31, 2006), http://www.webcitation.org.

129 "Masxadova Zastrelil Okrannik," Agentura.ru, http://www.agentura.ru/news
/21800/.

130 "March 8, 2005: Day of Martyrdom of Chechen President Aslan Maskhadov,"
Kavkaz Center, http://www.kavkazcenter.com.

131 "New Chechen Leader Vows No More Hostage Takings," Radio Free Europe/
Radio Liberty, June 3, 2005.

132 Ibid.

133 "Russia Braces for Terrorism's Return as 38 Die in Subway Bombings," *Washington Post*, March 30, 2010.

134 Dimitri Shlapentokh, "The Rise of the Chechen Emirate?" *Middle East Quarterly* (summer 2008).

135 Tom Parfitt, "The Battle for the Soul of Chechnya," *Guardian*, November 22,
2007, http://www.theguardian.com.

136 "Is the Caucasian Emirate a Threat to the Western World?" *North Caucasus Weekly*, December 7, 2007, http://www.jamestown.org.

137 "Za Nevskii Ekspress Obvinili i Opravdali" (Charges and Acquittals for Nevsky Express), *Kommersant*, January 4, 2010, http://www.kommersant.ru/doc
/1346687.

138 "Second Moscow Bomber Identified," BBC News, April 6, 2010, http://news.bbc
.co.uk.

139 "Chechen Rebel Says He Ordered Moscow Metro Attacks," BBC News, March 31,
2010, http://news.bbc.co.uk.

140 "North Caucasus Insurgency Leader Seeks to Prevent Sochi Olympics," Radio
Free Europe/Radio Liberty, March 17, 2014.

141 "Doku Umarov, Top Chechen Rebel Leader Who Threatened Olympics, Reportedly Killed by Russian Forces," CBS News, January 17, 2014.

142 "Shamil Became a Shaheed (*insha'Allah*)," Kavkaz Center, July 10, 2006, http://
www.webcitation.org/60XaWcGhR.

143 "Shamilya Basaeva Uznaut po Rukam i Noge," *Kommersant*, July 12, 2006, http://
www.webcitation.org/60XiDbiTP.

144 "Chechen Rebel Chief Basayev Dies," BBC News, July 10, 2006, http://news.bbc
.co.uk.

145 "Rebels' Dilemma after Basayev's Death," BBC News, July 12, 2006, http://news .bbc.co.uk.

146 "Shamil Basayev," *Economist*, June 13, 2006, http://www.economist.com/node /7160644.

147 "Chechnya Vow Casts Long Shadow," *Moscow Times*, February 26, 2008.

148 "Chechnya's Pro-Moscow President Rebuilds Nation," NPR, November 13, 2007.

149 "Chechens Now Fighting on Both Sides in the Ukraine," Radio Free Europe/ Radio Liberty, August 30, 2014.

150 "In Rebuilt Grozny, an Awkward Peace with Russia," *Globe and Mail*, March 9, 2012.

151 "Chechnya Vow Casts a Long Shadow," *Moscow Times*, February 26, 2008.

152 "Rebels' Dilemma after Basayev's Death," BBC News, July 12, 2006, http://news .bbc.co.uk.

CHAPTER 7. THE CHECHEN GHOST ARMY OF AFGHANISTAN AND SYRIAN BATTALION

1 C. J. Chivers, "Boston Attacks Turn Spotlight on Troubled Region of Chechnya," New York Times, April 20, 2013.

2 Sharon LaFraniere, "Moscow Eager to Tie Rebels in Chechnya to Bin Laden," *Washington Post*, September 26, 2001, http://www.washingtonpost.com.

3 Brian Glyn Williams, "From Secessionist 'Rebels' to 'Al Qaeda Shock Brigades': Critically Assessing Russia's Efforts to Extend the Post-September 11th War on Terror to Chechnya," *Comparative Studies on South Asia, Africa, and the Middle East* 23, no. 2 (2003), http://www.brianglynwilliams.com.

4 Ibid.

5 Ibid.

6 Ibid.

7 Brian Glyn Williams, "Shattering the Chechen Al Qaeda Myth: Part I," *Terrorism Monitor* 4, no. 35 (October 2, 2003), http://www.jamestown.org.

8 Bennett Roth, "White House Officials Temper Russian Criticism, Blast Chechens," *Houston Chronicle*, September 27, 2001, http://www.chron.com.

9 Williams, "From Secessionist 'Rebels' to 'Al Qaeda Shock Brigades.'"

10 "Chechen Insurgents Assisting Taliban against US, Afghan Forces," Breitbart. com, May 30, 2013, http://www.breitbart.com.

11 "Bin Laden's Cook Spills Beans on Escape to Chechnya," *Telegraph*, February 6, 2002, http://www.telegraph.co.uk.

12 This preposterous accusation was made, along with many others, in Yossef Bodansky's footnote-free flight of fantasy titled *Chechen Jihad: Al Qaeda's Training Ground and the Next Wave of Terror* (New York: HarperCollins, 2007), 103–105.

13 Khaled Dawoud, "Doomed Arab Units Prepared for Final Battle against the Odds," *Guardian*, November 20, 2001, http://www.theguardian.com.

14 Williams, "From Secessionist 'Rebels' to 'Al Qaeda Shock Brigades.'"

15 Conversations carried out at Harvard University, 2003.

16 Hughes, *Chechnya*, 101.

17 "Obituary: Shamil Basayev," BBC News, July 10, 2006, http://news.bbc.co.uk.

18 Hughes, *Chechnya*, 158.

19 Williams, "Allah's Foot Soldiers."

20 Shermatova, "Tak Nazyvaemye Vakhkhabity," 412.

21 Paul Tumelty, "The Rise and Fall of Foreign Fighters in Chechnya," *Terrorism Monitor* 4, no. 2 (January 31, 2006).

22 Brian Glyn Williams, "El Kaide Turka: Tracing an Al Qaeda Splinter Cell," *Terrorism Monitor* 2, no. 22 (November 18, 2004). Brian Glyn Williams, "Turkish Volunteers in Chechnya," *Terrorism Monitor* 7, no. 3 (April 7, 2005), http://www.jamestown.org.

23 Brian Glyn Williams, "The 'Chechen Arabs': An Introduction to the Real Al Qaeda Terrorists from Chechnya," *Terrorism Monitor* 1, no. 9 (January 15, 2004), http://www.jamestown.org.

24 Dore Gold, *Hatred's Kingdom* (Washington, DC: Regnery Publishing, 2003), 137.

25 Lawrence Wright, "The Man Behind Bin Laden," *New Yorker*, Sept. 9, 2002.

26 Jane Corbin, *The Base: In Search of Al Qaeda* (London: Simon and Shuster, 2002), 55.

27 "Before Boston, Warning Signs Chechen Extremists Were Plotting beyond Russia," Fox News, April 22, 2013, http://www.foxnews.com.

28 James Gordon Meeks, "The Secret Battles between US Forces and Chechen Terrorists," ABC News, February 19, 2014, http://abcnews.go.com.

29 "No Chechens at Guantanamo Bay," *Moscow Times*, April 5, 2002, http://www.themoscowtimes.com.

30 Williams, "Shattering the Chechen Al Qaeda Myth: Part I."

31 Carlotta Gall, "Fighters Were Lured to Afghanistan by Islam, Holy War, and Promise of Escape," *New York Times*, January 1, 2002.

32 For more on General Dostum, see Brian Glyn Williams, *The Last Warlord: The Life and Legend of Dostum, the Afghan Warrior Who Led US Special Forces to Topple the Taliban Regime* (Chicago: University of Chicago Press, 2013).

33 Chris Otton, "Americans Hunt for Chechens in Afghanistan," *American Free Press*, March 22, 2002; reprinted in *Dawn*, http://www.dawn.com.

34 Jonathan Kay, "How Did Chechnya's Culture of Terror Come to Boston?" *National Post*, April 19, 2013.

35 James Gordon Meeks, "The Secret Battles between US Forces and Chechen Terrorists," ABC News, February 19, 2014, http://abcnews.go.com.

36 Brian Glyn Williams, *Predators: The CIA's Drone War on Al Qaeda* (Philadelphia: Potomac Press, 2013), 84–85 and 147.

37 Joshua Foust, "Army Major Disputes Story of Chechens in Afghanistan," Registan.net, July 3, 2009, http://registan.net.

38 Meeks, "The Secret Battles between US Forces and Chechen Terrorists."

39 Ibid.

40 *Afghanistan behind Resistance Lines: Part 3*, http://www.youtube.com.

41 For more on foreign fighters in Afghanistan, see Brian Glyn Williams, "On the Trail of the 'Lions of Islam': A History of Foreign Fighters in Afghanistan and Pakistan, 1980–2010," *Orbis* 55, no. 2 (spring 2011).

42 "The Chechen Jihadist Fighting in Syria," BBC News, December 16, 2013, http://www.bbc.co.uk.

43 Derek Henry Flood, "The Caucasus Emirate: From Anti-Colonialist Roots to Salafi-Jihad," *Counter Terrorism Sentinel*, March 26, 2014, http://www.ctc.usma.edu/posts/the-caucasus-emirate-from-anti-colonialist-roots-to-salafi-jihad.

44 Alan Cullison, "Meet the Rebel Commander in Syria That Assad, Russia and the U.S. All Fear," *Wall Street Journal*, November 19, 2013, http://online.wsj.com.

45 Murad Batal al Shishani, "'Obliged to Unite under One Banner': A Profile of Syria's Jaysh al-Muhajireen wa'l-Ansar," *Terrorism Monitor* 11, no. 8 (April 19, 2013).

46 Ghaith Abdul-Ahad, "Syria: The Foreign Fighters Joining the War against Bashar al-Assad," *Guardian*, September 23, 2012, http://www.theguardian.com.

47 "Gulf States Recruit Chechen Veterans for War against Syria's Assad," *World Tribune*, March 27, 2013, http://www.worldtribune.com.

48 Bill Roggio, "Chechen Commander Leads Muhajireen Brigade in Syria," *Long War Journal*, February 20, 2013, http://www.longwarjournal.org.

49 Bill Roggio, "Al Nusrah Front Commanded Free Syrian Army Unit, 'Chechen Emigrants,' in Assault on Syrian Air Defense Base," *Long War Journal*, October 19, 2012, http://www.longwarjournal.org.

50 Cullison, "Meet the Rebel Commander in Syria That Assad, Russia and the U.S. All Fear."

51 Nicholas Clayton, "Portrait of a Chechen Jihadist," *Foreign Policy*, April 19, 2013, http://www.foreignpolicy.com.

52 Bill Roggio, "Al Nusrah Front Praises Chechen Commander Killed in Aleppo," *Long War Journal*, February 10, 2014, http://www.longwarjournal.org.

53 "Chempion po Boksu ili Mudzhahid?" http://fisyria.com/?p=3531.

54 See the image of a red-bearded Chechen dying here to chants of *Allahu Akbar!* Live Leak, http://www.liveleak.com/view?i=39f_1361378819.

55 Murad Batal al-Shishani, "Omar Shishani, Chechen Jihadist leader," BBC News, December 3, 2013, http://www.bbc.com. "Posol: Boeviki iz Rossii, Boiuiiushchie v Sirii, Otbyvaiut Nakazanie v Strane," *RIA Novosti*, December 12, 2013. "V Sirii Voiuiut Otriady im. Dzhokara Dudayeva, Kattaba i Shamilia Basaeva," Kavkaz Center, October 16, 2012, http://www.kavkazcenter.com.

CHAPTER 8. THE STRANGE SAGA OF THE BOSTON MARATHON BOMBERS

1 Carol Williams, "Festering Chechen Militancy Not Just Russia's Problem," *Los Angeles Times*, April 19, 2013.

2 "Tamerlan Tsarnaev: Experts Puzzled as Hunt for Terror Links Gleans Little," *Guardian*, April 23, 2013.

3 "Kyrgyz Former Neighbors Talk about Tsarnaevs, North Caucasus Ties," Radio Free Europe/Radio Liberty, April 17, 2014.

4 Associated Press, "Boston Suspects' Family Traveled Long Road," April 20, 2013, http://news.yahoo.com.

5 Aaron Davis, "The Tsarnaev Family: A Faded Portrait of an Immigrant's American Dream," *Washington Post*, April 27, 2014, http://www.washingtonpost.com.

6 Ibid.

7 Ibid.

8 "Chechnya to Boston: A Family History," *Los Angeles Times*, April 22, 2013, http://timelines.latimes.com/boston-bombing-suspects/.

9 Ibid.

10 Ibid.

11 Gamzat Izudinov, "In Dagestan, US Blamed for Boston Bombing," *Global Post*, April 24, 2013.

12 Scott Helman and Jenna Russell, *The Long Mile Home* (New York: Penguin, 2014).

13 "Boston Bombing Suspects' Father 'a Good Man,' Neighbors in Dagestan Say," NBCnews.com, April 21, 2013, http://worldnews.nbcnews.com.

14 Ibid.

15 "A Good Decision," *Washington Post*, August 10, 2004.

16 "Few Chechen Immigrants Make It to U.S.," *USA Today*, April 20, 2013. Carl Schreck, "In Small Boston Diaspora, Echoes of Chechnya," *RIA Novosti*, April 22, 2014, http://en.ria.ru/world/.

17 Ibid.

18 "Remembering Tsarnaev as a New Immigrant," Eurasia.org, July 9, 2013.

19 Sally Jacobs et al., "The Fall of the House of Tsarnaev," *Boston Globe*, December 15, 2013, http://www.bostonglobe.com.

20 Davis, "The Tsarnaev Family."

21 Ibid.

22 Gregory Feifer, "Boston Bombing's Chechen Connection," *Global Post*, April 19, 2013.

23 Davis, "The Tsarnaev Family."

24 Janet Reitman, "Jahar's World," *Rolling Stone*, July 17, 2013.

25 Ibid.

26 "April 19 Updates on Aftermath of Boston Marathon Explosions," *New York Times*, April 19, 2014.

27 "Tsarnaevs' News Conference: A Transcript," *New York Times*, April 26, 2013.

28 Reitman, "Jahar's World."

29 Kim Murphy, Joseph Tanfani, and Sergei L. Loiko, "The Tsarnaev Brothers' Troubled Trail to Boston," *Los Angeles Times*, April 28, 2013.

30 "Dzhokhar A. Tsarnaev's Chechnya: 'These People Are Killers,' Diplomat John Bolton Says," *Washington Times*, April 19, 2013.

31 Scott Shane, "Agents Pore over Suspect's Trip to Russia," *New York Times*, April 28, 2013, http://www.nytimes.com.

32 "The Chechen People: A Fierce Resistance," *USA Today*, April 21, 2013.

33 Jonathan Kay, "How Did Chechnya's Culture of Terror Come to Boston?" *National Post*, April 19, 2013, http://fullcomment.nationalpost.com.

34 "In Small Boston Diaspora, Echoes of Chechnya," *RIA Novosti*, April 22, 2013, http://en.ria.ru/world/.

35 "The Boston Case from Many Angles," *New York Times*, April 22, 2013, http://www.nytimes.com.

36 Ibid.

37 Michael Martinez, "Uncle Calls Boston Marathon Bombers 'Losers,'" CNN, April 20, 2013.

38 Ibid. Sarah Kendzior, "The Wrong Kind of Caucasian," *Al Jazeera*, April 21, 2013, http://www.aljazeera.com.

39 Ibid.

40 "Struggle at Home Intrudes on Chechen Haven in America," *New York Times*, April 21, 2013.

41 Inspectors General of the Intelligence Community, Central Intelligence Agency, Department of Justice, and Department of Homeland Security, "Unclassified Summary of Information Handling and Sharing Prior to the April 15, 2013 Boston Marathon Bombing," April 10, 2014, http://www.justice.gov/oig/reports/2014/s1404.pdf.

42 Thomas Joscelyn, "Dagestani Jihadist Group Issues Statement on Boston Bombings," *Long War Journal*, April 21, 2013, http://www.longwarjournal.org.

43 "FBI Interviewed Tamerlan Tsarnaev after 2011 Tip," Associated Press, April 20, 2013.

44 Inspectors General of the Intelligence Community, "Unclassified Summary."

45 "Turn to Religion Split Suspects' Home," *Wall Street Journal*, April 22, 2013, http://online.wsj.com.

46 Ibid.

47 "Dagestan, Family and Neighbours of Boston Suspects Describe Shock," *Guardian*, April 20, 2013.

48 Eric Thayer, "Bombing Inquiry Turns to Motive and Russian Trip," *New York Times*, April 20, 2013.

49 "2011 Request for Information on Tamerlan Tsarnaev from Foreign Government," FBI.gov, http://www.fbi.gov/news/pressrel/press-releases/.

50 "Timeline: A Look at Tamerlan Tsarnaev's Past," CNN, April 22, 2013.

51 "Tsarnaev Neighbors: Older Bombing Suspect Spent Time in Dagestan Helping Dad with Construction," *Time*, April 21, 2013, http://world.time.com.

52 "Tamerlan Tsarnaev in Dagestan: The Unanswered Questions," *Guardian*, April 22, 2013.

53 "Deadly Blast Hits Russian Parade," BBC News, May 9, 2002, http://news.bbc.co.uk/2/hi/europe/1976776.stm.

54 "A Russian Region Neither at War nor at Peace, but Facing a Crackdown," *New York Times*, October 9, 2013.

55 Allan Cullison, "Tsarnaev's Six-Month Visit to Dagestan Is Scrutinized," *Wall Street Journal*, April 24, 2013, http://online.wsj.com.

56 Ibid.

57 Arsen Mollayev, "Tsarnaev's Russian Trip under Scrutiny," *Sydney Morning Herald*, April 22, 2013, http://www.smh.com.au/world/.

58 Ibid.

59 Davis, "The Tsarnaev Family."

60 Reuters, "The Radicalization of Tamerlan Tsarnaev — Profile Slowly Emerges of Boston Marathon Bomber," April 23, 2013, http://www.nydailynews.com/news/national/.

61 Jacobs et al., "The Fall of the House of Tsarnaev."

62 "A Russian Region Neither at War Nor at Peace."

63 Mairbek Vatchagaev, "International Islamist Movement Spreads to the North Caucasus," *Eurasia Daily Monitor*, May 16, 2013, www.jamestown.org.

64 Simon Shuster, "Exclusive: Dagestani Relative of Tamerlan Tsarnaev Is a Prominent Islamist," *Time*, May 8, 2013.

65 Rohan Gunaratna and Cleo Haynal, "Current and Emerging Threats of Homegrown Terrorism: The Case of the Boston Bombings," *Perspectives on Terrorism* 7, no. 3 (2013).

66 "Canadian Boxer Had Links to Boston Bomber," *Sydney Morning Herald*, April 29, 2013.

67 Shane, "Agents Pore over Suspect's Trip to Russia."

68 Ibid.

69 Izudinov, "In Dagestan."

70 Ibid.

71 "A Dead Militant in Dagestan: Did This Slain Jihadi Meet Tamerlan Tsarnaev?" CNN, May 1, 2013, http://www.cnn.com.

72 Allison Cullison, "Dagestan Islamists Were Uneasy about Boston Bombing Suspect," *Wall Street Journal*, May 9, 2013.

73 Stewart Bell, "The Canadian Who Converted to Jihad: Boxer Turned Militant Killed in Dagestan," *National Post*, August 20, 2012.

74 Ibid.

75 Ibid.

76 "Canadian Boxer Had Links to Boston Bomber."

77 Bell, "The Canadian Who Converted to Jihad."

78 "Canadian Boxer Had Links to Boston Bomber."

79 Ellen Barry, "Boston Bomb Inquiry Looks Closely at Russia Trip," *New York Times*, May 8, 2013.

80 "Investigators Explore Possible Link between Boston Bombing Suspect and Extremist Group," Fox News, April 20, 2013.

81 Izudinov, "In Dagestan."

82 "Tamerlan Tsarnaev's Dagestan Mystery," *Global Post*, April 23, 2013, http://www.globalpost.com.

83 Michael Schmidt, "Russia Didn't Share All Details on Boston Bombing Suspect, Report Says," *New York Times*, April 9, 2014.

84 "Statement of the Command of Mujahideen of Caucasus Emirate's Dagestan Province in Relation to Events in Boston," Kavkaz Center, April 21, 2013, http://www.kavkazcenter.com.

85 Shane, "Agents Pore Over Suspect's Trip to Russia."

86 Ellen Barry, "Suspect in Boston Bombing Talked Jihad in Russia," *New York Times*, May 9, 2013.

87 Cullison, "Dagestan Islamists Were Uneasy about Boston Bombing Suspect."

88 "Tsarnaev Neighbors: Older Bombing Suspect Spent Time in Dagestan Helping Dad with Construction."

89 "Chechnya President, Islamic Rebels Deny Ties to Boston Suspects," *Washington Times*, April 19, 2013.

90 Alan Cullison, "Tsarnaev's Six-Month Visit to Dagestan Is Scrutinized," *Wall Street Journal*, April 24, 2013, http://online.wsj.com.

91 Simon Schuster, "Exclusive: Dagestani Relative of Tamerlan Tsarnaev Is a Prominent Islamist," *Time*, May 8, 2013, http://world.time.com.

92 Schuster, "Exclusive."

93 Barry, "Boston Bomb Inquiry Looks Closely at Russia Trip."

94 Barry, "Suspect in Boston Bombing Talked Jihad in Russia."

95 Reitman, "Jahar's World."

96 Schuster, "Exclusive."

97 Ibid.

98 Ibid.

99 Arsen Mollayev, "Parents of Boston Suspect Describe His Russia Trip," Associated Press, April 22, 2013.

100 "In Dagestan, Family and Neighbours of Boston Suspects Describe Shock," *Guardian*, April 20, 2013.

101 Cullison, "Tsarnaev's Six-Month Visit to Dagestan Is Scrutinized."

102 Cullison, "Dagestan Islamists Were Uneasy about Boston Bombing Suspect."

103 Jacobs et al., "The Fall of the House of Tsarnaev."

104 Ibid.

105 Cullison, "Dagestan Islamists Were Uneasy about Boston Bombing Suspect."

106 James Meek, "Fort Hood Gunman Nidal Hassan 'Is a Hero,'" *Daily News*, November 9, 2009.

107 Brian Glyn Williams, *Predators: The CIA's Drone War on Al Qaeda* (Washington, DC: Potomac, 2013): 138–44.

108 Reuters, "The Radicalization of Tamerlan Tsarnaev." Inspectors General of the Intelligence Community, "Unclassified Summary of Information Handling and Sharing Prior to the April 15, 2013 Boston Marathon Bombing."

109 "Tamerlan Tsarnaev: Experts Puzzled as Hunt for Terror Links Gleans Little," *Guardian*, April 23, 2013.

110 "The Obscure Russian Jihadist Whom Tamerlan Tsarnaev Followed Online," *Washington Post*, April 24, 2013.

111 Rohan Gunaratna and Cleo Haynal, "Current and Emerging Threats of Home-grown Terrorism: The Case of the Boston Bombings," *Perspectives on Terrorism* 7, no. 3 (2013).

112 This video or one like it is still accessible on YouTube as "The Army of Khorosan: Prophecy Emerging True," https://www.youtube.com/watch?v=-1zFVqjWTPI.

113 Reitman, "Jahar's World."

114 Inspectors General of the Intelligence Community, "Unclassified Summary of Information Handling and Sharing Prior to the April 15, 2013 Boston Marathon Bombing."

115 Peter Bergen and Jennifer Rowland, "Four Things We Learned about the Boston Bombing," CNN, April 15, 2014.

116 Reitman, "Jahar's World."

117 Kendzior, "The Wrong Kind of Caucasian."

Index

ABOUT THE AUTHOR

Dr. Brian Glyn Williams is professor of Islamic history at the University of Massachusetts-Dartmouth, where he received tenure in 2006 and teaches courses on warfare and terrorism in Islamic Eurasia. Prior to teaching at UMass-Dartmouth he taught Ottoman history at the University of London's School of Oriental and African Studies. He has carried out fieldwork in Islamic Eurasia ranging from Kosovo to the Caucasus to Kazakhstan to Kashmir to Afghanistan to tribal regions of Pakistan. This fieldwork has helped him write *The Crimean Tatars: From Soviet Genocide to Putin's Conquest* (2015); *The Last Warlord: The Life and Legend of Dostum, the Afghan Warrior who Led* US Special Forces in Toppling the Taliban Regime (2013); *Predators: The* CIA's Drone War on Al Qaeda (2013), and *Afghanistan Declassified: A Guide to America's Longest War* (2011).

Dr. Williams earned his PhD in Central Asian history at the University of Wisconsin in 1999, a master's degree in Russian history at Indiana University in 1992, and a master's in Central Eurasian studies at Indiana University in 1990. He has published articles in journals such as *Journal of the Royal Asiatic Society, Central Asian Survey, Small Wars and Insurgencies, Terrorism Monitor, West Point's Counter Terrorism Sentinel, Jane's Intelligence Review, Militant Leadership Monitor, Jane's Terrorism and Security Monitor, Middle East Policy, Foreign Policy*, and is a regular contributor to the *Huffington Post*.

Dr. Williams can be reached at bwilliams@umassd.edu, and he has photographs and articles from his fieldwork on his website at brianglynwilliams.com.